IMAGES
of America

MIDDLESEX COUNTY

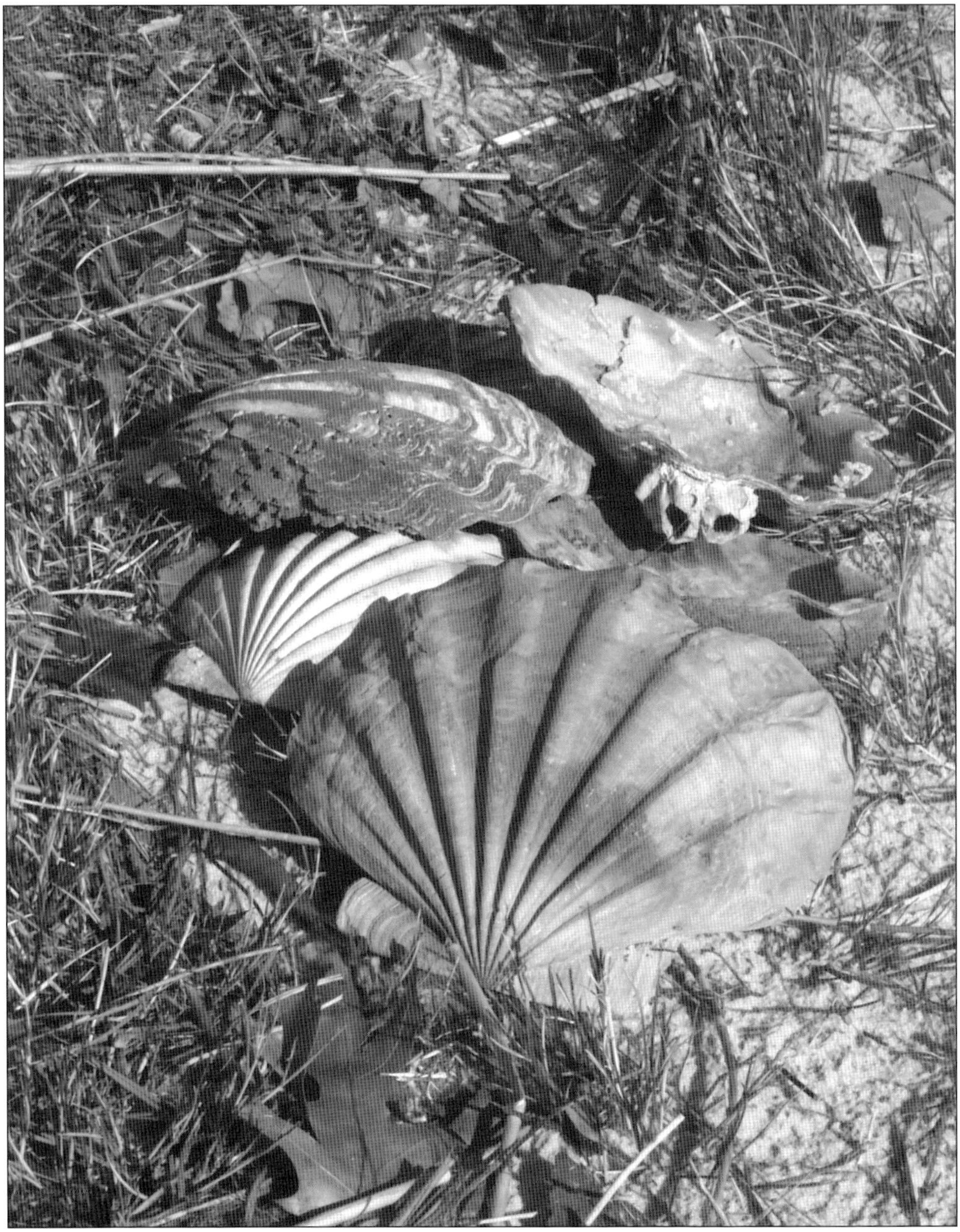

Fossilized scallop shells dating to the Miocene Epoch, 5 to 23 million years ago, are found in the high river banks on the Rappahannock River and Urbanna Creek. The scallop species in this photograph was first discovered in 1936 and named *Chesapecten middlesexensis* after Middlesex County, where it was found. (Courtesy of Mark and Julie Bray.)

ON THE COVER: John Hinton Pitts Sr. founded Pitts Lumber Company near Saluda in 1898. At that time, there were dozens of sawmills in the county. Pitts started with a few oxen used to haul trees out of the forest and a portable steam-powered sawmill. He timbered land in the Dragon Run region, which provided cypress, oak, poplar, spruce pine, and maple woods along with the water needed to operate his mill. (Courtesy of Jimmy Pitts.)

IMAGES
of America

MIDDLESEX COUNTY

Larry S. Chowning

ARCADIA
PUBLISHING

ISBN 978-1-4671-0250-6

Published by Arcadia Publishing
Charleston, South Carolina

Printed in the United States of America

Library of Congress Control Number: 2018946440

For all general information, please contact Arcadia Publishing:
Telephone 843-853-2070
Fax 843-853-0044
E-mail sales@arcadiapublishing.com
For customer service and orders:
Toll-Free 1-888-313-2665

Visit us on the Internet at www.arcadiapublishing.com

On January 21, 1651, less than two years after permanent English settlement in Middlesex County, Virginia, Robert Chowning of Kent, England, arrived in what was then Lancaster County, Virginia, and received two land grants amounting to 300 acres at the head of what is today LaGrange Creek in Middlesex County. Chownings have lived in Middlesex ever since. This book is dedicated to the memory of Caleb Shepherd Chowning, grandson of the author, who died of cancer at the age of seven on May 16, 2017.

Contents

Acknowledgments

I want to thank all those who have assisted me in this effort to produce a photographic history book of Middlesex County, Virginia. Without your help, this would not have been possible. I also want to thank the Middlesex County Board of Supervisors and the Jamestown 2007 Middlesex Book Committee, who partnered in publishing *Signatures in Time: A Living History of Middlesex County, Virginia*, the first definitive history written on the 350-year-old county. I was the author of the book; research on the book, along with a lifetime of living in Middlesex County, led to the culmination of this project. I also want to thank past and present historians who over the years kept our history alive. Carroll C. Chowning Sr., Rutherford Snell, Cora Marchant, Louise Gray, Jessie DeBusk, Evelyn Q. Ryland, Bettie Simmons, Sherman and Easter Holmes, Pat and Bert Perkinson, Claudia and Archie Soucek, Julie Bray, Pat DePina, Raynell Smith, Dan Gill, Bob Montague, and Bill Powell have all, in their own way, contributed to this work. I personally want to thank Jane Mason, Gray Wyatt, Carroll Davies, Alva and Jerry Bray, Nola Watson, Jean Holman, Wanda Hollberg, and Mary and Danny Loving, who brought in boxes and albums of old photographs, which greatly enhanced this book. I am also thankful to Fred and Bettie Lee Gaskins and editor Tom Hardin of the *Southside Sentinel* for providing me with an avenue to work and write about my community. Marilyn South and Tyler Radabaugh of the Middlesex County Museum were always helpful in filling historical holes with appropriate photos. Vera England graciously provides me with editorial assistance, for which I am forever grateful. Finally, I want to thank my wife, Dee, and my mother, Emily Chowning, for encouraging me to continue to write about things I love.

INTRODUCTION

Middlesex County's history evolved from the natural development of the Chesapeake Bay, the arrival of the first inhabitants of North America, and English settlement by the Virginia Company of London.

For centuries, the area's waterways and the land near to the water have defined the way people have lived in the area we now call Middlesex. Scientists believe that about 35 million years ago a comet or meteor, called a bolide (Greek for missile), hit the area that is now the lower tip of the Delmarva Peninsula. The bolide created what geologists call the Exmore Crater, which they believe was as large as the state of Rhode Island and as deep as the Grand Canyon.

The outer edge of the crater touched the eastern end of what would become Middlesex County. While the object did not actually create the Chesapeake, it did help determine that a shallow-water bay would eventually be located there. Scientists believe the crater acted like the drain in a bathtub. When sea levels were low, it gave the region's rivers a single outlet to the ocean, creating the Bay's broad, shallow waters. It is believed that the crater shaped the channels of the Piankatank and Rappahannock Rivers and Dragon Run, the bodies of water that touch the shores of Middlesex on its northern and southern boundaries.

To this day, there is evidence of life here not long after the crater struck. The landscape of some areas along the high southern banks of the Rappahannock includes high clay and sandy banks with millions of white-colored, chalky-looking fossil shells protruding from the gray-colored mix of mud and sand. The fossil beds are predominately from the Miocene Epoch, 5 to 23 million years ago. The Miocene was a time of wildly fluctuating climate here, when the Chesapeake Bay region went through subtropical, cold, and temperate periods. This resulted in rapid evolution and extinction of species found today in large deposits of fossil shells in the river and creek banks and in the bottom of Middlesex County wells.

In 1936, paleontologist Wendell C. Mansfield of the US Geological Survey of the Smithsonian Institution visited these fossil beds and discovered a large extinct species of scallop, never seen before, that he named *Chesapecten middlesexensis* after Middlesex County. Mansfield had visited the creek banks on Urbanna Creek earlier in 1929 and found a new species of shell, which he named *Carolinapecten urbannansis*, after the Town of Urbanna, located in the county.

The first inhabitants of North America, later known as Native Americans, entered the continent sometime during the Ice Age, which began 2.6 million years ago. A hunting culture, it is believed that they crossed the Bering Strait from Russia into North America by way of an ice and land bridge, while over the centuries they found their way to the East Coast of America and to Middlesex. Prior to English settlement in 1642, generations of Virginia's Native Americans lived here. Arrowheads, spearheads, and stone relics are often found in fields and along the beaches.

The English arrived on Middlesex shores in the 17th century, bringing Capt. John Smith and a band of explorers in 1608. When Smith's famous map of the Chesapeake was published in 1612, it showed two locations of Native American villages in the county: "Opiscopank," a village on Urbanna Creek, and "Parankatank," located on the Piankatank River. The two rivers on each side of the county are named for ancient tribes. The Piankatank River on the north side of Middlesex is named for the Piankatank tribe and the Rappahannock River for the Rappahannock tribe that was located across that river on what is today the Northern Neck. The Piankatanks, believed to be a peaceful tribe, were part of the larger Algonquian-speaking culture ruled by Chief Powhatan, chief of the Powhatan Confederation, whose main village was on York River. Around 1608, Chief Powhatan's warriors punished the Piankatanks by ambushing and annihilating them, perhaps over issues of disobedience or failure to pay tribute. It is likely that those left alive fled to the northern shores of the Rappahannock. This may have contributed to the fact that there were so few Native Americans living on Middlesex soil in 1649, the first year of permanent English settlement.

Just a year after the English settlement of Jamestown on May 13, 1607, Capt. John Smith touched the shores of the far eastern end of Middlesex in the Chesapeake Bay. Smith and his band of explorers fished with swords in shallow water. Smith speared a stingray, and when he pulled it to the surface, it jabbed its poisonous barb into his arm. Since he was thought to be dying, a grave was dug for him on Middlesex soil. However, he recovered, and the location has ever since been known as Stingray Point.

The first of seven English land grants were issued in 1642 along the Piankatank River. Another grant was issued in 1643 for 2,000 acres to Sir Francis Wyatt, the first English royal governor of Virginia. The next year in 1644, Opechancanought, then chief of the Powhatan Confederacy, attacked and massacred English settlers. This prompted the assembly in Jamestown to have all settlers living on the eastern frontier, which included Middlesex, move back to the north side of the York River. The war lasted until 1646, when Opechancanought was captured and killed. After this, treaties with Native Americans provided a safe pathway for English settlement into Middlesex County. Although it is not known for certain how long Native Americans made Middlesex their home, thousands of relics have been found on county soil, which speaks to generations and generations having lived here.

After John Smith's map entry, the next reference to a Native American village was on June 16, 1649, when Capt. Ralph Wormeley was issued a patent for 3,200 acres of land, which he named Rosegill. The patent states that it includes lands once known as "old & new Nimcock towne."

In 1649, English land grants were issued that led to a plantation-based agricultural lifestyle supported by the growing of sweet-scented tobacco. Growing tobacco required a large labor force, and enslaved Africans provided the manpower to support this lifestyle. Slavery was a part of the county's culture for the next 216 years. The first African slaves were brought to Middlesex in 1649. The Rosegill land grant stated that Ralph Wormeley secured his 3,200 acres by providing cost of transportation for 64 persons (headrights). The government granted land according to the headright system—50 acres per person. The Wormeley grant included 17 slaves, believed to be the first Africans in the county.

The land that is now Middlesex County was established in 1651 as part of Lancaster County. After a petition from landowners was presented before the assembly in 1668 to create a separate county on the south side of the Rappahannock River, the assembly voted to create Middlesex County, with 131 square miles of land and 80 square miles of waterfront. The county is named after the historic Middlesex County in southeast England, today part of the City of London.

The Church of England, also known as the Anglican Church, brought Christianity to the shores of Middlesex. The county was divided into two parishes until 1666, when Christ Church Parish was established by combining Piankatank and Lancaster Parishes. The Baptist movement started in the county in 1770 when the Anglican resistance resulted in the jailing of Baptist preacher John Waller in the county jail in Urbanna. Waller preached from a jailhouse window, and the Baptist movement took off like wildfire. Early Methodists arrived in the county in 1763, but it took over 65 years before Forest Chapel Methodist Church (1829), the mother church of all Methodist churches in the county, was organized.

Issues over slavery and states' rights eventually led to the American Civil War, which, after a Union victory in 1865, freed Middlesex slaves. After slavery, the socioeconomic issues between whites and blacks were played out in Civil Rights conflicts ranging from the passing of local Jim Crow Laws (1902); desegregation of schools (1963); and the US Supreme Court trial of Morgan vs. Virginia (1944). Irene Morgan, a Gloucester County resident, was a pioneer in the American Civil Rights movement. Her fight for equality happened in Middlesex. When passing through Saluda on a Greyhound bus, she refused to give up her seat to a white couple. The bus driver called Middlesex sheriff R. Beverley Segar, who arrested Morgan. The Supreme Court ruled by a 6-1 vote that Virginia law requiring blacks to give up their seats to whites on commercial interstate passenger buses was unconstitutional. This happened nearly a decade before Civil Rights icon Rosa Parks refused to give up her seat in 1955 on a bus in Montgomery, Alabama.

Rebellions and wars fought on American soil—from Bacon's Rebellion (1675–1676), the Tobacco Cutting Rebellion (1681), the Revolutionary War (1775–1783), the War of 1812, (1812–1815) and the Civil War (1861–1865)—directly affected the people of Middlesex, and at times resulted in bloodshed and death on county soil.

Throughout Middlesex County's history, the Chesapeake Bay, the Rappahannock and Piankatank Rivers, and Dragon Run have positively impacted county life, bringing sustenance and economic gain by the harvesting and selling of crabs, fish, and oysters. The county's maritime heritage is steeped in the tradition of boatbuilding and boats. First, the rivers provided an avenue for the comings and goings of ships from England, bringing goods from the mother country and returning to Britain with holds full of Middlesex tobacco. During the Civil War, the waters provided a pathway to freedom for slaves who rowed out in skiffs or swam to waiting Union ships. Many Middlesex lads spent careers as captains or mates aboard sailing schooners that sailed the bay, hauling lumber, watermelons, and freight. The rivers, creeks, and streams have provided opportunities that have often led to a better way of life.

Today, the Chesapeake Bay and the waters that feed it provide a natural, beautiful environment that contributes greatly to the county's economic life, to waterfront landowners who come down on weekends to enjoy their second homes, and boat owners who rent slips at the county's many marinas. This new age of economic growth led to Deltaville, at the far eastern end of the county and on the Chesapeake Bay, being called "the Boating Capital of Chesapeake Bay."

The county's oyster past is remembered and honored each year on the first weekend in November at the Urbanna Oyster Festival. The festival was named the official oyster festival of Virginia in 1985 under an act of the Virginia General Assembly. It draws over 60,000 people over the two-day event and celebrates the county's rich seafood heritage.

One

Colonial Life

Middlesex County, Virginia, was established during the English colonization of North America that started at Jamestown in 1607. Royal governor Sir William Berkeley arrived in the colony in 1642, the same year English settlement began on land that would become Middlesex County. Berkeley was born and raised in Middlesex, England, and is believed to have encouraged Virginia's Royal Assembly to name the county after his home. It is one of 25 Virginia counties that, by 1703, was established with an English royalist name.

The first English land grant issued for Middlesex land was for 1,900 acres awarded to John Matrum. The grant, known as "Matrums Mount," was issued July 20, 1642.

The Virginia Assembly established Lancaster County, which included future lands known as Middlesex, in 1651. Seventeen years later, in 1668, Middlesex County was shaved out of Lancaster's south side of the Rappahannock River.

The colonial period was marked by the establishment of the English court system, the Anglican Church, and an infrastructure designed to grow the economy by farming tobacco.

The Town of Urbanna on the Rappahannock River and Kempts on the Piankatank River were established as official colonial ports and customhouses where tobacco was graded, priced, and shipped to England. Ships annually arrived in March from England and Scotland with goods and supplies to support the colonists and to transport tobacco back to England.

Colonial living was hard, as day-to-day life centered around the grit and grind of plantation life—a hard life for most with little medical assistance available when sick and few schools to provide hope for a better life for tomorrow. People did not live long, and most of the population could not read or write. As colonial life advanced into the 1700s, life improved some with each generation.

Middlesex County's economic underpinning was strongly tied to what was referred to as the South's "peculiar institution." Slavery provided the labor force for the county to grow and prosper but raised moral and social issues that would haunt the people of Middlesex—white and black—for generations.

The colonial period ended in 1776 with the establishment of the Commonwealth of Virginia. James Montague and Edmund Berkeley IV were Middlesex County's representatives to the Virginia Conventions that ended the colonial period and brought forth a revolutionary spirit that, in 1781, culminated in an American victory over the English at Yorktown.

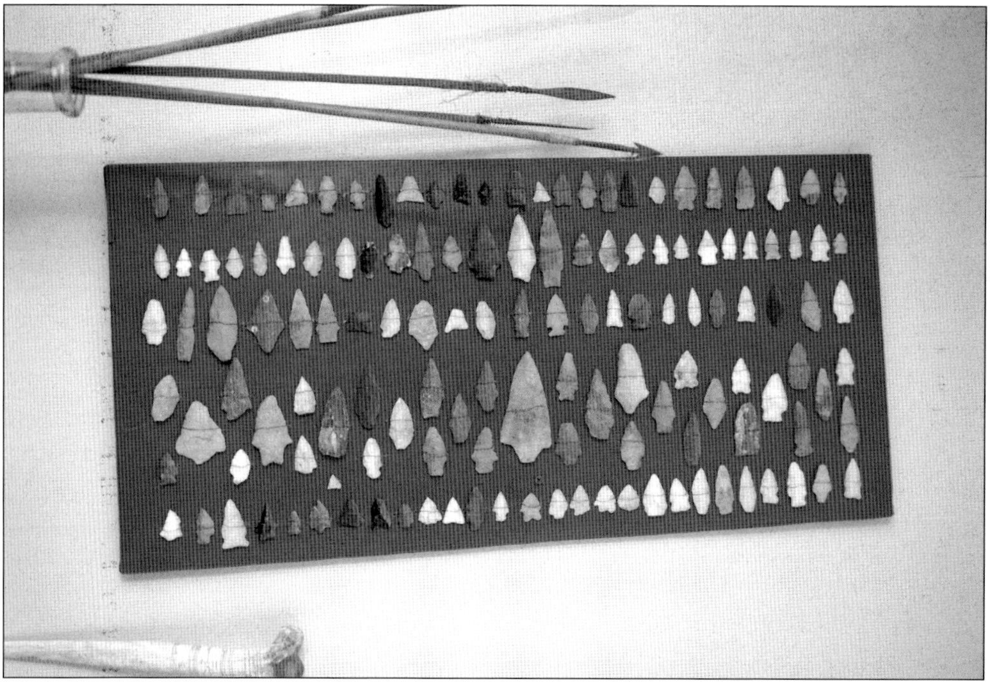

These Native American artifacts were found in Middlesex County. John Smith's 1612 map of the Chesapeake Bay showed two Indian "townes" in what is now Middlesex County. They were "Opiscopank," located on the shores of Urbanna Creek, and the "Paranktanks," on the Piankatank River. Today, the names of the Rappahannock and Piankatank Rivers are reminders that Native Americans were living in Middlesex long before English settlement. (Courtesy of Stan Dameron.)

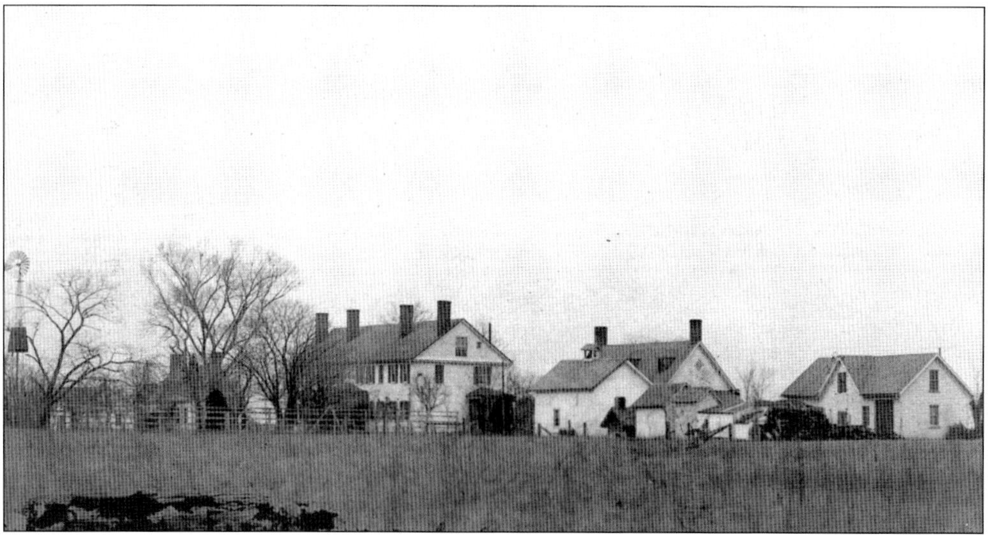

Rosegill Plantation was the colonial home of the Wormeley family. Capt. Ralph Wormeley received a grant of 3,200 acres on June 16, 1649, for land that would eventually become part of Middlesex County. The Wormeley grant mentioned the "Indian townes of old and new Nimcock." It was the only time Nimcock Indians were mentioned in colonial writings. (Courtesy of Emily Chowning.)

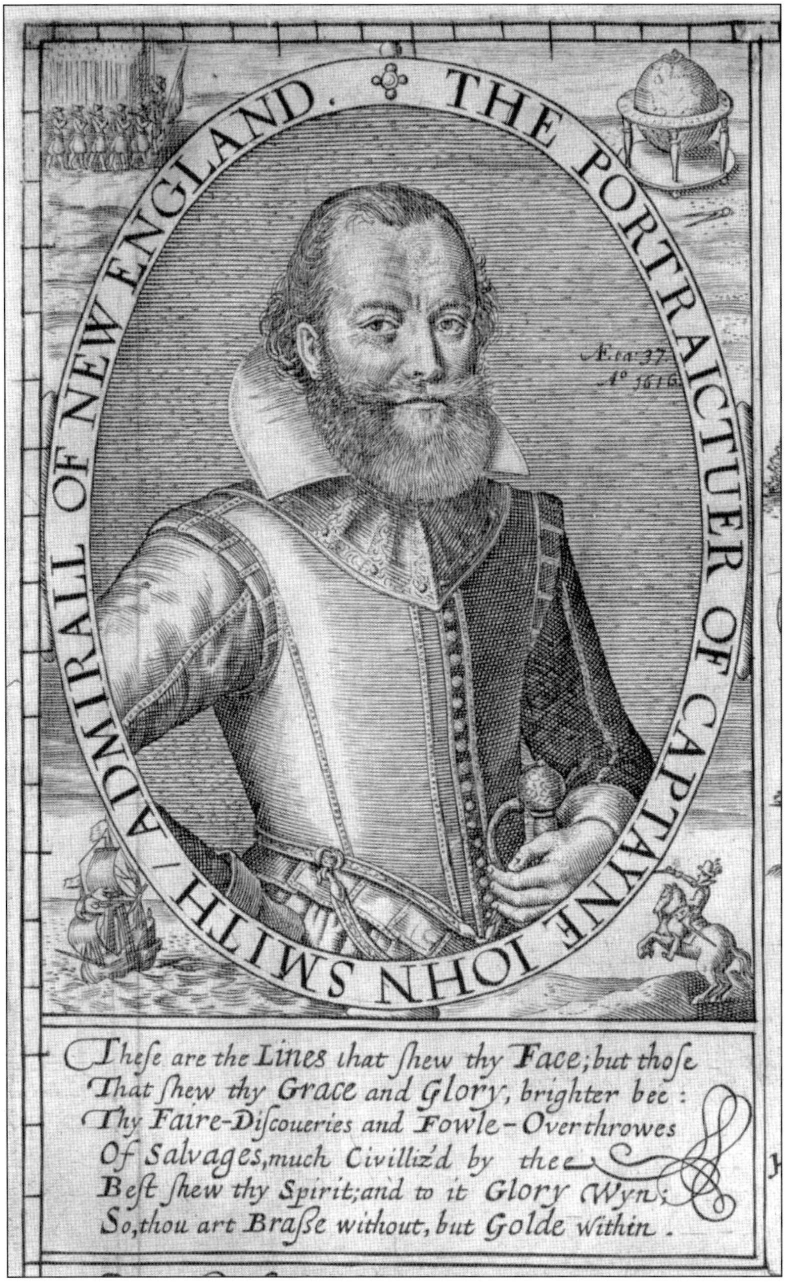

On July 17, 1608, the English explorer Capt. John Smith was nearly killed by a stingray when he and a group of 14 men from Jamestown were charting the Chesapeake Bay in a shallop. When Smith and his group sailed into shoal waters at the mouth of the Rappahannock River to go fishing with their swords, Smith brought up a stingray. The fish stabbed its venomous barb into Smith's arm. His men thought he was dying, so they dug a grave. Smith did not die and, after recovering, continued to map the bay region and to accomplish other significant deeds. When he published his famous map of Virginia in 1612, he named the spot where he was nearly killed "Stingray Isle." The location is at the far eastern end of Middlesex County and is named Stingray Point today. (Courtesy of Virginia Historical Society.)

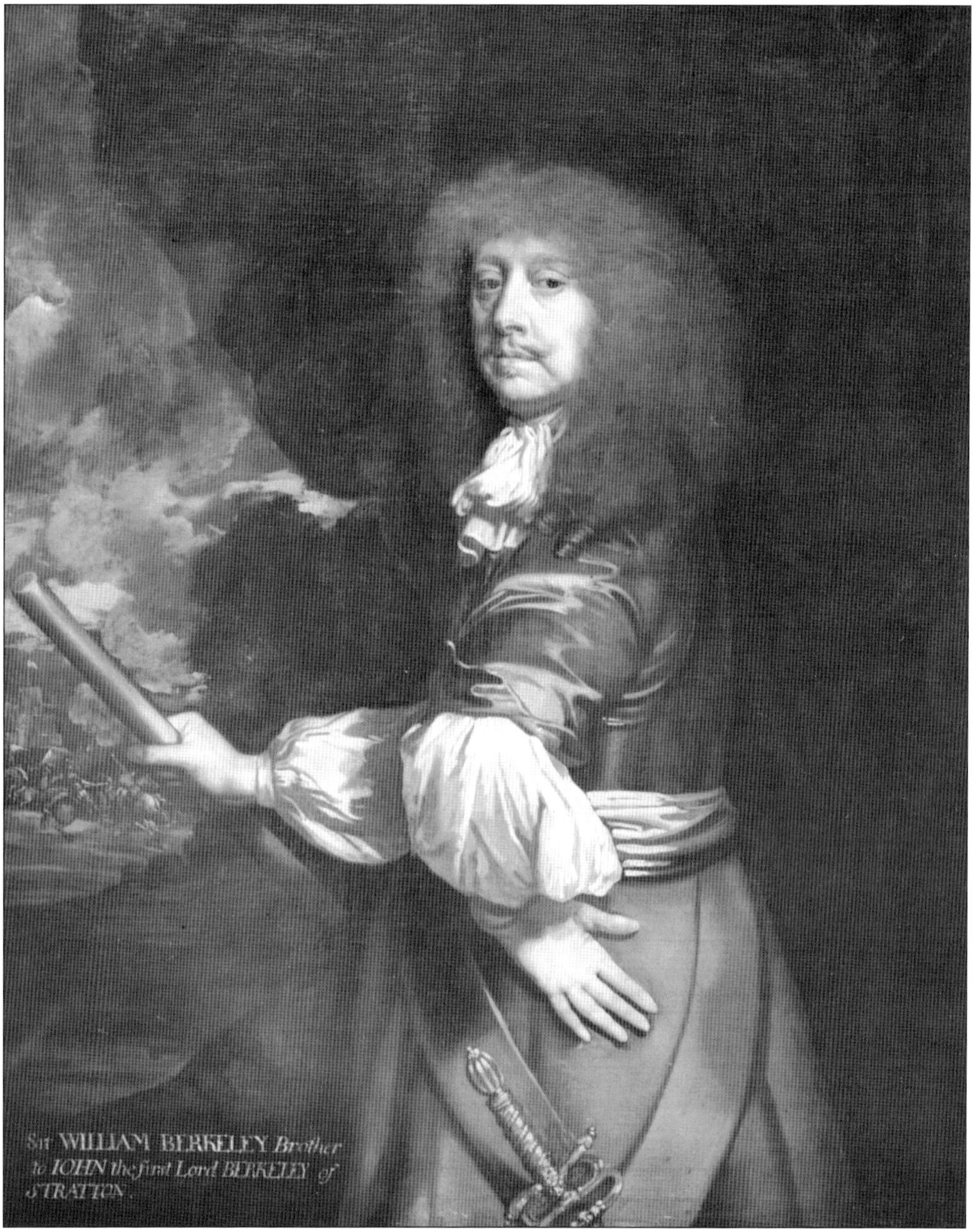

The English began settlement of Middlesex County in 1642, the same year Sir William Berkeley arrived as the new royal governor of Virginia. Berkeley was born in 1605 at Hanworth Manor in Middlesex, England, the home of his maternal grandparents. It is believed that in 1668 when the Virginia Assembly agreed to split Lancaster County in two to create Middlesex, Berkeley was influential in giving the county its name. He was the longest serving royal governor in Virginia. He was involved in the first American rebellion, known as Bacon's Rebellion. When the rebel Nathaniel Bacon died in October 1676 of natural causes, Berkeley rounded up rebels with help from loyalist Henry Corbin of Buckingham in Middlesex. Three rebels were hung at Royal Oak on Corbin's land in the county. (Courtesy of Virginia Historical Society.)

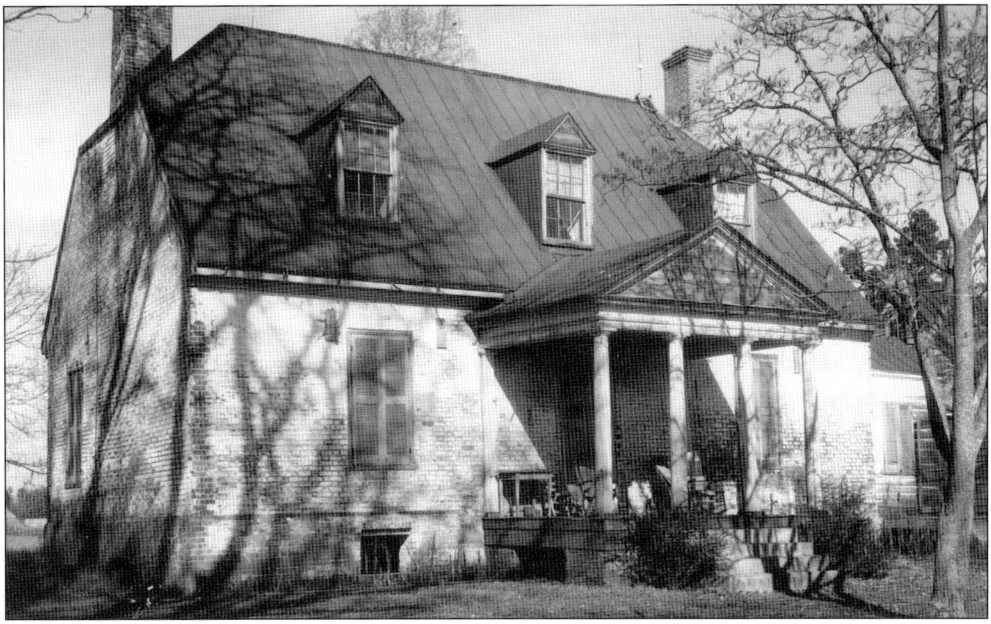

The original Deer Chase was built around 1690. A fire destroyed the interior, and sometime later, the home was rebuilt within the original walls. An examination of the upstairs woodwork by a specialist in colonial architecture suggests the rebuild was around 1725. Deer Chase had many outbuildings, with its most noted being Deer Chase Academy. Early inventory records of the estate of Thomas Kempt date a school there to 1772. (C.C. Chowning collection.)

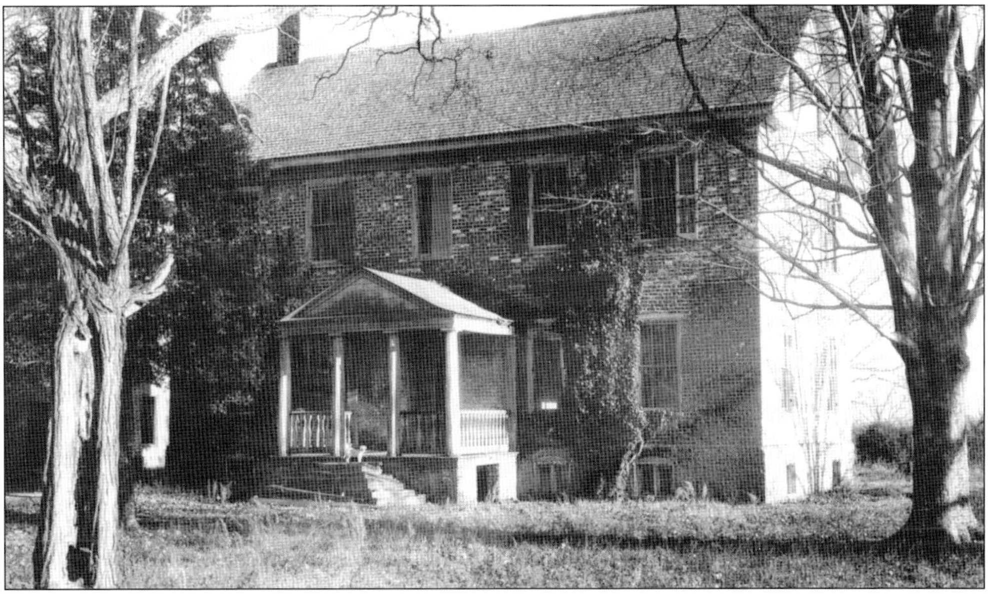

Barn Elms was the home of the Middlesex Berkeley family and was located near Hartfield. The home was on land that was originally part of the first English land grant here, issued to John Matram in 1642. Barn Elms was home to Edmund Berkeley IV, a Middlesex County burgess from 1773 to 1776. Berkeley and representative James Montague were the key people in bringing the revolutionary spirit to Middlesex and conveying that spirit to other Virginians. (C.C. Chowning collection.)

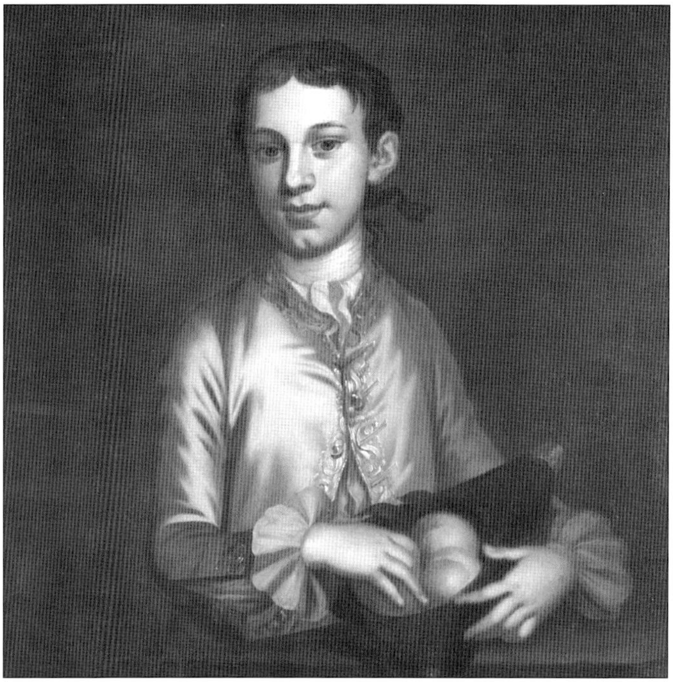

Ralph Wormeley V was the last of his name to live at Rosegill. He was born at Lansdowne in Urbanna in 1744. During the American Revolution, he was a tory and became a target of concern for American patriots. On May 13, 1776, Wormeley was placed under house arrest at Rosegill and later sent to his father's estate in Berkeley and Frederick Counties, where he was confined for two years. He died in 1806, ending that family's long social and political dynasty in Middlesex and Virginia. (Courtesy of Virginia Historical Society.)

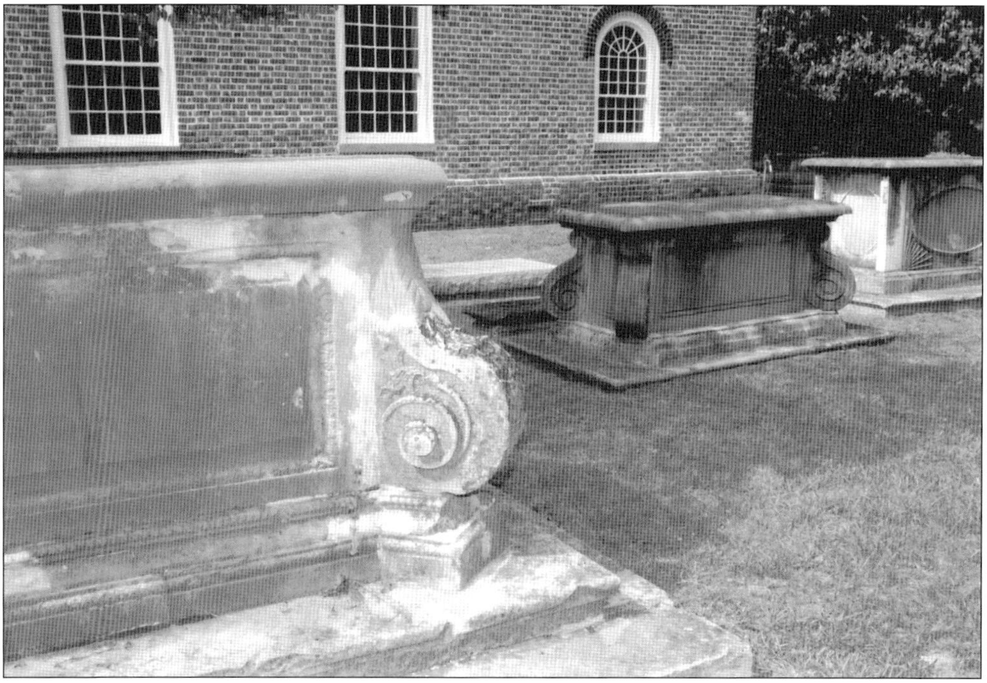

The Grymes and Wormeley family crypts at Christ Church cemetery speak to the wealth and power of these two families in colonial Middlesex. Virginia's English social order was well defined when settlement began in Middlesex. The Church of England encouraged a social order where a few dictated the way life was to be lived. The first church vestries in Virginia were elected, but that soon changed to appointed members, further encouraging a social elite society. (Author's collection.)

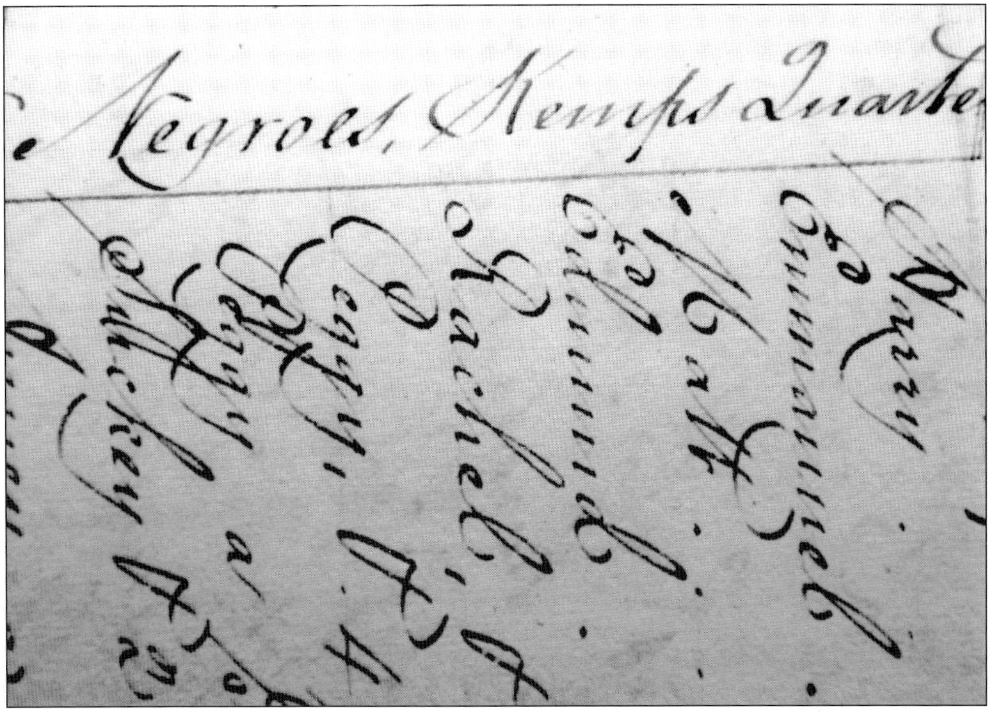

Old Middlesex court records contain inventories of properties, which include slaves. Colonial landowners with large tracts divided their land into quarters to more efficiently raise tobacco. Each quarter was a working community run by a white overseer and worked by slaves who lived on the quarter. Harry, Emmanuel, Matt, Edmund, Rachel, Peggy P., Peggy A., Zachery, and Jinney were slaves of Matthew Kempt and worked "Kempts Quarter." Slavery was a part of Middlesex's history for 216 years. (Courtesy of Middlesex County Circuit Court.)

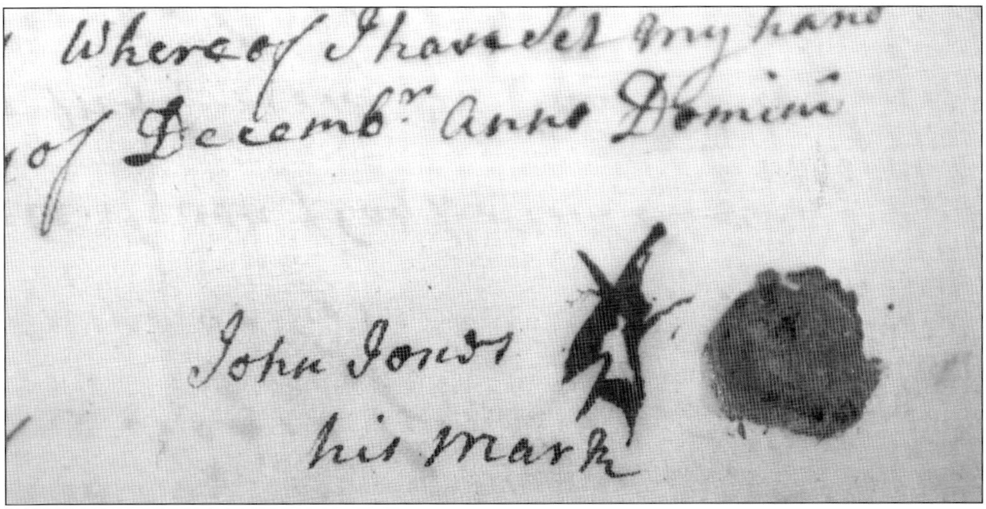

During colonial times, most Middlesex men and women were unable to read or write and used their mark to denote their signature. John Jones had a rather distinct mark that he used beside a red wax seal and his name, which was written out by the county clerk. Most letters, wills, and deeds from the colonial period contain an official red wax seal next to the name, which denotes authenticity. (Courtesy of Middlesex County Circuit Court.)

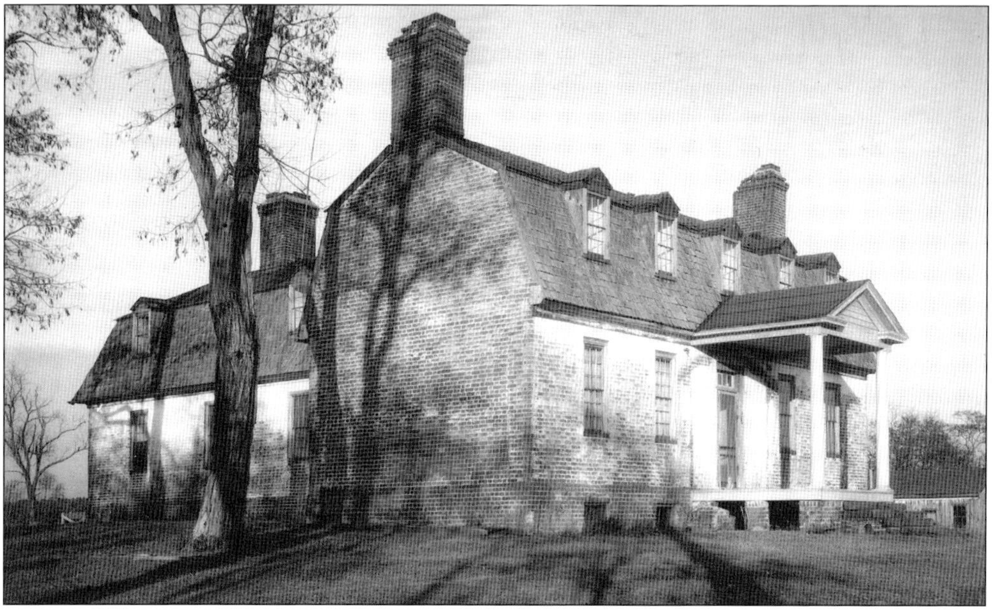

The immigrant William Churchill came to Middlesex in 1688 and established a plantation on the Rappahannock River known as Churchill and later Bushy Park. When the manor house burned around 1760, the family moved to this house called Wilton on the Piankatank. During the Revolutionary War, English sailors plundered Wilton and captured patriot Col. William Churchill. He survived and would serve as clerk of Middlesex courts from 1772 to 1799. (C.C. Chowning collection.)

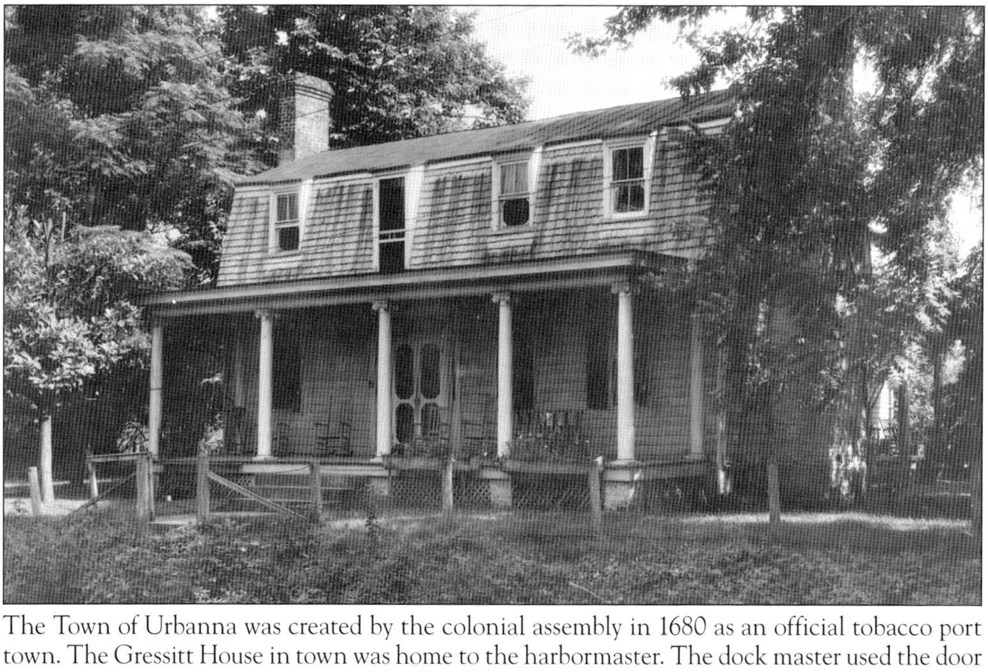

The Town of Urbanna was created by the colonial assembly in 1680 as an official tobacco port town. The Gressitt House in town was home to the harbormaster. The dock master used the door on the second floor to walk out on the roof to view ships in the harbor. A plaque once hung near the front door of the house commemorating William Clark's departure from the house in 1804 to join Meriwether Lewis for their expedition westward. (Courtesy of Amy Denney.)

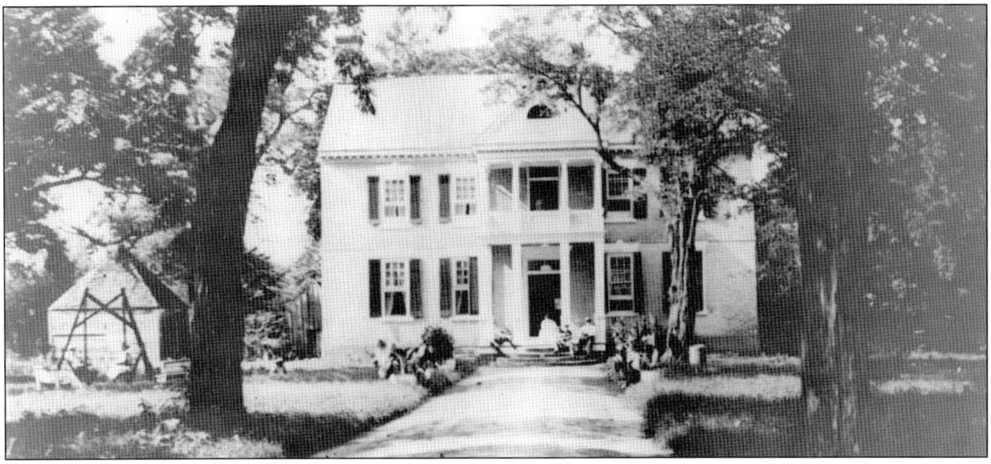

Lansdowne dates to about 1740. The most famous owner was Dr. Arthur Lee, a Revolutionary War patriot and diplomat. Dr. Lee purchased Lansdowne in 1791 and named it for his friend, the Earl of Landsdowne. Dr. Lee, along with Benjamin Franklin and Silas Deane, negotiated the Treaty of Alliance with France, which ultimately aided in the American victory and independence at Yorktown. He died in December 1792 in Urbanna and is buried in the cemetery behind Lansdowne. (Courtesy of the Town of Urbanna.)

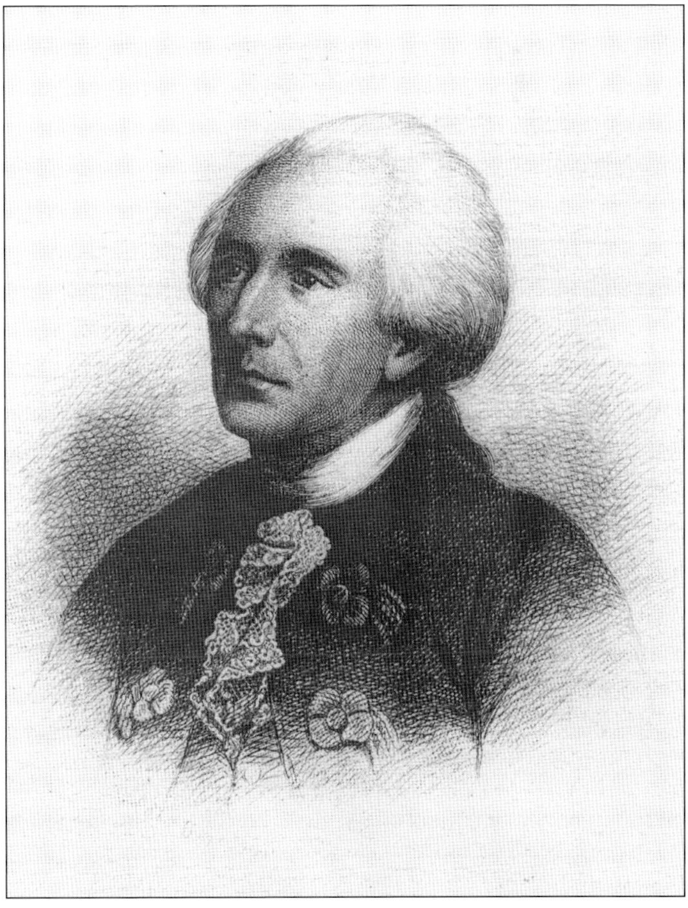

Arthur Lee is buried in Urbanna in an unmarked grave. His will is in the Middlesex County courthouse and states, "My wish is that . . . my remains be interred in the vault of my dear parents unless I should die at an inconvenient distance." His brother Richard Henry Lee, signer of the Declaration of Independence, offered the will to probate 12 days after his death, leading some to speculate that he arrived after his brother had already been buried. (Courtesy of Virginia Historical Society.)

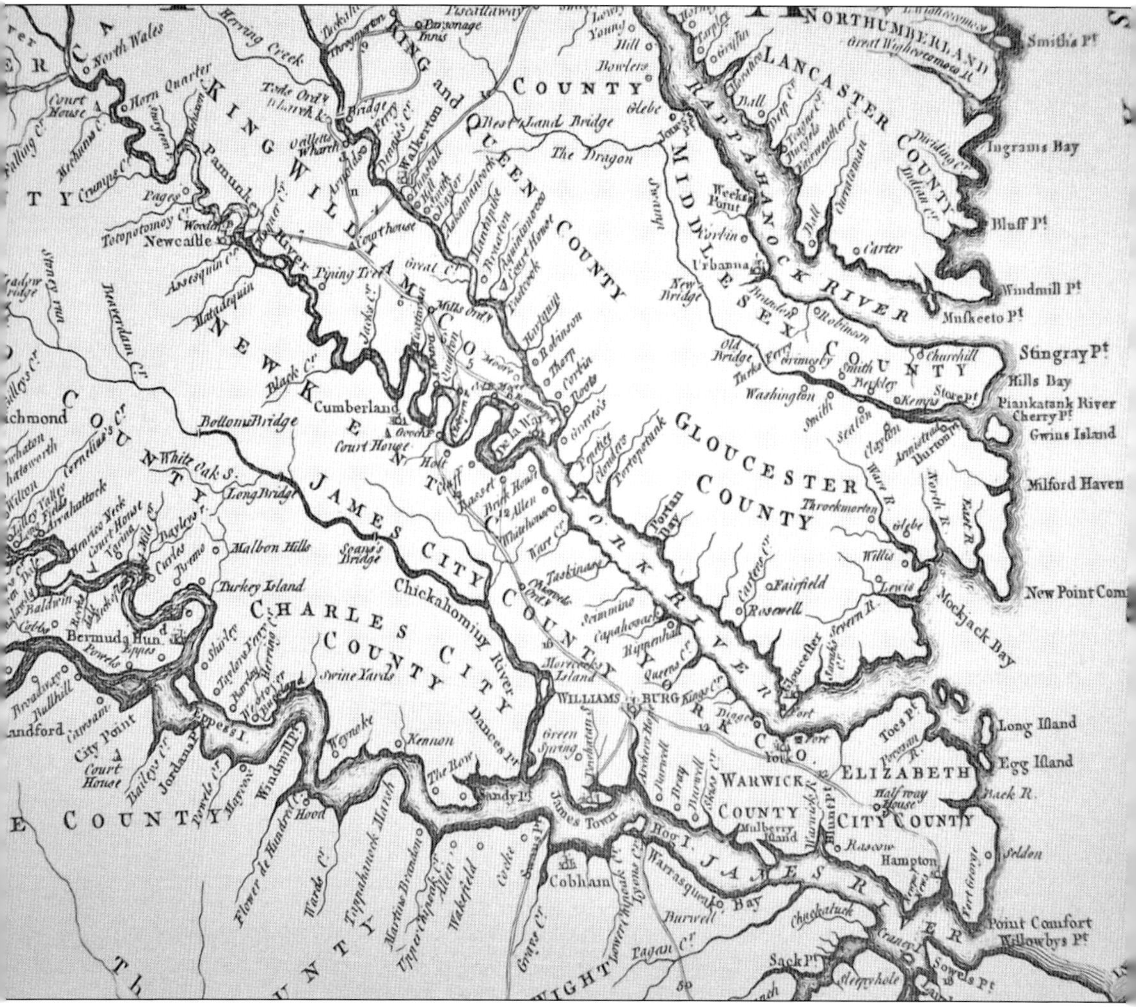

The Fry-Jefferson Map of Virginia, first published in 1751, was a definitive map used for travel and exploration of the state in the 18th and 19th centuries. Middlesex place names on the map, other than Urbanna, show that formations of towns and villages were still some years down the road. The named locations were of plantations identified by the last names of their owners. Kemps, Berkeley, Smith, Grymes, Corbin, Weeks, Robinson, and Churchill were all large landowners in Middlesex. The map shows that by the mid-1700s, two bridges crossed Dragon Run, one from Gloucester County, and another from King and Queen County into Middlesex. The colonial Turks Ferry was operating across the Piankatank River as it is shown on the map. (Courtesy of Virginia Historical Society.)

Two

Buildings and Structures

Middlesex County has a variety of styles and shapes of structures going all the way back to the beginning of the county. There are, however, few wooden buildings left from the 1600s. One of the oldest is Nesting in the western end of Middlesex. The land was patented by Richard Perrott on March 13, 1649. It is believed that the north wing of this two-story building was built between 1649 and 1655. Most likely, however, there are other old structures buried beneath the woodwork. A reason that so few, if any, 17th-century wooden structures survived was because homes and buildings were built using foundation wood pier construction. This involved using Dragon Run cypress and cedar blocks as foundation pieces instead of longer-lasting bricks. As brick construction and raised wooden floors took the place of wooden walls and dirt floors over the next centuries, buildings became more substantial and longer-lasting.

The county has wonderful examples of colonial plantation homes and sundry 18th-, 19th-, and 20th-century homes, outbuildings, school buildings, slave quarters, barns, and other types of structures reflective of lifestyles during the period they were built.

The Town of Urbanna was founded in 1680 as a port of call for regulating and transporting tobacco from the new world to England. The town has several 18th-century structures that rival those in Williamsburg. The village of Saluda was established in the late 1840s and has the 1852 county courthouse and other homes and buildings of that time.

Many old buildings and structures along the roads and highways of Middlesex give us insight into how the county grew and developed from a colonial tobacco culture through today.

Smokehouses, barns, log corncribs, antebellum school houses, late 19th and early-20th-century stores at crossroads, and abandoned oyster shucking houses and boatbuilding sheds along creek banks all reflect how Middlesex County folk traveled through time.

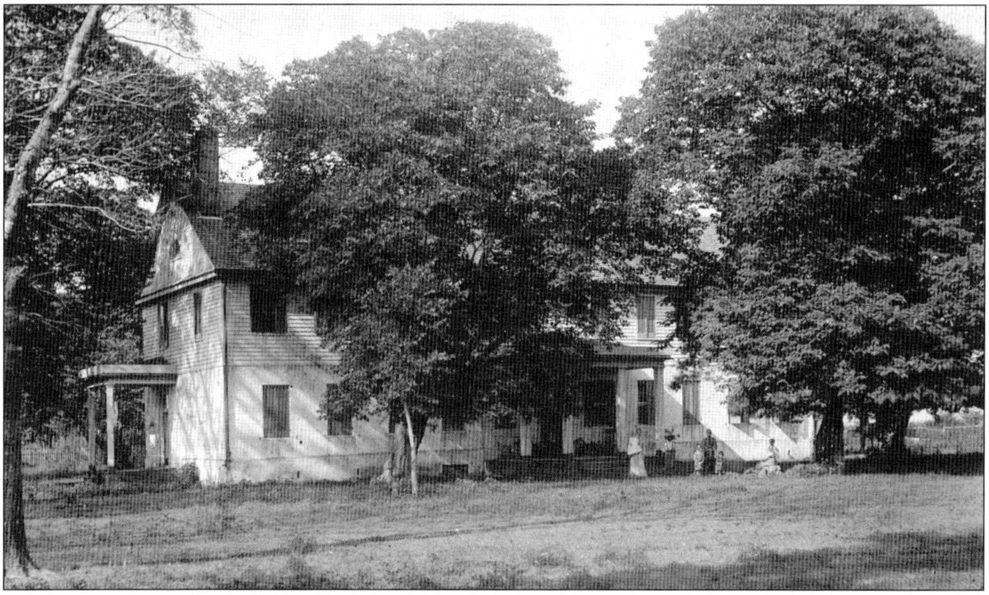

Although Ralph Wormeley IV and V were loyalists to the crown during the Revolutionary War, their home, Rosegill, was plundered by British privateers. During the Civil War, John Taylor Wood, a nephew of Confederate president Jefferson Davis, launched a series of daring naval raids, capturing, killing, and wounding Union soldiers and runaway slaves. Rosegill was transformed into a hospital to nurse Confederate and Union sailors and former slaves wounded in the conflict. (Courtesy of George Temple.)

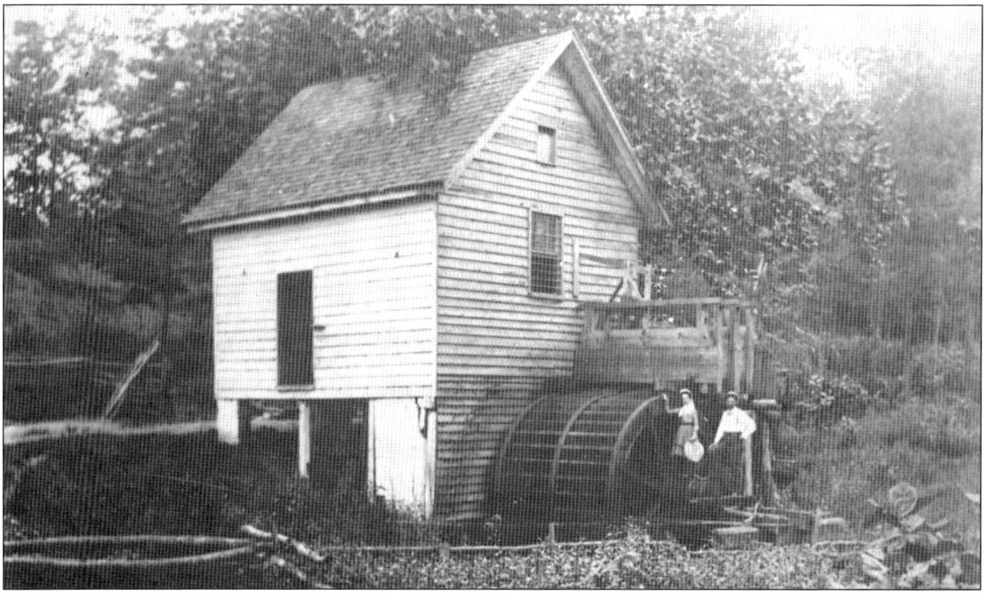

Conrad Mill near Hartfield was named for William Conrad, who purchased Woodport-on-the-Piankatank in 1868. There had been a gristmill on this site since colonial days. It had been named Kempts Mill after the family who owned it then. Middlesex had numerous gristmills up and down the county located on freshwater man-made ponds. Farmers brought wheat and corn to the mill and had it ground into meal or flour, minus a percentage called the "miller's toll," which amounted to wages for the miller. (Courtesy of Violene Jackson.)

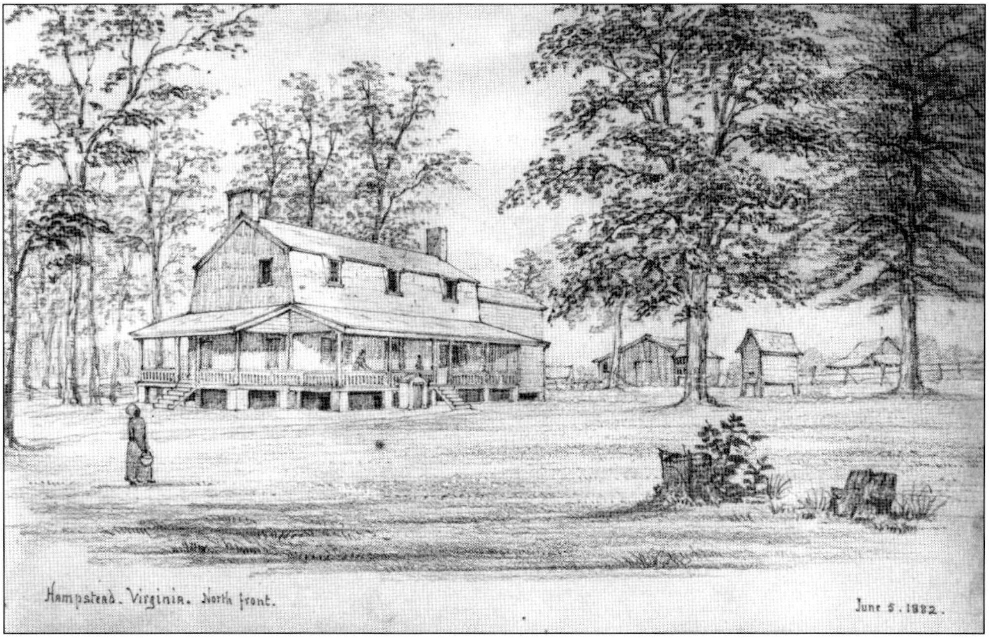

On June 5, 1882, artist George Monier Williams did several sketches of Hampstead Farm. At the time of the drawings, Hampstead was owned by G.T. Williams. It is assumed the artist was a relative. The outbuildings in his sketch reflect the agricultural lifestyle of that era. Hampstead was owned in 1750 by Capt. Henry Washington, a cousin of George Washington. A gristmill on the property was named Washington's Mill. (Courtesy of Virginia Historical Society.)

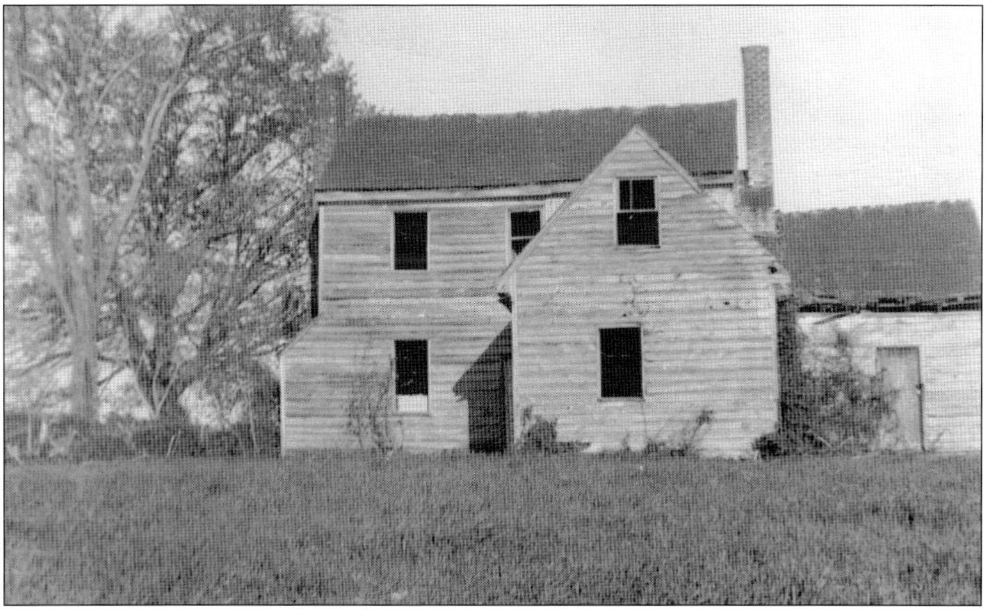

In 1695, George Wortham conveyed to the justices of Middlesex County a house to be used as a courthouse that had belonged to his late brother John. It is believed that this house near Stormont was the first public-owned courthouse building in the county. It was to remain the county courthouse until 1748, when the county seat was moved to Urbanna. The building burned sometime in the 1950s. (Courtesy of Webster Brooke.)

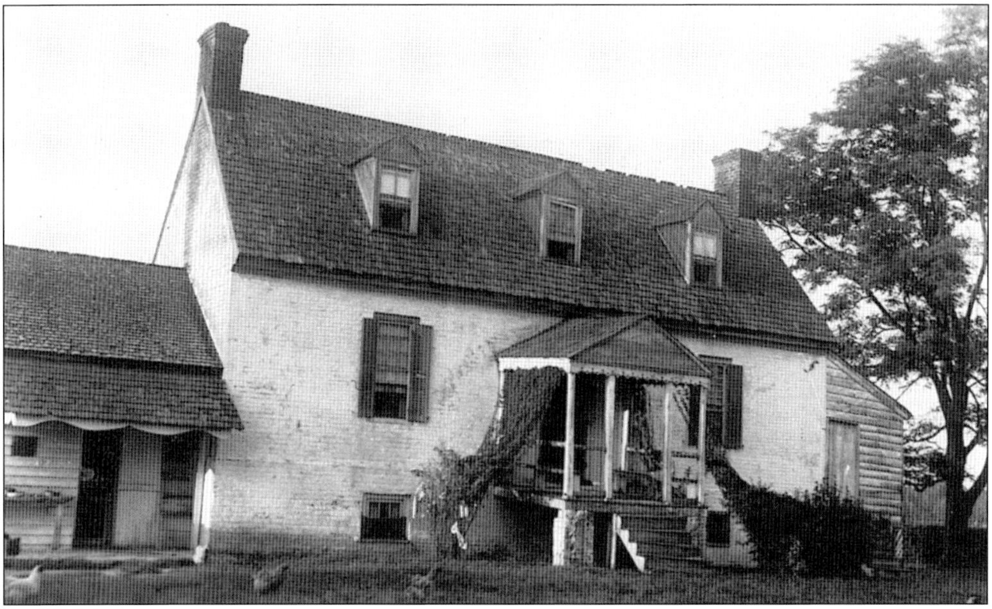

Although unclear when Providence was built, a brick bears the date 1760. Also etched in a window pane is "Dec. 1 1771—Hard and deep snow." Providence was raided during the Revolutionary and Civil Wars by British and Union troops. During a Union raid, two Confederate soldiers home on leave were executed at the front gate of Providence and buried in the Vaughan family cemetery. (C.C. Chowning collection.)

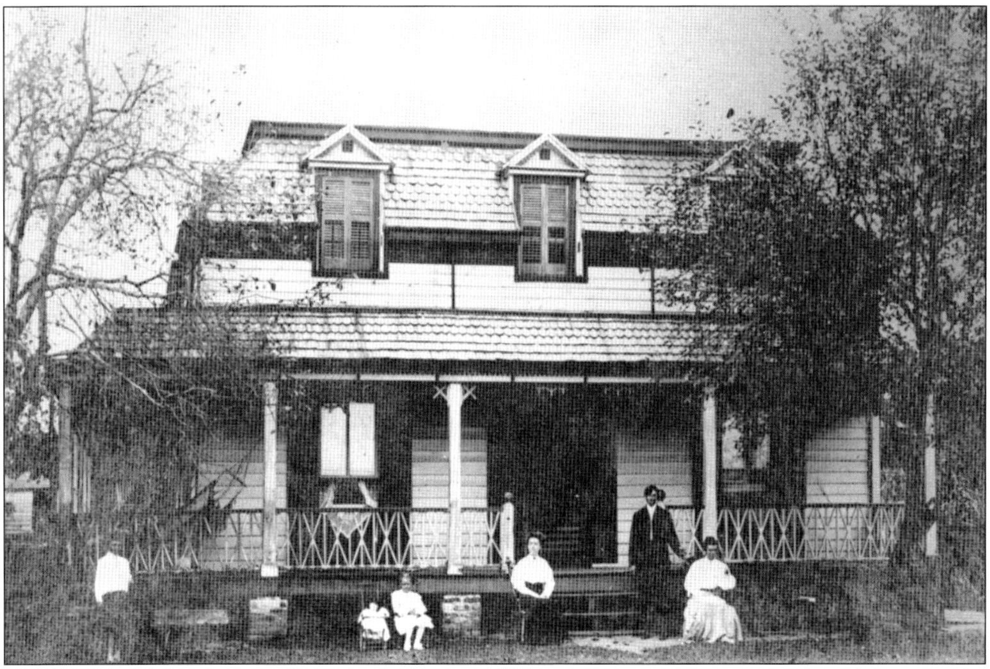

Turk's Ferry Farm was built as a home and tavern at Turk's Ferry on the Piankatank River. The ferry was established in 1664 and remained a ferry until a bridge was built there around 1910. In 1900, C.E. Nauman operated the ferry and charged 20¢ for a one-horse buggy, 25¢ for a two-horse buggy, 5¢ for each person in a vehicle, and 5¢ each for walkers. (Courtesy of Louise E. Feitig.)

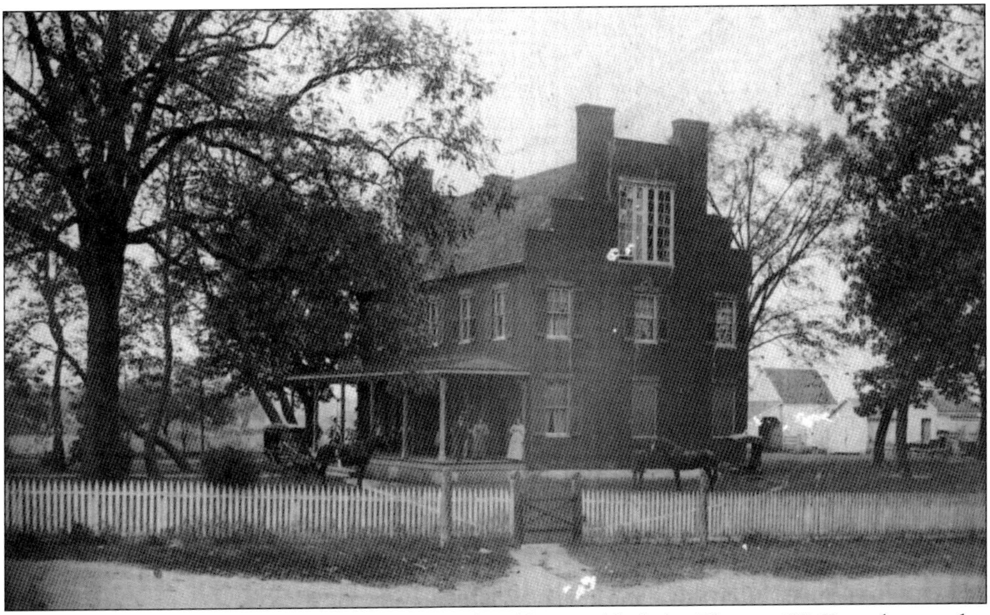

The three-story Saluda hotel was built around 1855, most likely by Thomas W. Fauntleroy, who was instrumental in establishing Saluda as the county seat of Middlesex County in 1852. The hotel reached its peak in the 1880s when its bar was a great attraction, as were the delicious meals served in the dining room. Croquet was a favorite outdoor sport, but the hotel's tennis court drew the largest number of spectators. (Courtesy of Jean Holman.)

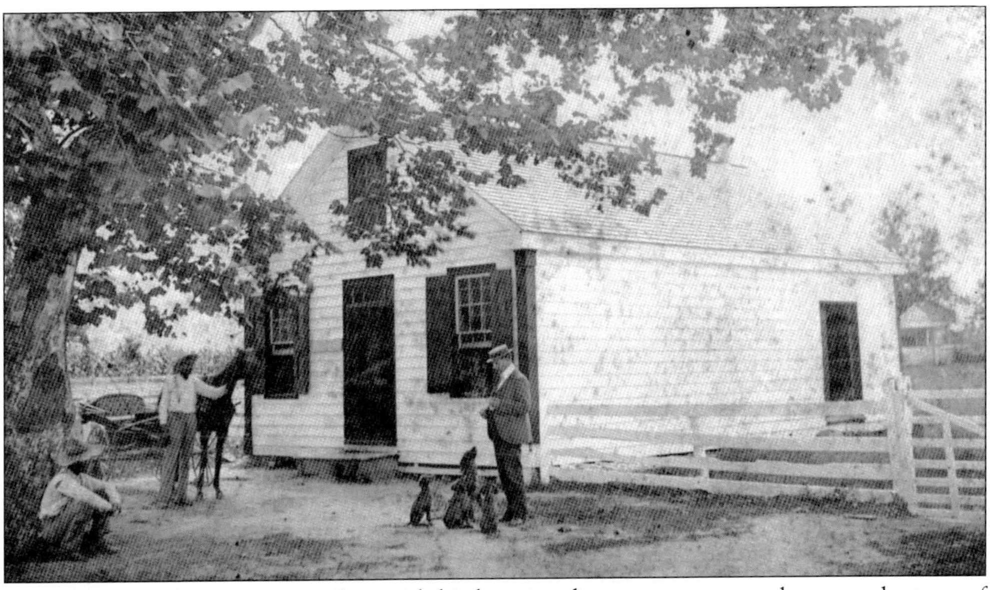

Dr. William R. Gwathmey, standing with his hunting dogs, was a country doctor at the turn of the 20th century at Ruark on Jackson Creek. His office building was located in the side yard of his home. The building is typical of the style built as an office in those days. However, many of Dr. Gwathmey's patients were served by house calls. He traveled to visit them by horse and buggy, automobile, and boat. (Courtesy of Caroline Gwathmey Jones.)

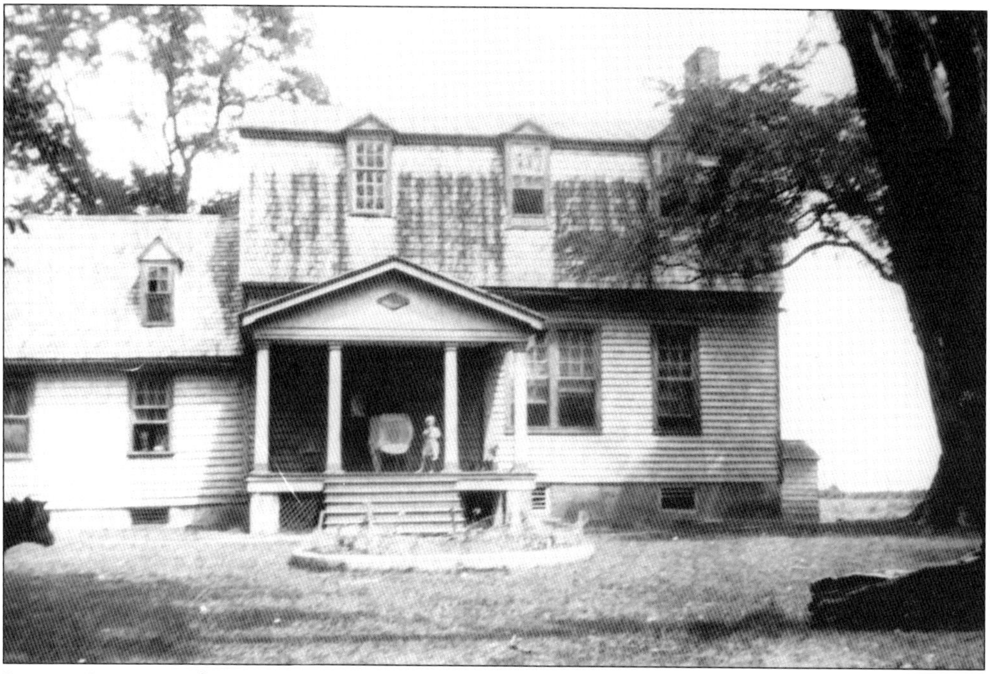

Locust Grove sits between Rappahannock River and Whitings Creek near Locust Hill and Topping. The 1751 Fry-Jefferson map of Virginia identified the area as "Robinson." Locust Grove was patented in 1690 by Capt. Christopher Robinson of Hewick and is one of the oldest wood-frame structures still standing in Middlesex. (Courtesy of Louise Gray.)

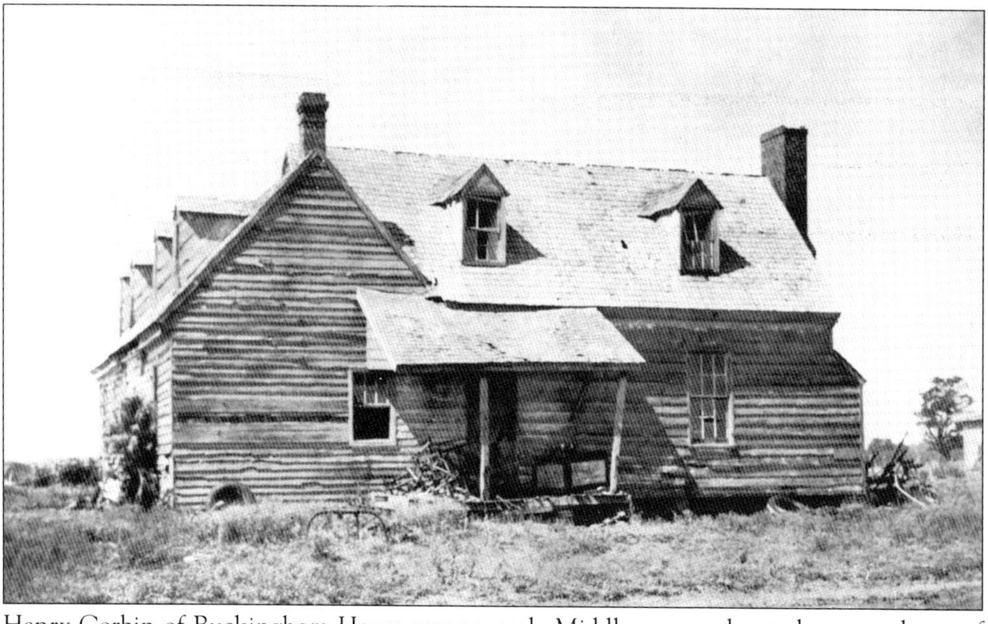

Henry Corbin of Buckingham House was an early Middlesex merchant-planter and one of the wealthiest men in Virginia. During the English Civil War, Corbin fought as a Cavalier in support of King Charles I. He was a 12-year member of the Council of Virginia and served in the House of Burgesses. One of his many plantations was Corbin Hall, just east across the road from Buckingham in Middlesex. (Courtesy of Lewis Wilkins.)

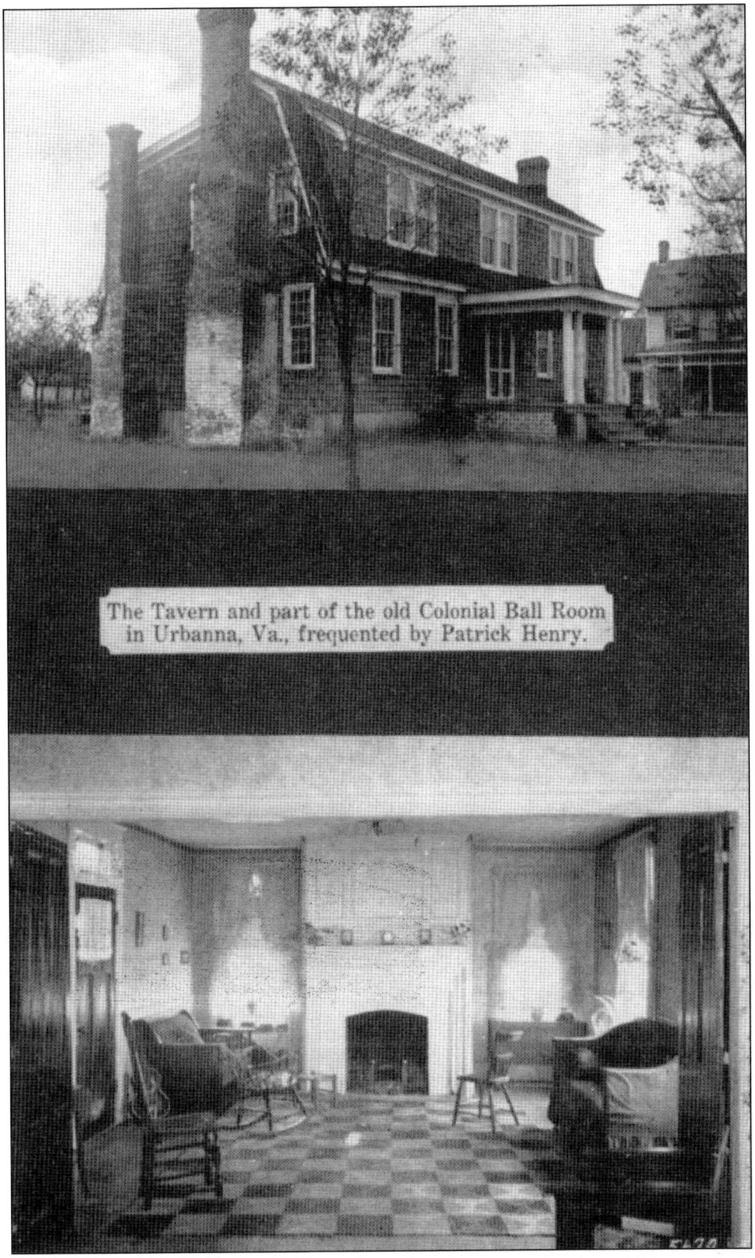

The Colonial tavern, or "ordinary," served as a boardinghouse and pub in Urbanna when the town was the county seat of Middlesex County. The tavern also was a place for dancing, fiddling, and drink, or "tipple." George Chowning and Benjamin Rhoads obtained a business license in 1765 to operate the tavern. The county court ordered that they provide "wholesome and cleanly Lodging and Diet for Travellers and Stableage, Fodder and Provender as the Seasons shall require for their horse. Also, "unlawful Gaming in the House . . . nor on the Sabbath Day suffer any person to tipple . . . any more than necessary" was not allowed. The county court set prices for beverages served there. In 1770, tavern keepers served Canary wine, Malaga, sherry, Madeira wine, claret, Rhenish, Fyall wine, Nants, French brandy, arrack, Caribbean rum, Virginia brandy, beer, and apple cider. (Courtesy of Middlesex County Public Library.)

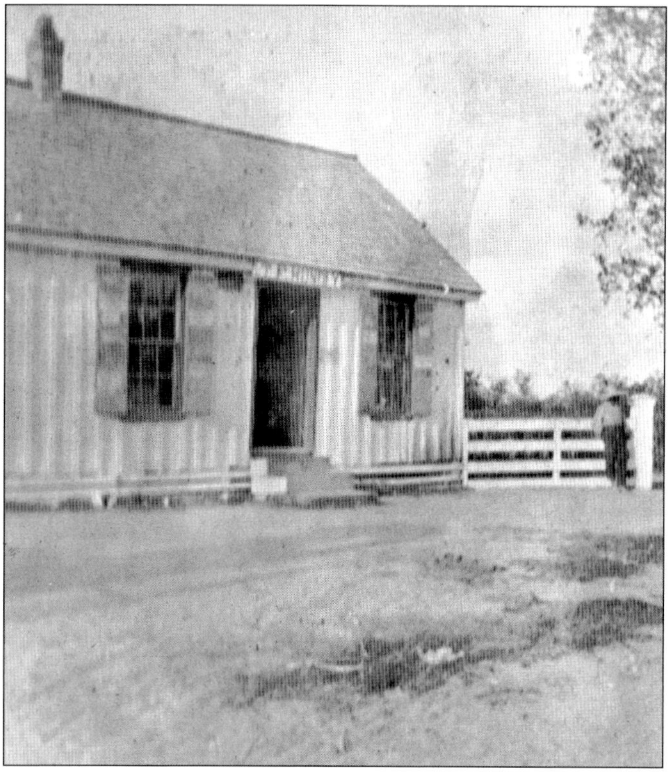

Library of Congress records state that Thomas F. Hundly was postmaster of Ambrug Post Office from June 1893 to March 1914. This photograph of his store and post office was taken sometime during that period. Amburg Post Office was established in March 1891. Matthew Glenn was the first postmaster. Early post offices were located in country stores. Merchants wanted a post office in their stores to encourage people to come in regularly. (Courtesy of Nola Watson.)

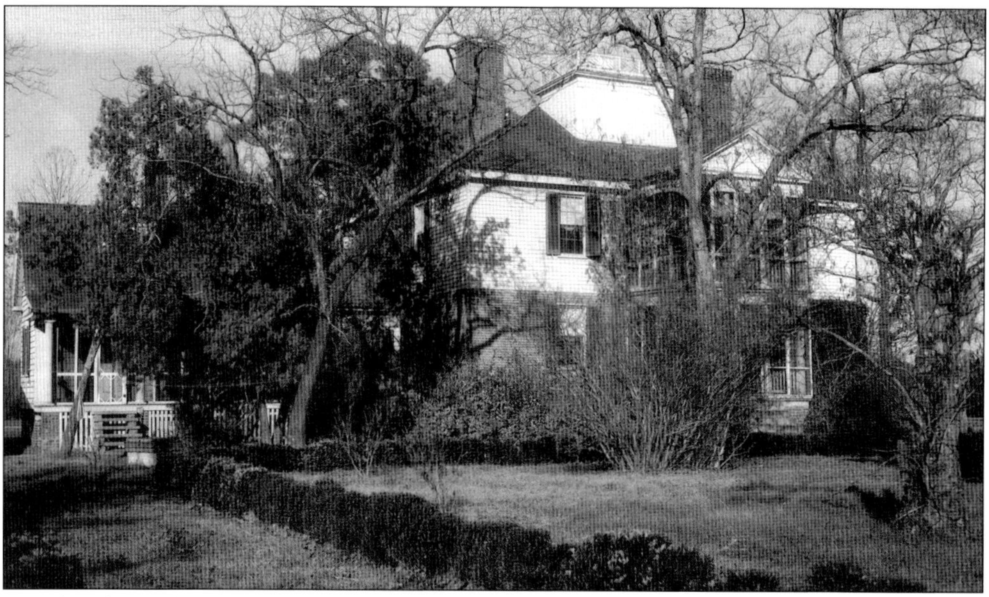

Woodstock on the Piankatank was built by Robert Healy in 1840. It was later owned by Jessie Lincoln Randolph, daughter of Robert Todd Lincoln, son of President Abraham Lincoln and Mary Todd Lincoln. While the Lincolns owned it, interior floors from three rooms were removed and used in developing the Lincoln Museum in Springfield, Illinois. The Lincoln family owned Woodstock until Robert Todd Lincoln Beckwith, great-grandson of Lincoln, died in 1985 in Saluda. (C.C. Chowning collection.)

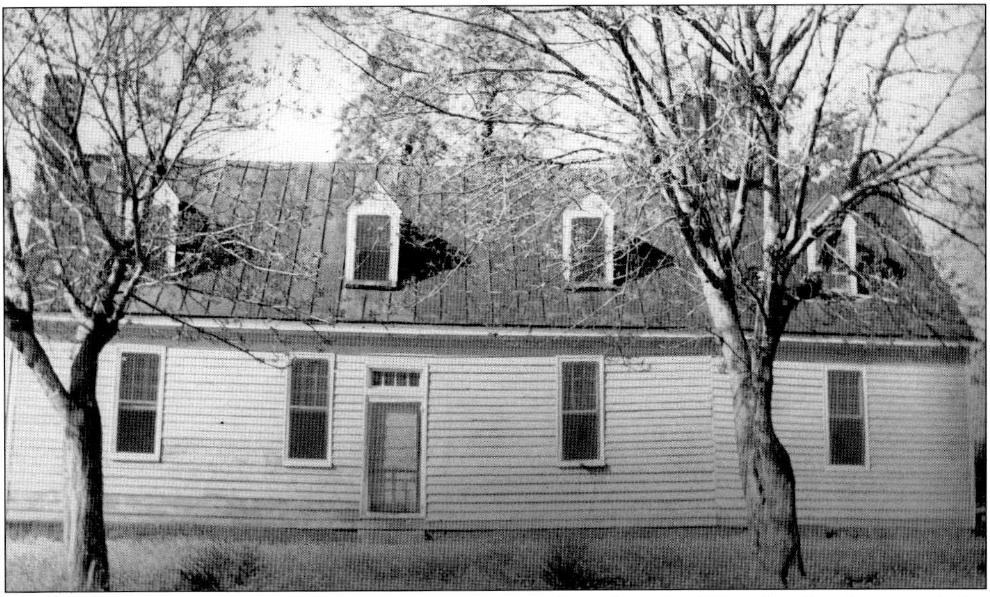

Piankatank was tied to the grand plantation Rosegill in that the Womeley family owned the property almost as long as they owned Rosegill. The property is on the dividing line of Piankatank River and Dragon Run. It is believed this structure was built between 1831 and 1834 by then-owner Thomas Woodward. (C.C. Chowning collection.)

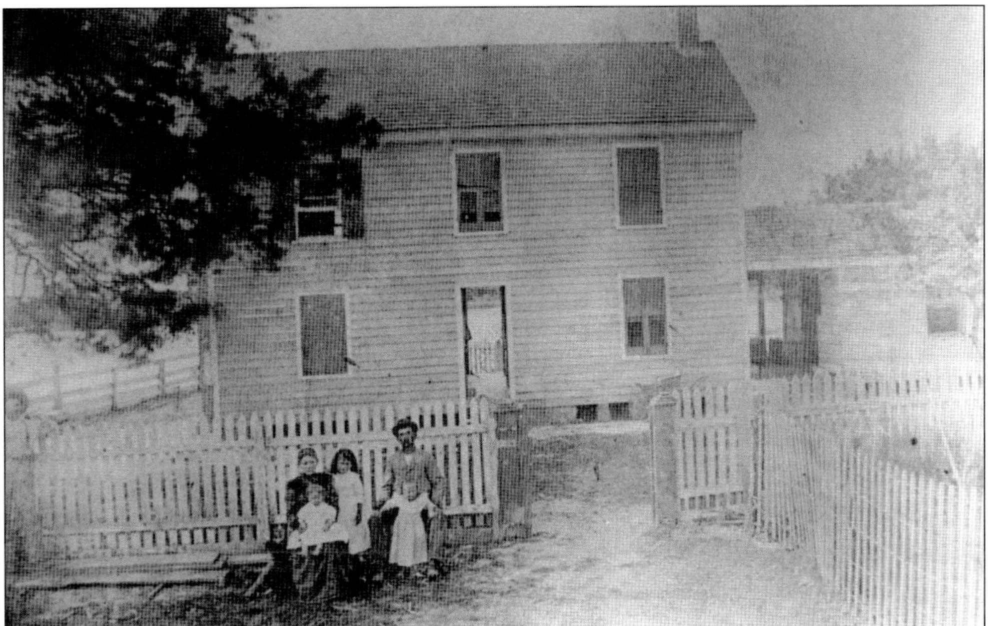

William Hervey Norton and his wife, Olivia Jane (Ailsworth) Norton, are shown here with three of their 12 children. The Nortons bought their home in Deltaville in the early 1890s with money made by oystering. This was a typical home of the times, with the kitchen attached by a dogtrot to the main house. Many Middlesex folk lost fathers in the Civil War. Hervey lost his at the Second Battle of Cold Harbor. (Courtesy of Randolph Norton.)

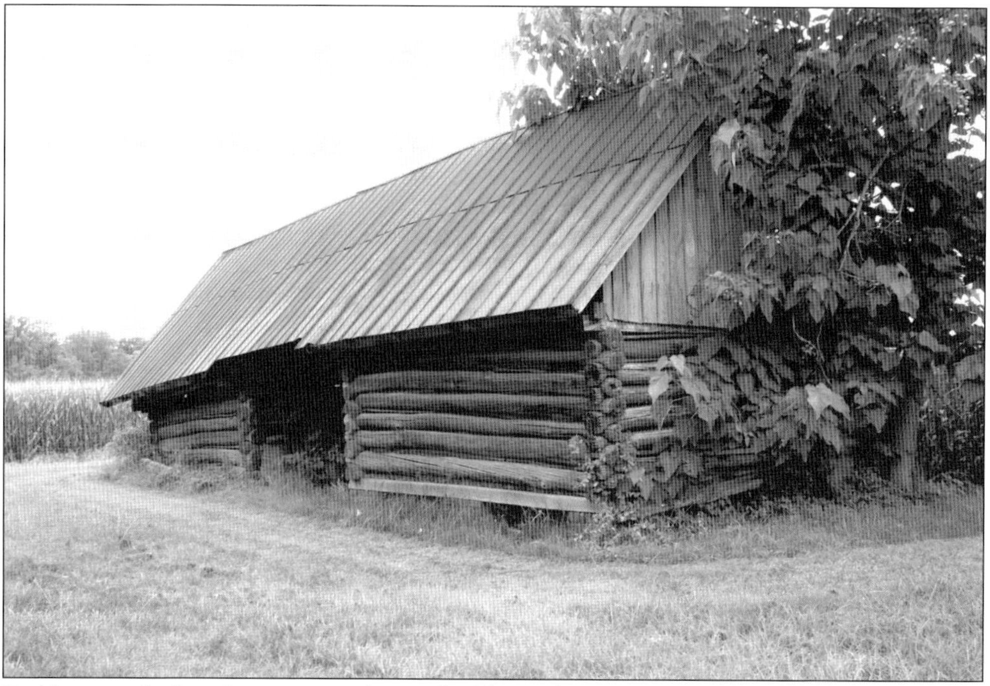

Buildings made from logs were used as outbuildings, slave quarters, and in this case, a corncrib for the storage of corn and fodder to feed livestock at Plaln View Farm near Saluda. The 1840s antebellum farmhouse and most of its outbuildings have been taken down. Although no longer there, this log corncrib was still standing into the early 2000s. (Author's collection.)

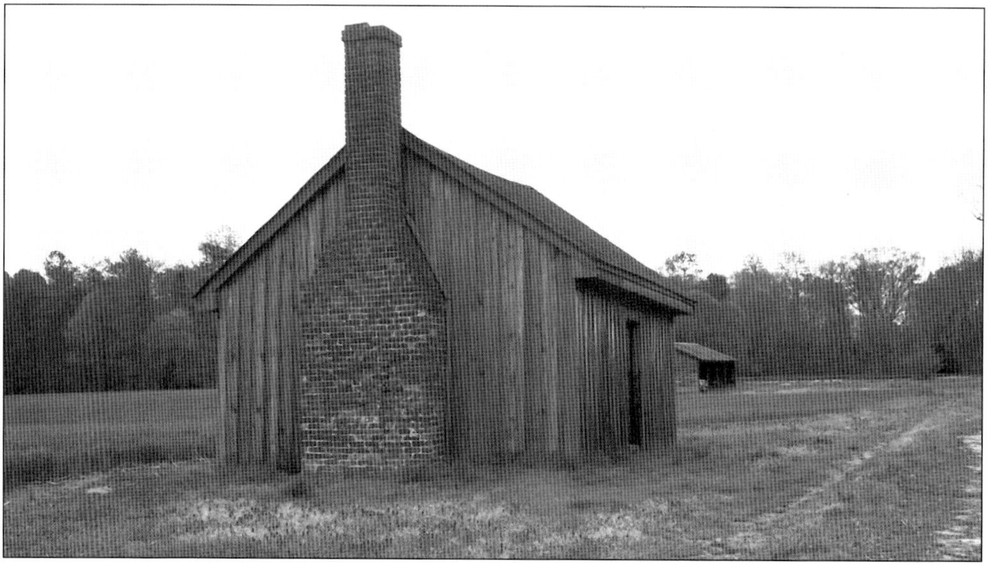

This slave house at Walboro near Saluda is one of the last standing from the days of slavery. The county's colonial tobacco economy necessitated a large slave population. Generations of African Americans lived here as slaves until freedom finally came April 9, 1865, with the surrender of Gen. Robert E. Lee at Appomattox. Although President Lincoln officially freed Middlesex slaves with his Emancipation Proclamation on January 1, 1863, slavery did not end until the war ended. (Author's collection.)

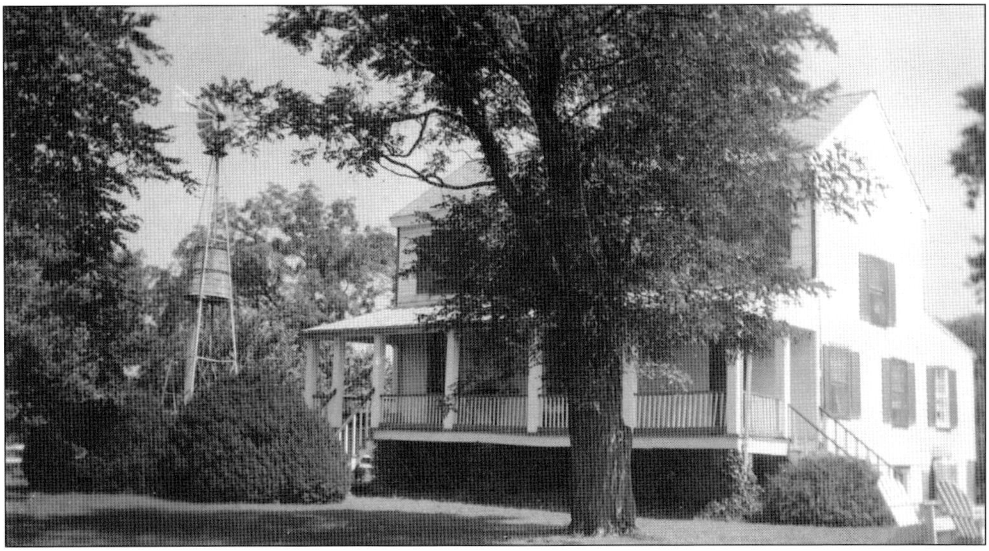

Providence near Water View was home for many generations of the McKann family. The house was built by Robert Henry McKann about 1856. The McKann family, however, goes back much further than that in Middlesex, as McKann Bay at the far western end of the county on the Rappahannock was named for them. Windmills were scattered up and down the county and used to provide running water inside the home. (Courtesy of Sue McKann Brown.)

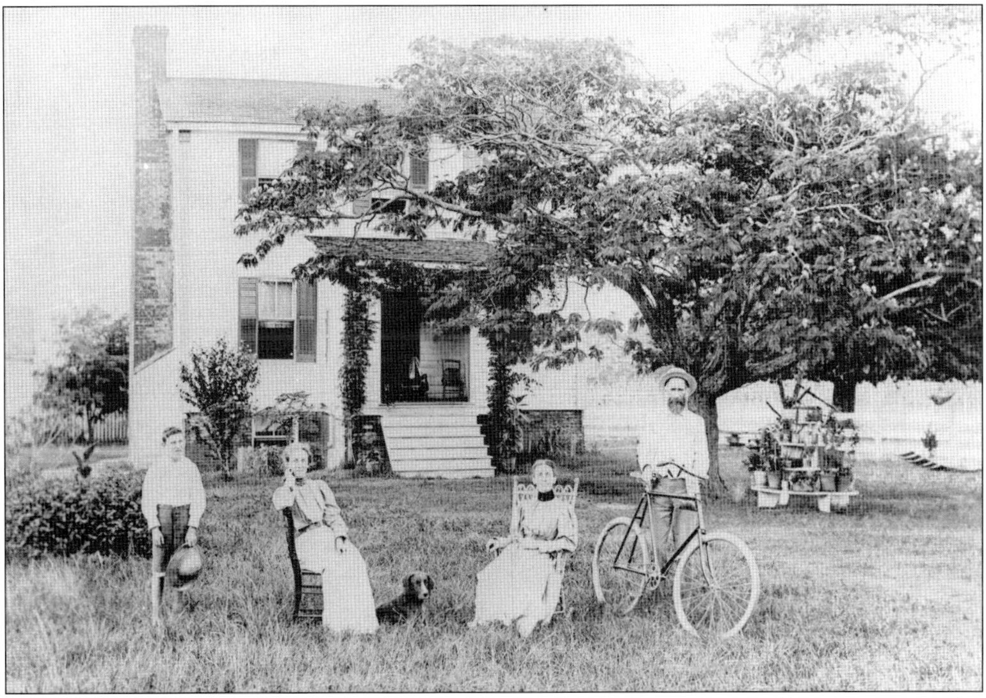

New Market was home of the Jackson family, some of whom are pictured here; some are the namesake of Jackson Creek in Deltaville. James H. Jackson is believed to have built New Market right after the Civil War. He ran a general merchandise store on the corner lot of the home. New Market was later owned by M.A. "Moat" Jackson, who ran a store and post office named Enoch on Jackson Creek steamboat wharf. (Courtesy of Jerome Jackson.)

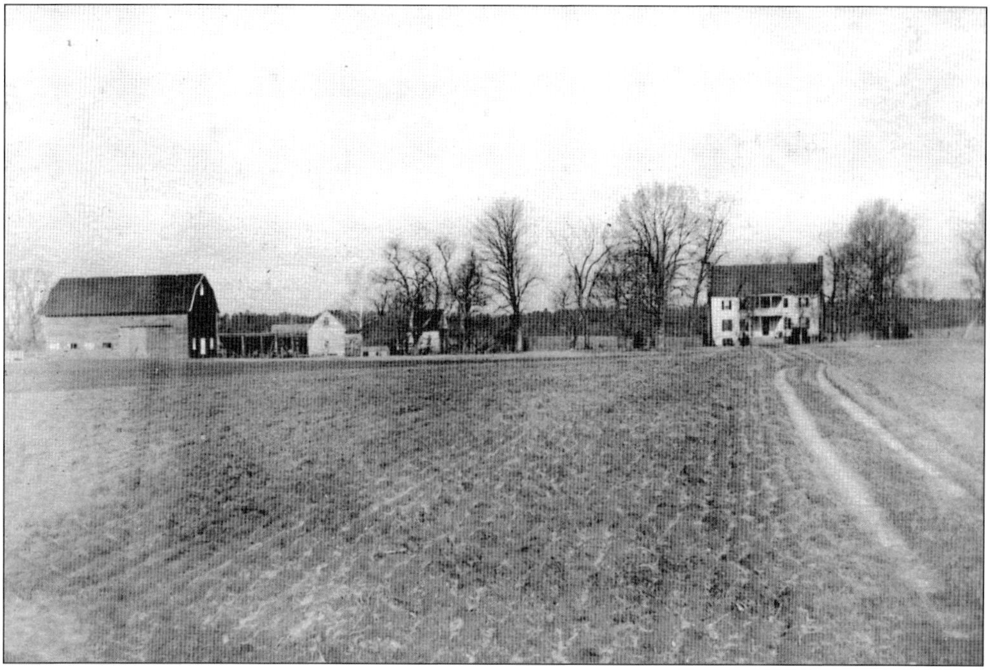

Oakenham was built by Thomas Waring Fauntleroy in 1837. Fauntleroy offered to donate land to Middlesex County in 1849 for a new courthouse. He encouraged that the county seat be moved from Urbanna to Saluda. In 1852, when the courthouse was nearly complete, he laid out the village and named it Saluda, which means "healthful." The name was suggested to him by relatives who lived on the Saluda River in South Carolina. (Courtesy of Middlesex County Museum.)

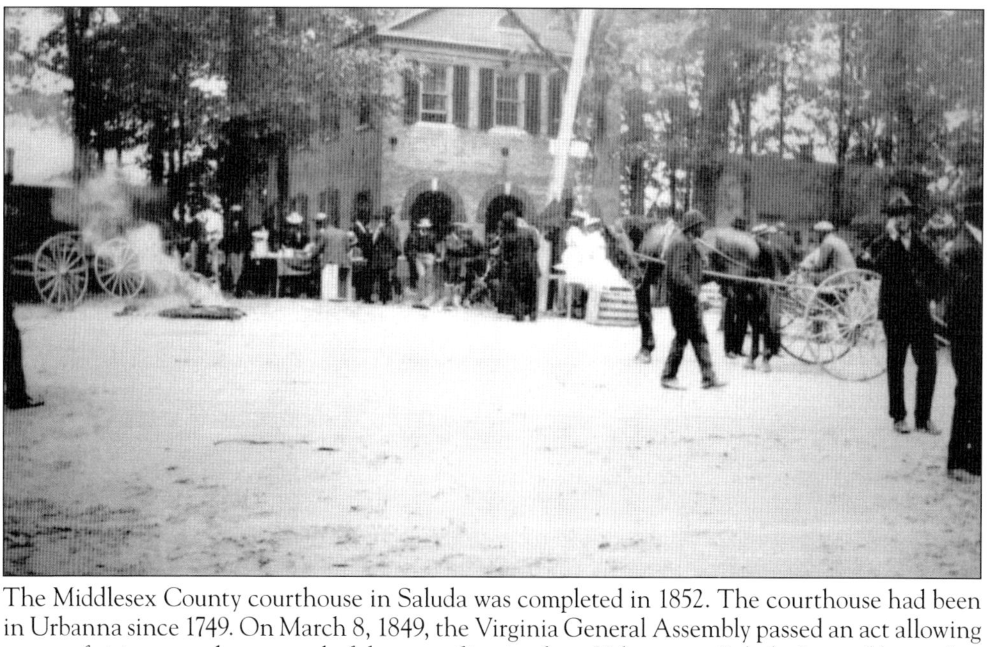

The Middlesex County courthouse in Saluda was completed in 1852. The courthouse had been in Urbanna since 1749. On March 8, 1849, the Virginia General Assembly passed an act allowing a vote of citizens on the removal of the seat of justice from Urbanna to Saluda. Legend has it that the deciding vote was cast by a bitter opponent of the Urbanna location who had to be brought in on a stretcher to cast his vote. (Courtesy of William C. Hight.)

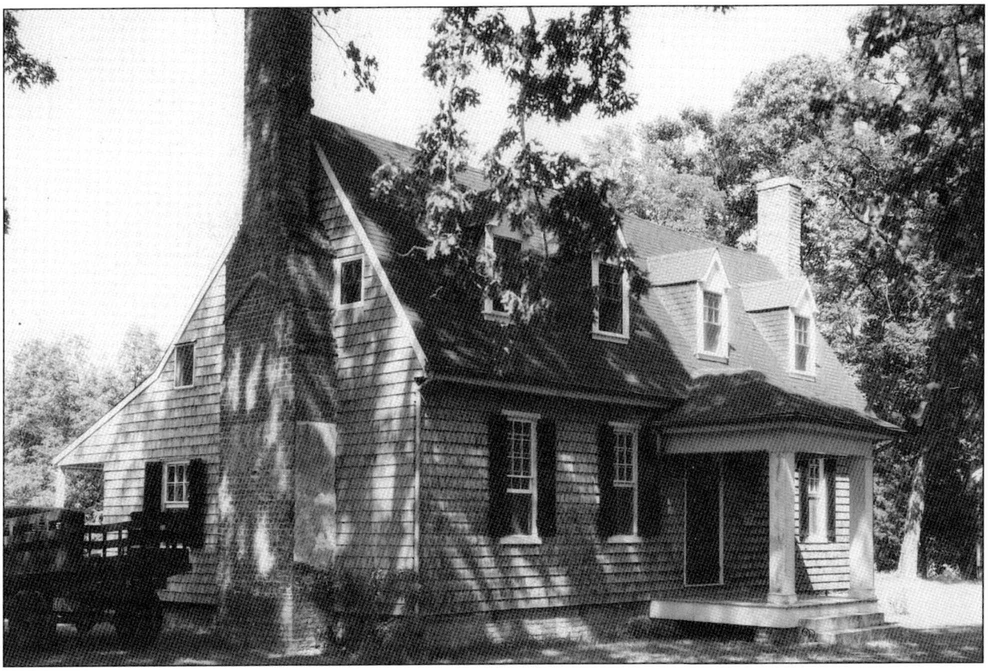

Beechwood near Warner was built between 1841 and 1843 by Walter Healy for his son Elliott Muse Healy. Elliott was a graduate of Columbia College and studied law at the University of Virginia. He was a practicing attorney in Middlesex when the Civil War broke out. He was killed in 1862 at the Second Battle of Bull Run. Walter was a large landowner who owned and lived at the Eminence near Pine Tree and owned Cedar Park Farm near Urbanna. (C.C. Chowning collection.)

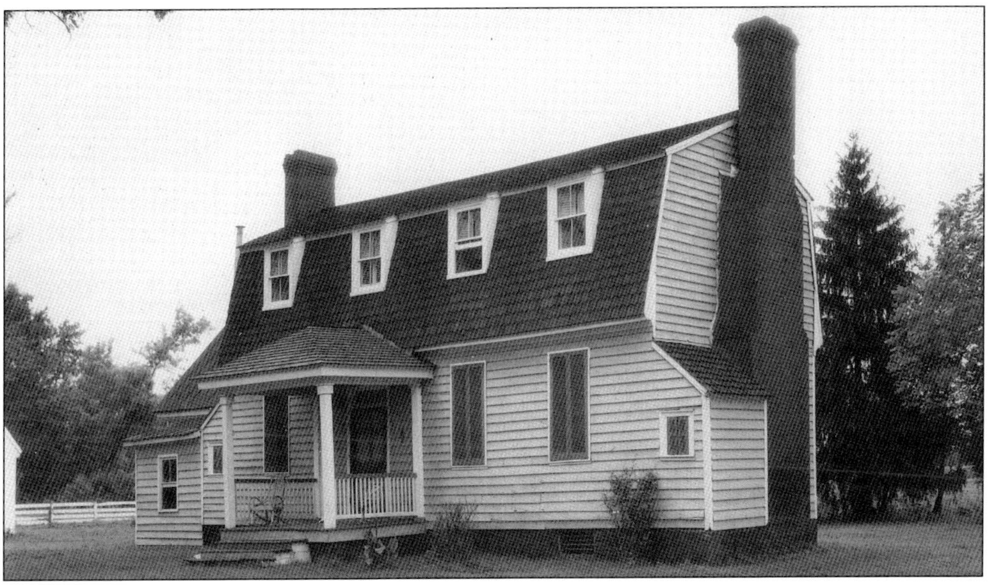

Cedar Park Plantation was built by James Ross in 1810. Portions of the property had once been owned by Richard Henry Lee and his brother Francis Lightfoot Lee, two signers of the Declaration of Independence. At his death in 1825, James Ross freed five of his slaves and, in an unprecedented move for the times, left the plantation and all his land holdings to descendants of his "mulatto" slave, Mary Woodford. (C.C. Chowning collection.)

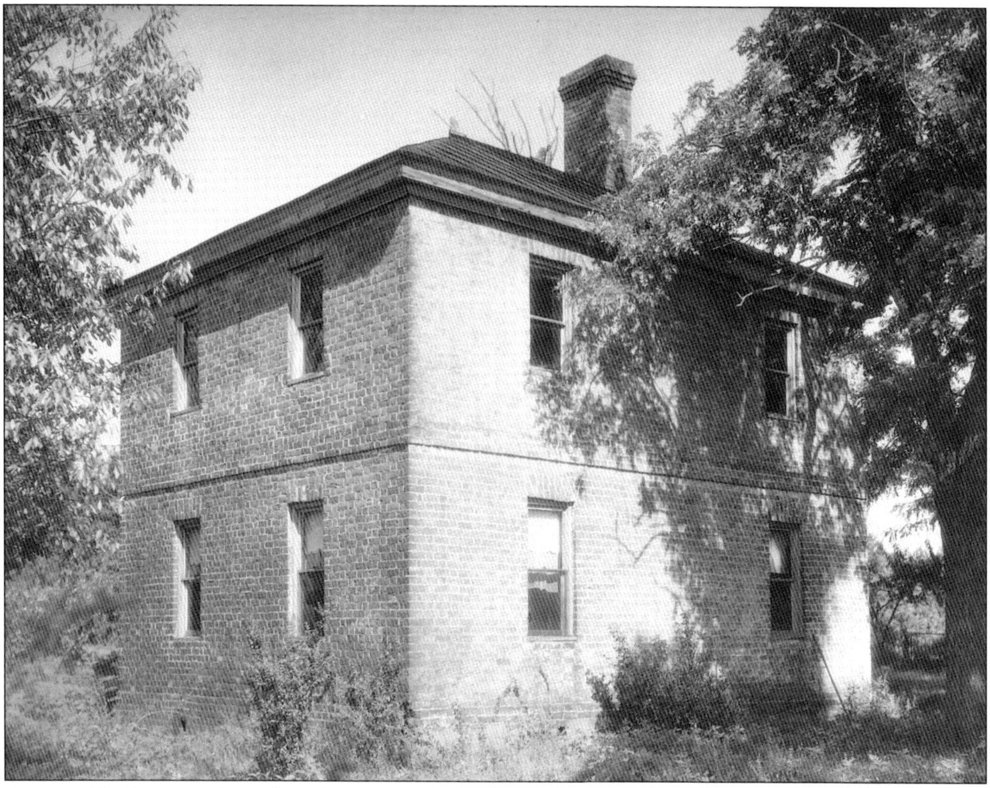

Francis Corbin purchased Gales in 1790. Corbin was elected in 1788 as Middlesex County's delegate to Virginia's Constitutional Convention. Befriended by James Madison, he supported Madison's belief in a national constitution. At the convention, Corbin debated Patrick Henry, who was opposed. On the floor, the famed orator made Corbin look a fool. Corbin, however, got the last laugh, as the assembly narrowly voted to ratify. (C.C. Chowning collection.)

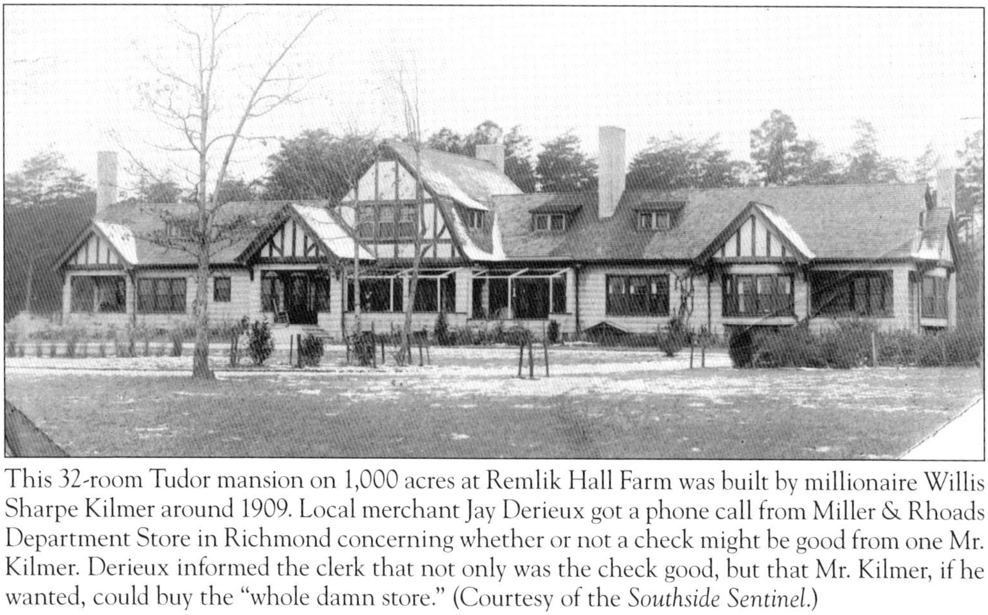

This 32-room Tudor mansion on 1,000 acres at Remlik Hall Farm was built by millionaire Willis Sharpe Kilmer around 1909. Local merchant Jay Derieux got a phone call from Miller & Rhoads Department Store in Richmond concerning whether or not a check might be good from one Mr. Kilmer. Derieux informed the clerk that not only was the check good, but that Mr. Kilmer, if he wanted, could buy the "whole damn store." (Courtesy of the *Southside Sentinel.*)

Three

Sailboats, Motorboats, and Boatbuilding

The county's proximity to the Chesapeake Bay, Rappahannock and Piankatank Rivers, and Dragon Run made it a prime area for the rise of a wooden boatbuilding culture. As neighborhoods developed along the rivers, creeks, and coves, commercial entities such as blacksmith shops, country stores, and woodworking shops sprang up throughout the county. Local smithies and woodworkers were closely tied to the agriculture and seafood commerce in the county.

The woodworkers made wooden shafts for oyster hand tongs, sculling paddles, masts for sailboats, wooden handles for scythes and plows, and oxen and cattle yokes. They also repaired and built small craft and larger boats shaped out of logs. Prior to the arrival of the English, Native Americans burned and hand-dug logs with sharp rocks and shells to shape canoes. When the first settlers came in 1642 from across the Piankatank, they came in small craft looking for land not yet patented. They crossed the river in Indian log boats and other small boats brought from England or built by area boatwrights. Colonial records state that in 1625, there were 25 English built small craft in Virginia; within a quarter of a century, there were hundreds of pinnaces, barks, and many other types of large and small boats. It was clear from the start that boatbuilding, and the maintenance of boats, was going to be of commercial value in Middlesex.

With the development of the oyster fisheries in the late 1700s and early 1800s, a strong, sturdy, fast sailing vessel was needed, and Chesapeake Bay log canoes met that challenge. Early county boatbuilders regularly built log canoes out of three and five logs attached together with trunnels made of locust wood and used as a platform in the gritty, hardworking oyster fishery.

As local forests became more and more depleted of good boatbuilding lumber, the secluded and forbidding Dragon Run Swamp continued to provide cypress, white oak, and spruce pine for building boats well into the 20th century. As the boatbuilding industry began the switch from logs to planks in the 1880s, Middlesex boatbuilders became pioneers in the development of the classic deadrise and cross-planked bottom style of boats. This led to an East Coast–wide demand for vessels built by Middlesex boatbuilders and eventually led to the noted "Deltaville Deadrise," a style of vessel built in Deltaville that was known far and wide. The wooden deadrise style reached its pinnacle on March 25, 1988, when Virginia's legislature named the deadrise vessel the official boat of the State of Virginia.

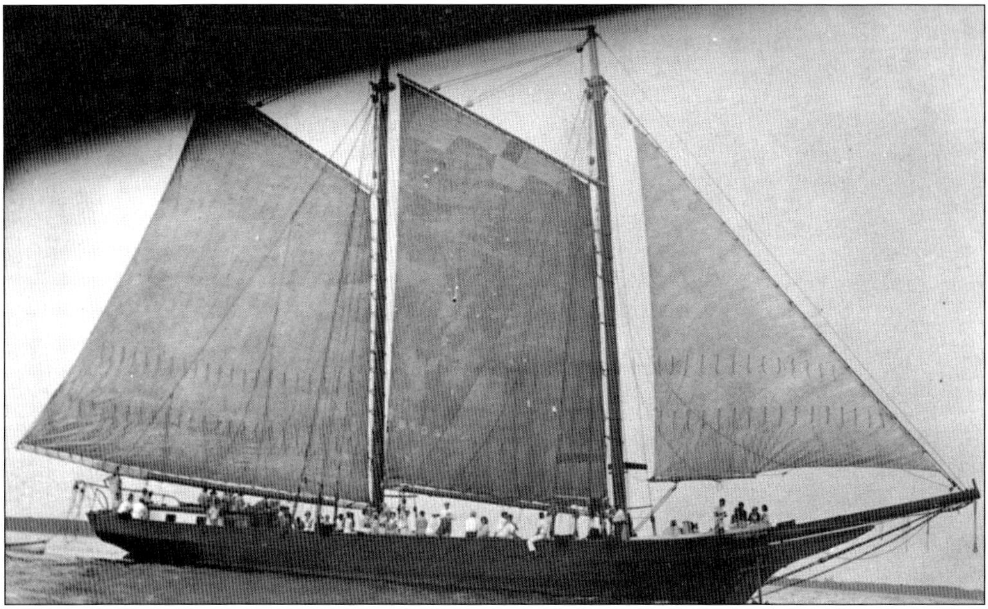

Urbanna Creek was home port to the two-masted schooner *Kate S. Tighlman*. She was owned by Saluda sea captain R.O. Smith Sr. After World War II, with the decline of the schooner era and rise of overland trucking, the vessel was left to die off Rosegill shore. This photograph was most likely taken on a Sunday summertime cruise, perhaps a church or masonic group, or a friends or family outing. (Dr. A.L. VanName collection.)

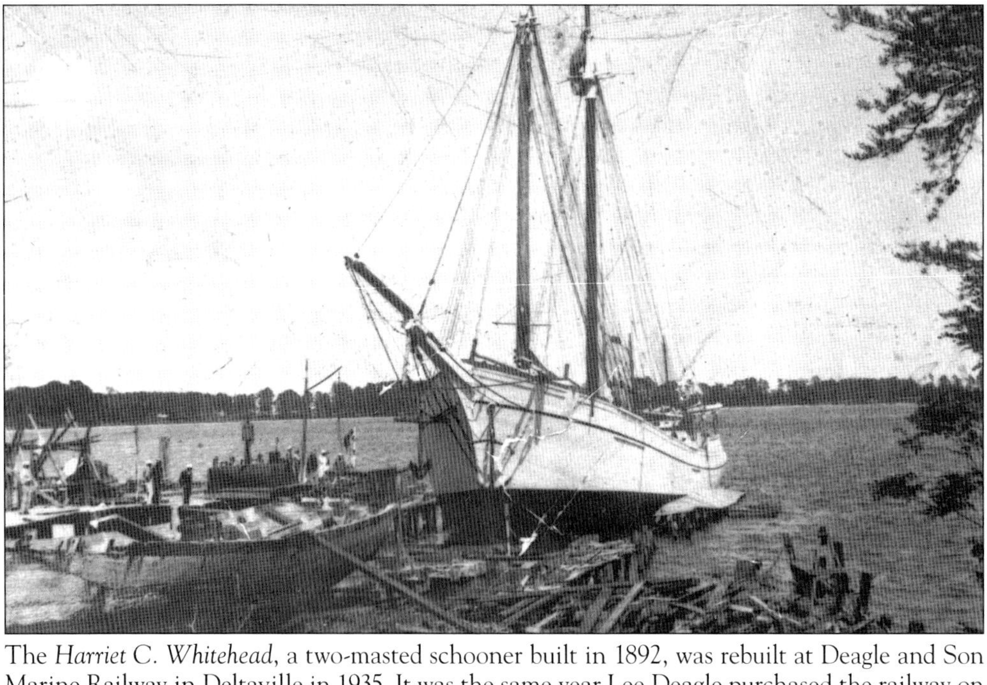

The *Harriet C. Whitehead*, a two-masted schooner built in 1892, was rebuilt at Deagle and Son Marine Railway in Deltaville in 1935. It was the same year Lee Deagle purchased the railway on Fishing Bay. The restoration of the *Whitehead* was Deagle's first job after taking over, and funds from that job led to many others. Lee and his son Ed became well known for having the ability to convert Chesapeake Bay sailing craft to powerboats. (Dr. A.L. VanName Jr. collection.)

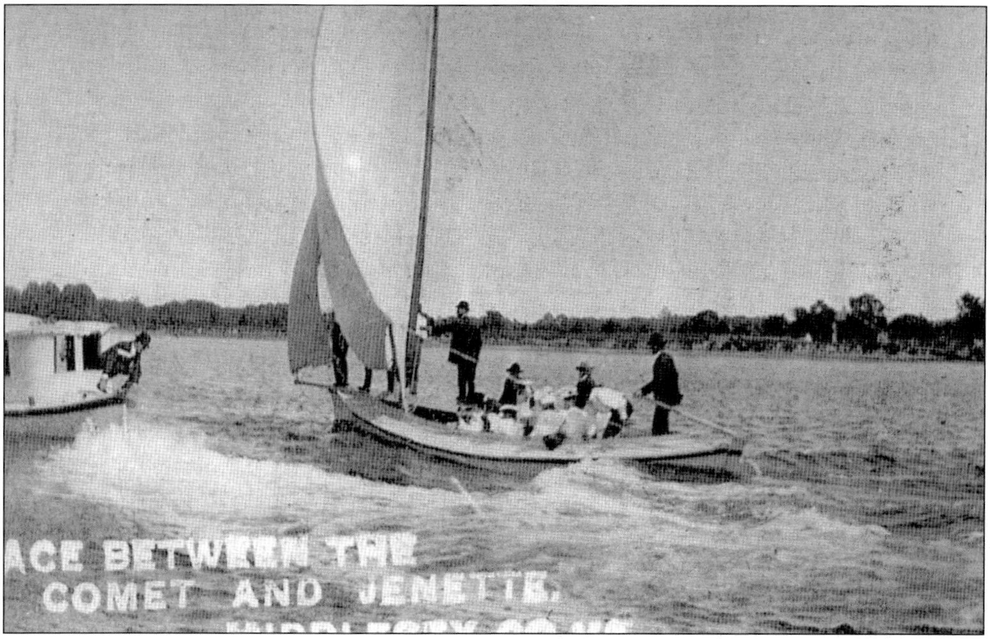

The first gasoline engines came along in the 1880s and were soon being installed in boats. The first engines lacked horsepower, and on days when there was a good breeze, sailboats could hold their own in a race with them. However, the advantage of being able to go from point A to point B with no wind encouraged many boat owners to switch from sail to motor power. (Courtesy of Deltaville Maritime Museum.)

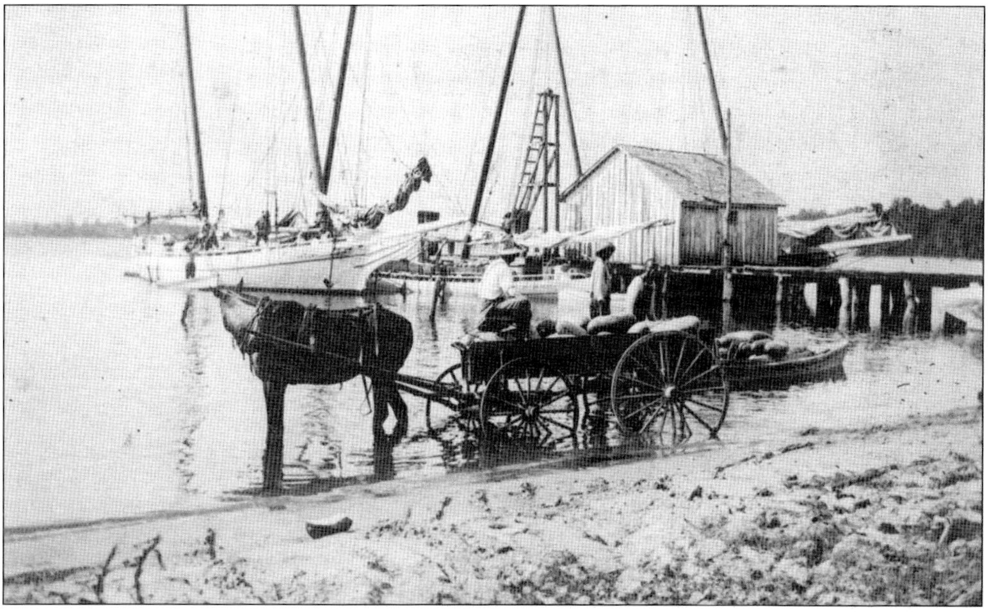

Watermelons were brought to river and creek landings in horse and wagon and loaded onto awaiting sailing schooners. This was a typical scene at Conrad's Steamboat Landing during melon harvest. Sailing vessels were used to haul the watermelons to docks in Washington, DC, and Baltimore, where melons were sold individually to customers coming down to the docks. (Courtesy of Nola Watson.)

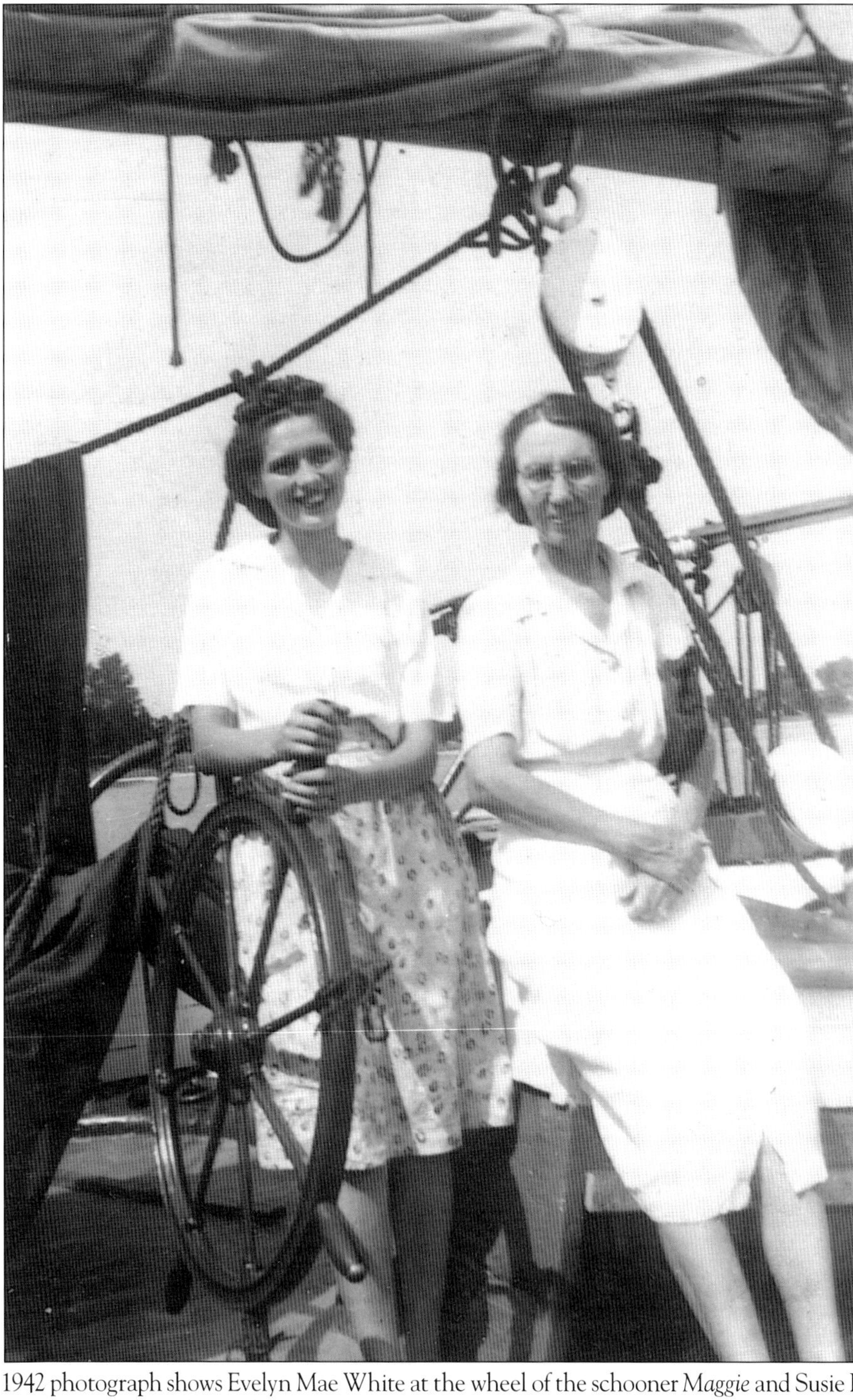

This 1942 photograph shows Evelyn Mae White at the wheel of the schooner *Maggie* and Susie Ruark Evelyn's soon to be mother-in-law. In a few years, Evelyn Mae married Susie's son Talmadge, and throughout their lives, they lived right beside the Ruark home on Jackson Creek. The women often sailed and cooked aboard the *Maggie* and *Columbia F.C.* The Ruark family owned and captained the last commercial sailing freight vessel in Middlesex. (Courtesy of Charles A. Ruark.)

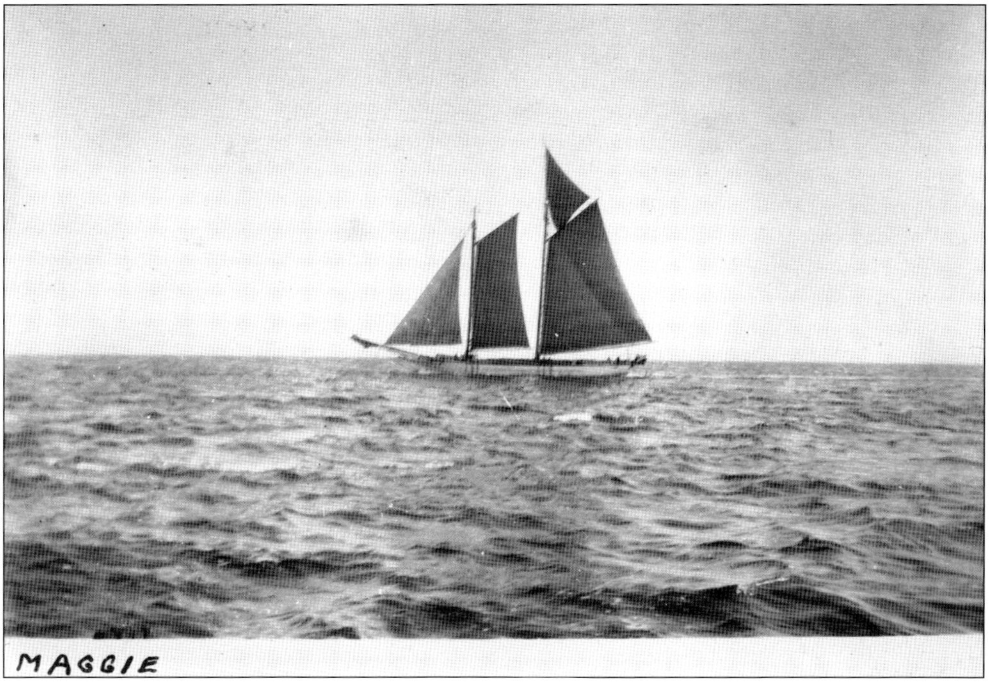

The schooner *Maggie* was built in 1871 in Dorchester, Maryland, and was abandoned at Rockland, Maine, in 1955. For most of her life, she sailed on the Chesapeake Bay. Tom Henry Ruark of Deltaville owned the *Maggie* in the 1940s, and her home port was Jackson Creek. Many a Deltaville lad found employment on the boats that hauled oysters and bulk freight. (Dr. A.L. VanName Jr. collection.)

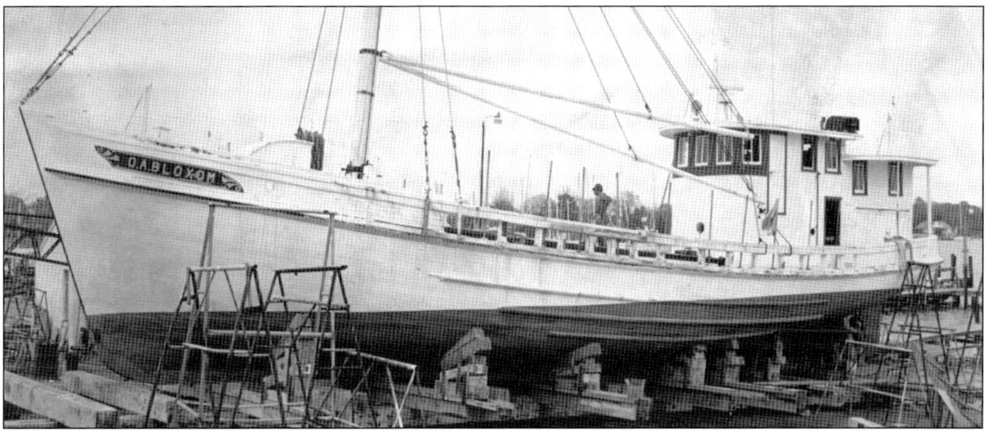

The O.A. *Bloxom* was built in 1901 as a two-masted sailing bugeye, 75 feet long and 21 feet wide. In 1948, the vessel was brought to Deagle & Son Marine Railway in Deltaville for a complete rebuilding. Deagle installed a round stern on her, cut her in two, and lengthened the vessel to 84 feet. This type of specialty work became a trademark of several Deltaville boatyards. (Author's collection.)

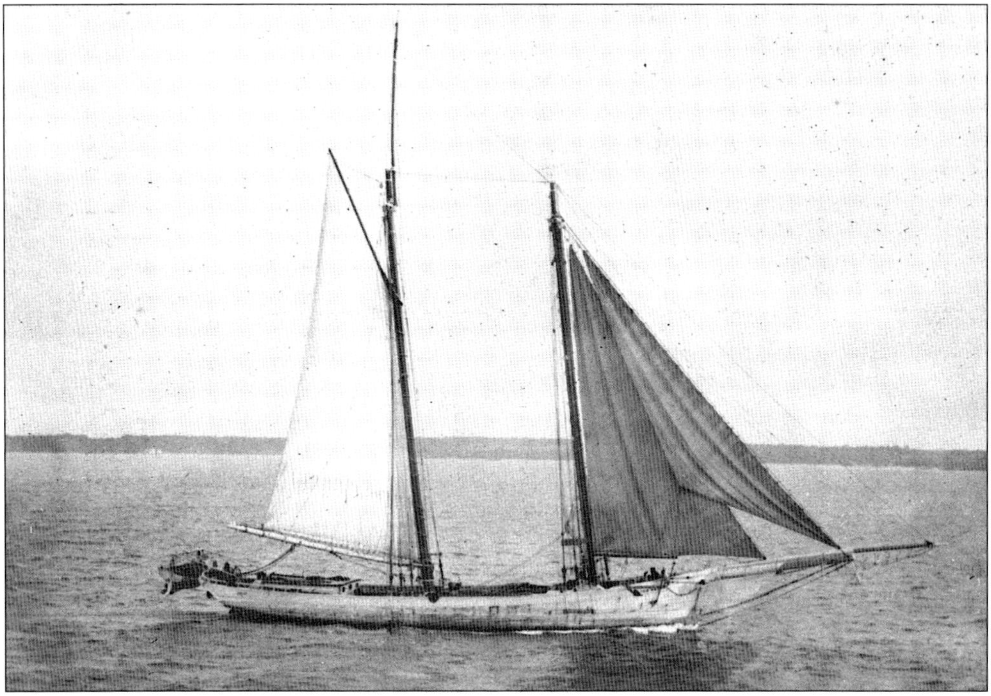

Ida Mae, pictured off Grey's Point, was previously the *Jacob S. Barnes*, but after Fred Ward of Urbanna rebuilt her from the keel up in 1898, she was renamed, and Ward registered as her builder. Capt. Charlie Christopher of Deltaville was her longtime captain, and she was owned for many years by Van Wagner Bros. of Urbanna. (Dr. A.L. VanName Jr. collection)

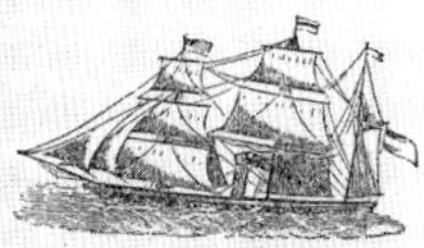

G. R. NORTHAM,

DEALER IN

WOOD AND SAWED LUMBER,

CHURCHVIEW, VIRGINIA.

Amount on Deck,__________

" Under Deck,__________

Total,__________

Received of__________

__________Dollars on acct. of freight

__________Master.

SHIPPED, in good order and condition, by Geo. R. Northam in and upon the good Schooner called the__________whereof __________is Master for the present voyage: now lying at the Port of__________and bound for__________ To say__________ft.__________lumber, more or less consisting of

Being marked and numbered as in the margin: to be delivered in like good order and condition, at the aforesaid Port of__________ (the danger of the seas only excepted, it being understood vessel to wait turn to discharge cargo,) unto__________or assigns, he or they paying freight for the said goods at the rate of__________ per thousand feet for all delivered without primage and average accustomed.

IN WITNESS WHEREOF, the Master or Purser of said vessel hath affirmed to__________Bills of Lading all of this tenor and date, one of which being accomplished the others to stand void.

Dated at__________the__________day of__________

__________Master.

Geo. R. Northam of Church View was in the lumber business in Middlesex County. Lumber was hauled by sailing vessels until trucks took over the business. This invoice speaks to the procedure used when shipping lumber by vessel. Northam owned a schooner and shipped lumber for himself and others. Most successful lumbermen owned a sailing vessel, which enabled them to get their product to market and haul freight for hire. Most hired a captain and crew to work the boat. (Courtesy of George Northam.)

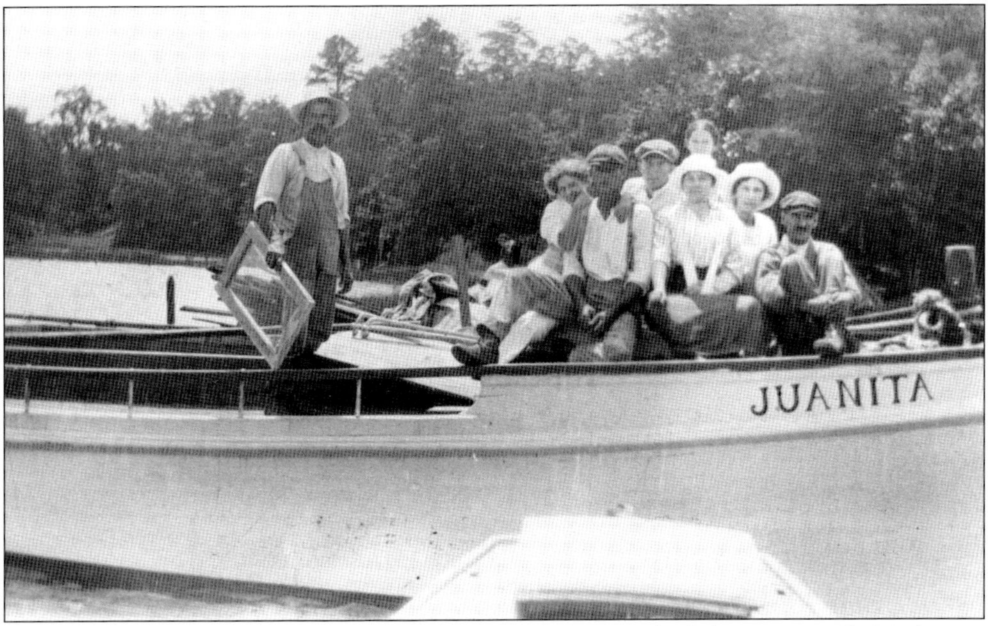

Russell Carroll Parker (standing) and his brother Lawrence built boats on Mill Creek near Wake. Parker built *Juanita* for himself in 1926 and named the boat after his daughter. He hauled watermelons and freight in the vessel. The brothers lived and built boats near Mill Creek Steamboat Wharf. (Author's collection.)

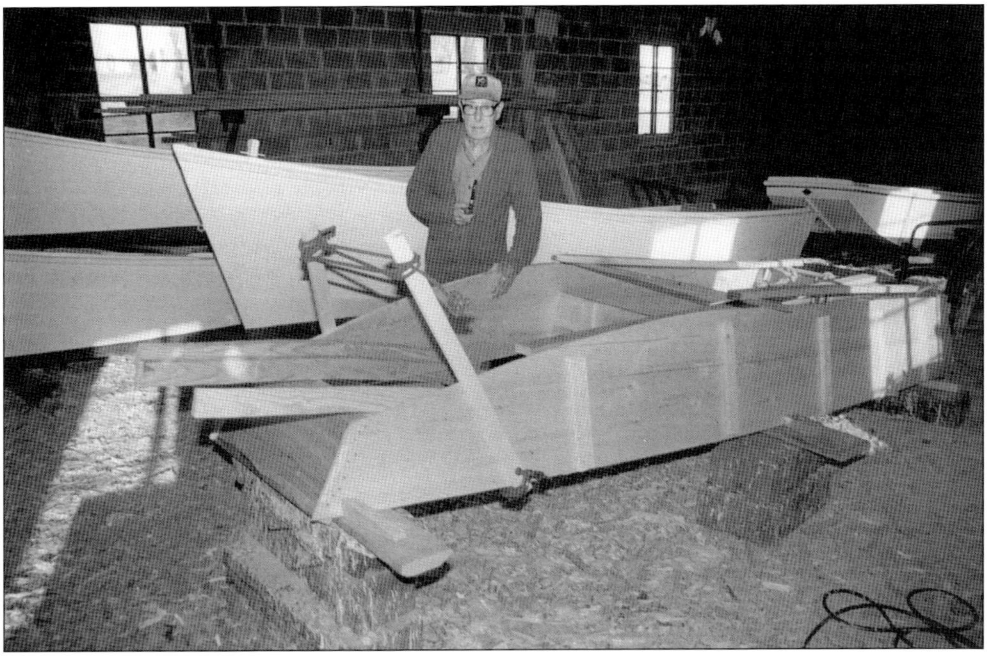

Lewis G. Wright was the son of Tom Wright, one of the early pioneers in Deltaville wooden deadrise and cross-planked boatbuilding. Wright built his first boat, a flat-bottomed skiff, in 1916. The boat was delivered to Baltimore on the deck of his uncle's sailing schooner, *Ester A. Waters*. Wright was still building boats well into his 80s at this boat shop on Lover's Lane when this photograph was taken in 1984. (Author's collection.)

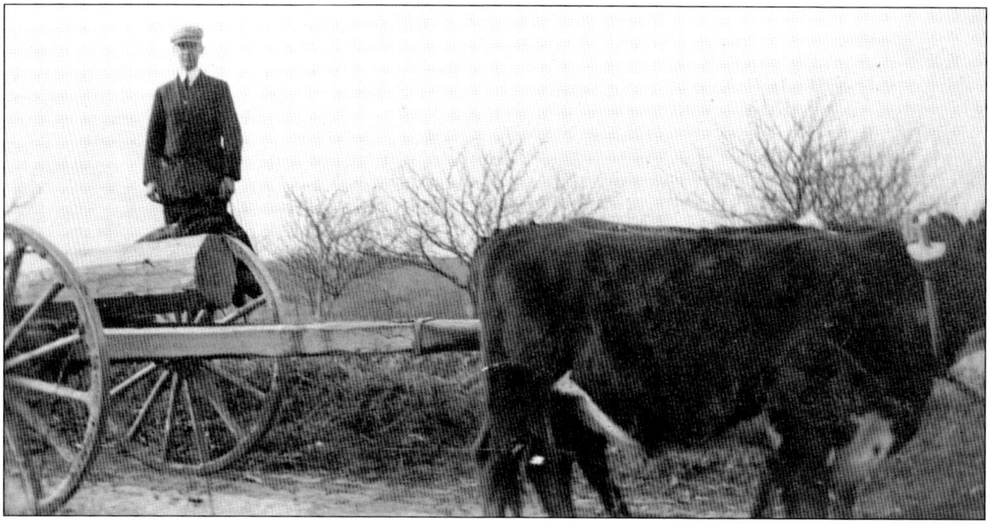

Sailboat masts were cut from Dragon Run and often rough-shaped by workers with foot adzes and broad axes along the shore. Masts were hauled out of the Dragon by oxen to a schooner landing, where the mast was lifted onto the deck of a schooner and hauled to a boatyard for finishing and installation. This photograph shows the bottom end of a mast that is being hauled by oxen from the Dragon. (Courtesy of Jean Holman.)

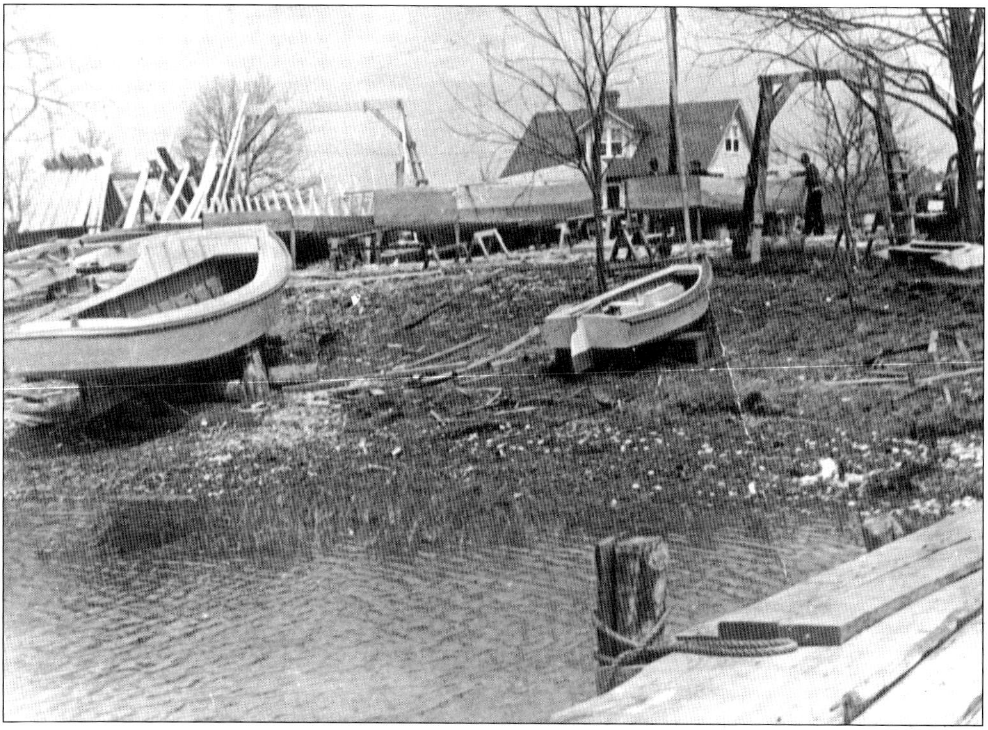

John Wright of Deltaville built wooden boats in his backyard off Lover's Lane on Jackson Creek. Pictured here in the 1940s is a Wright-built sailboat in the foreground constructed for pleasure, and to the left is a round-stern commercial fishing powerboat. Wright built in the classic deadrise and cross-planked style and was a pioneer in the development of that style of boatbuilding on the Chesapeake Bay. (Courtesy of Bob Walker.)

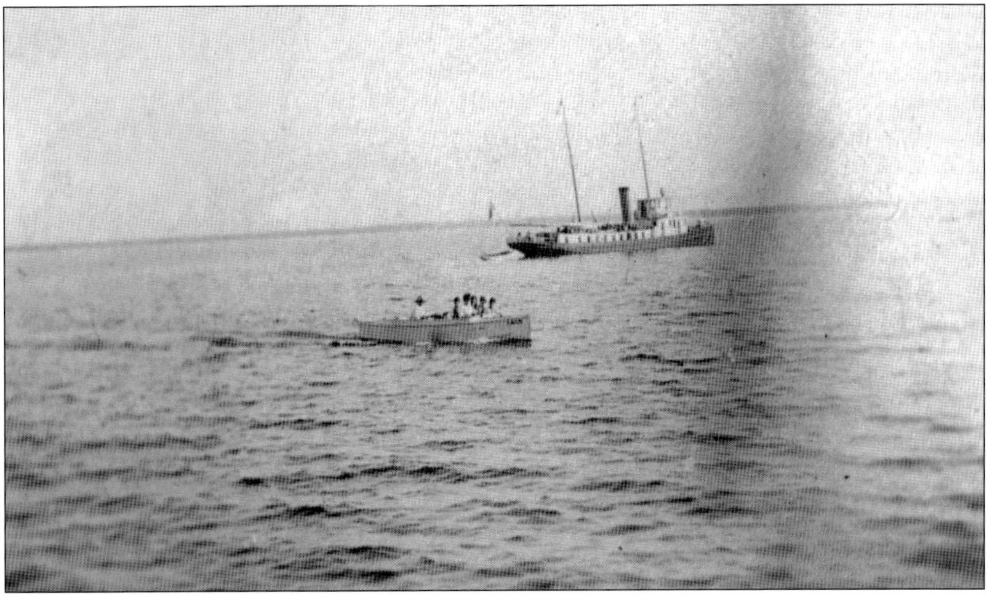

The steam-powered yacht *Remlik*, in the background off Balls Point in the Rappahannock River, belonged to millionaire Willis Sharpe Kilmer of Binghamton, New York. Kilmer made a fortune marketing Dr. Kilmer's Swamp Root, a patent medicine. In 1909, he bought a 1,000-acre farm near Streets and built a 32-room Tudor mansion. Shortly after Kilmer moved to Streets, the name was changed to Remlik—Kilmer spelled backward. (Courtesy of Mary and Danny Loving.)

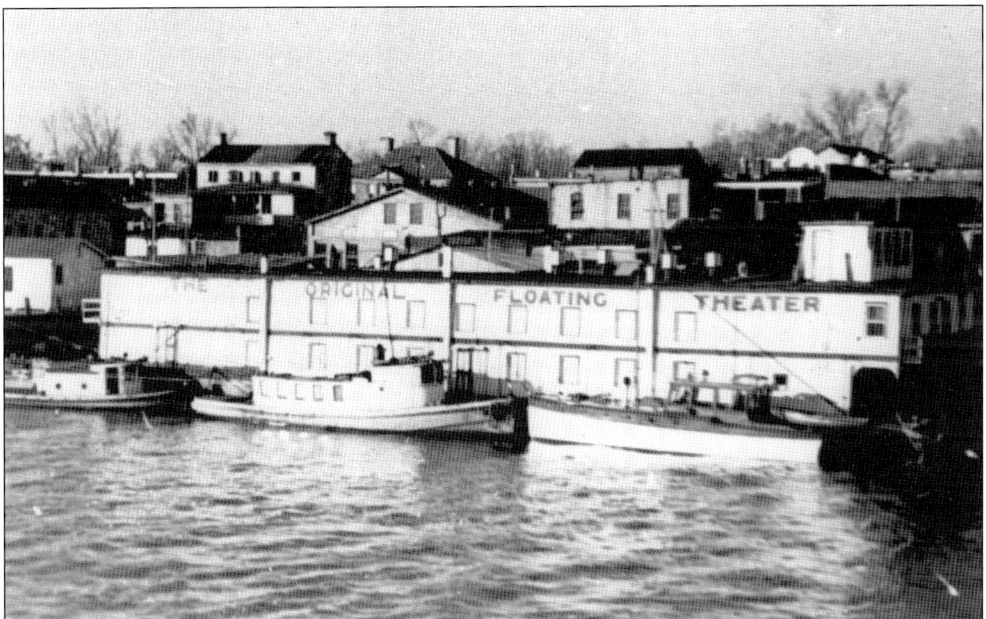

The James Adams Original Floating Theater came annually to Urbanna and Ruark on Fishing Bay. The weeklong visit brought New York–style theater to Middlesex. On the day the showboat arrived, the communities of Urbanna and Deltaville were humming with anticipation. Crowds gathered to welcome the annual event that brought excitement to rural, quiet Middlesex. (Courtesy of Virginia Burton.)

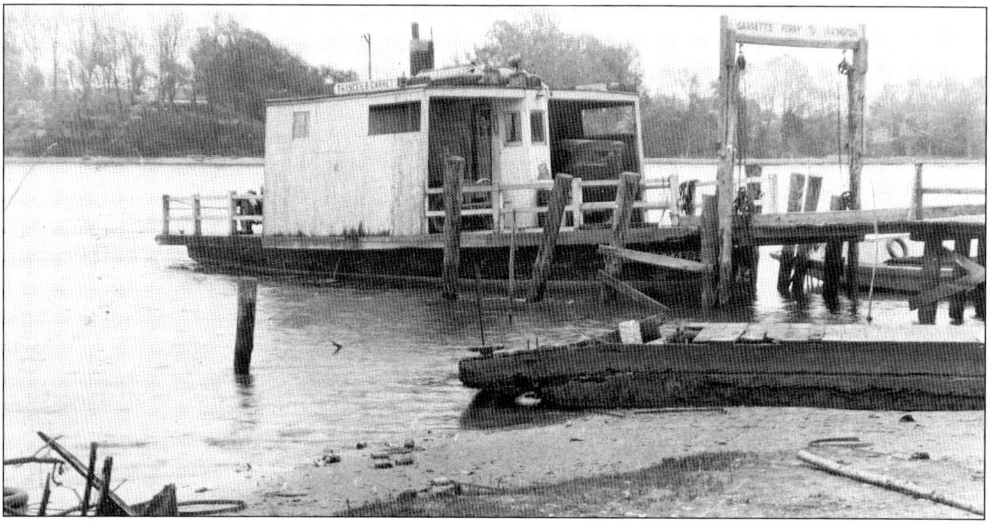

Harry L. Garrett had the ferryboat *Frances B. Garrett*, named after his wife, built in 1924 and started a car ferry that ran from Irvington to Locklies Creek and later to Urbanna. The maiden trip came on May 15, 1924, from Irvington to Archie Segar's landing on Locklies Creek in Middlesex. Around 1930, he moved his landing sites from Locklies and Urbanna to Grey's Point and from Irvington to White Stone. It cut the water travel time from 1.5 hours to 18 minutes. (Author's collection.)

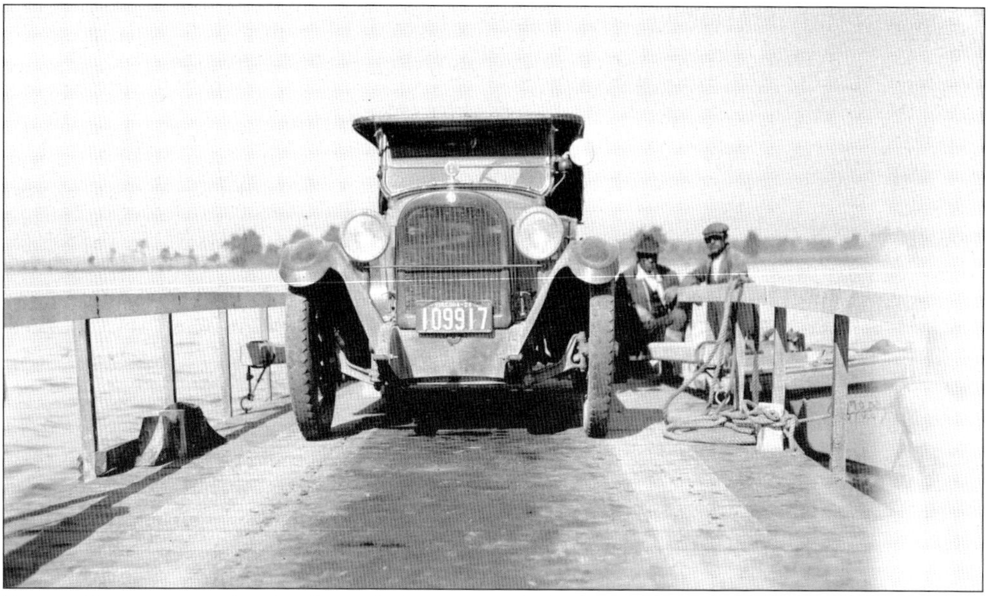

Tippits Ferry crossed the Piankatank River near the location of the current Piankatank bridge and was known in 1924 as part of Route 225. The Piankatank and Rappahannock Rivers had ferries across them until the John Andrew Twigg Bridge was built over the Piankatank in 1953 and Robert O. Norris Bridge over the Rappahannock in 1957. For generations prior to bridges, ferries bridged the waters between Middlesex, Lancaster, Mathews, and Gloucester Counties. (Courtesy of Dick Murray)

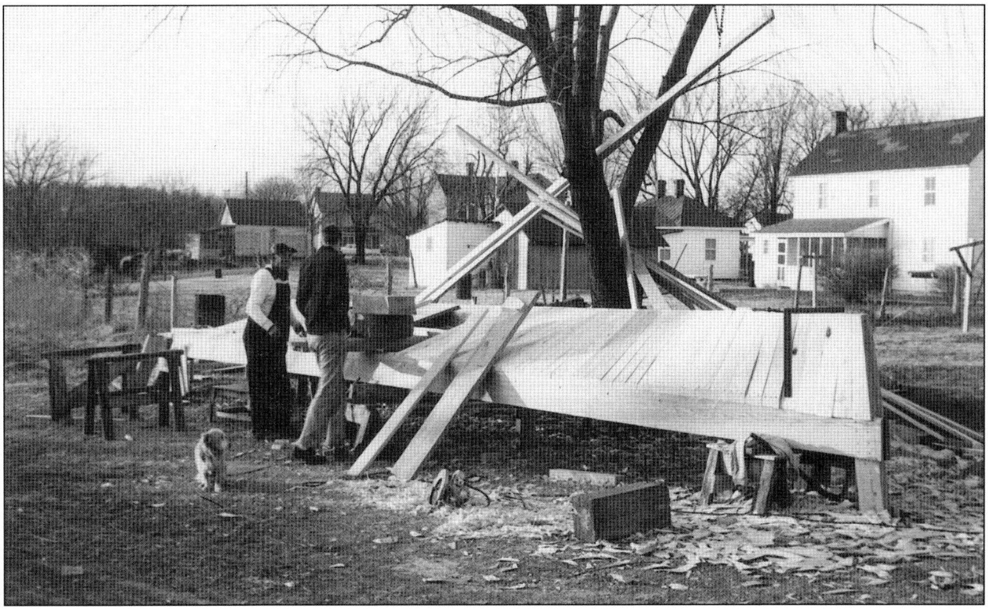

In March 1964, boatbuilder Tom Treviilan, left, has a 40-foot deadrise workboat underway behind his home on Rappahannock Avenue in Urbanna. The homes in the background are on the backside of Howard Street. Howard Street was named for Howard Bristow, who was killed in World War II. Although Deltaville was a wooden boatbuilding center, backyard boatbuilding was a cottage industry throughout Middlesex County. (Courtesy of Joe Conboy.)

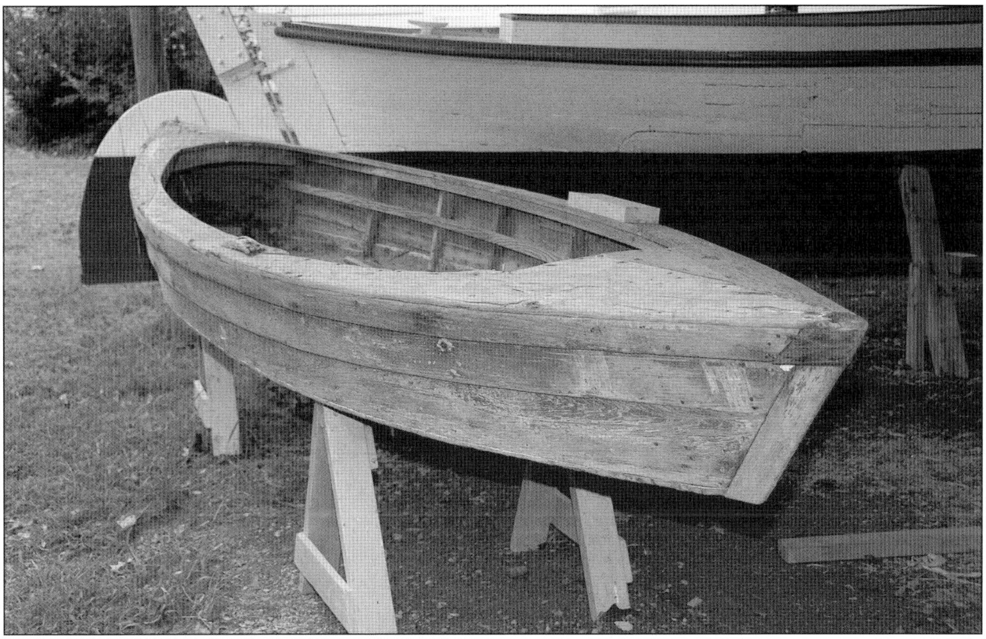

This skiff used for hunting sora came from Wood Farm on the Piankatank River. The banks of the farm are situated on brackish waters near where the Piankatank and Dragon Run converge. Soras feed in marshes off plant seed, insects, and snails. A "sora tide" is an unusually high tide that floods the marshes, taking away the cover of marsh grass and giving the hunter an edge over the elusive sora. (Author's collection.)

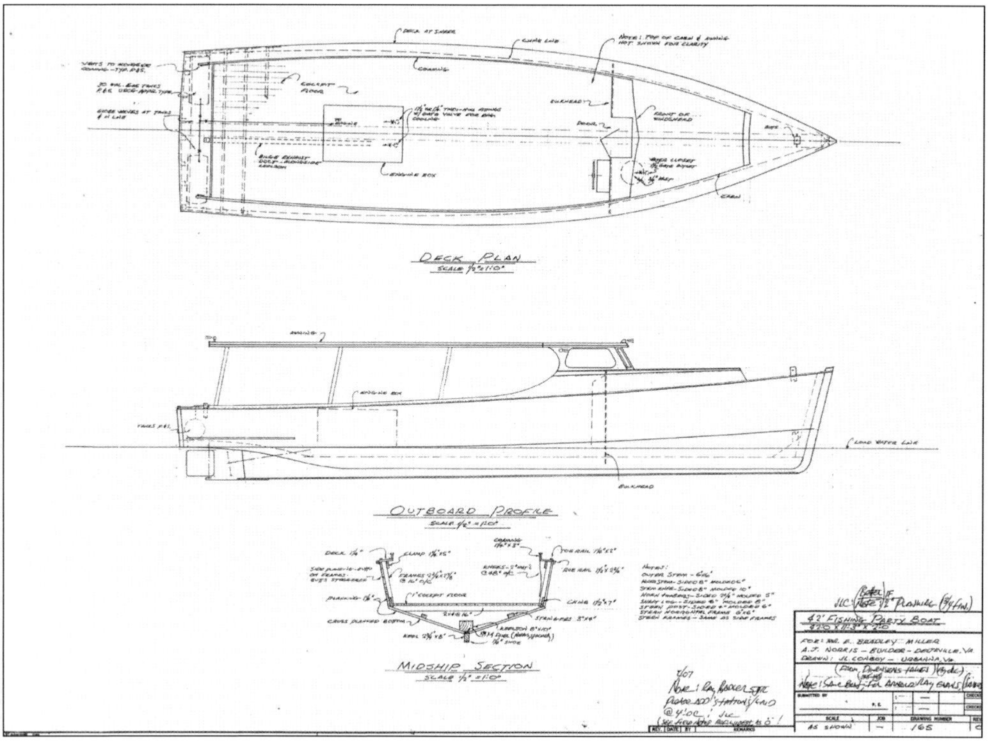

John, Ladd, Tom, and Lewis Wright; Rob Dudley; Hugh, Willard, and Alfred Norris; Ed and Pete Deagle; Edmond Harrow; Willie Marchant; and Bez and Jim Cornelius all built wooden boats on Lovers Lane in Deltaville. All of these builders built their boats without professional plans using what is referred to as "rack of eye." The 42-foot Deltaville deadrise-style boat in this drawing was built by Alfred Norris. (Courtesy of Joe Conboy.)

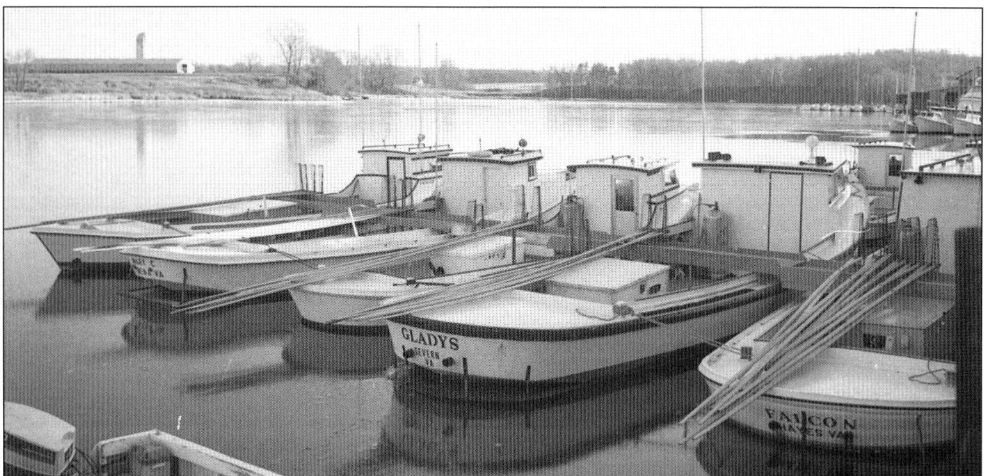

During the winter oyster season, Urbanna Creek had a fleet of oyster boats for the fall and winter hand tong season on Rappahannock River. The oyster business fueled the area's boatbuilding business, as these styles of boats were built by hand, locally, out of wood and provided an ideal platform for tonging oysters. This photograph was taken in 1973, before hand tongs used on public oyster grounds were replaced by 22-inch-wide dredges. (Author's collection.)

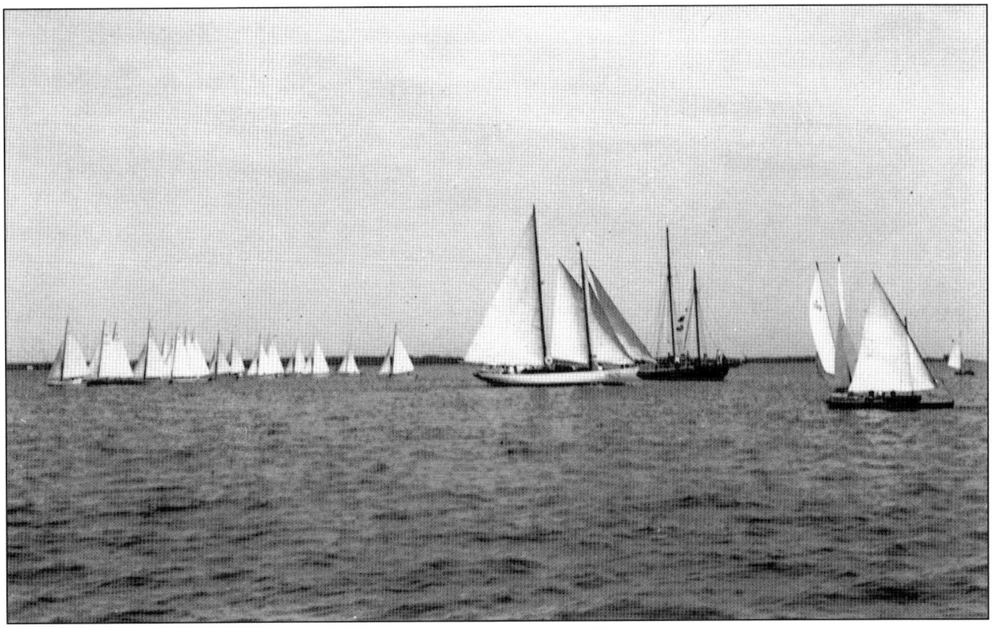

The Urbanna Sailing Association was founded in 1939. The organization sponsored an annual small-craft sailing regatta. This photograph of the event was taken around 1942, with two sailing yachts, white-hulled *Quail* and black-hulled *Nighthawk*, competing in the last race of the day. The two boats sailed to the mouth of Carters Creek and back to the finish line at Urbanna Creek. Hundreds of spectators stood on the riverbanks and watched. (C.C. Chowning collection.)

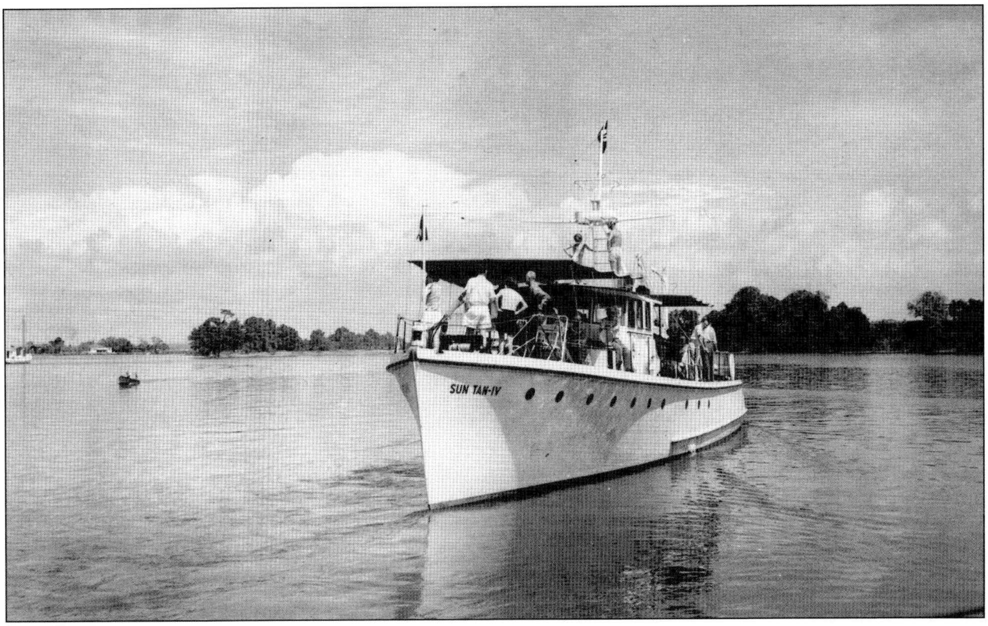

The Tides Inn, a luxury hotel, opened in 1947 in Irvington in Lancaster County. Lancaster was a dry (alcohol-free) county. However, because private clubs were not bound by the same constraints, the Tides owners formed the Chesapeake Club. Middlesex was a wet county, so the inn purchased a yacht that made Saturday runs across the river to Urbanna's liquor store. It was known as the "whiskey run." An early yacht used was the *Sun Tan-IV*. (C.C. Chowning collection.)

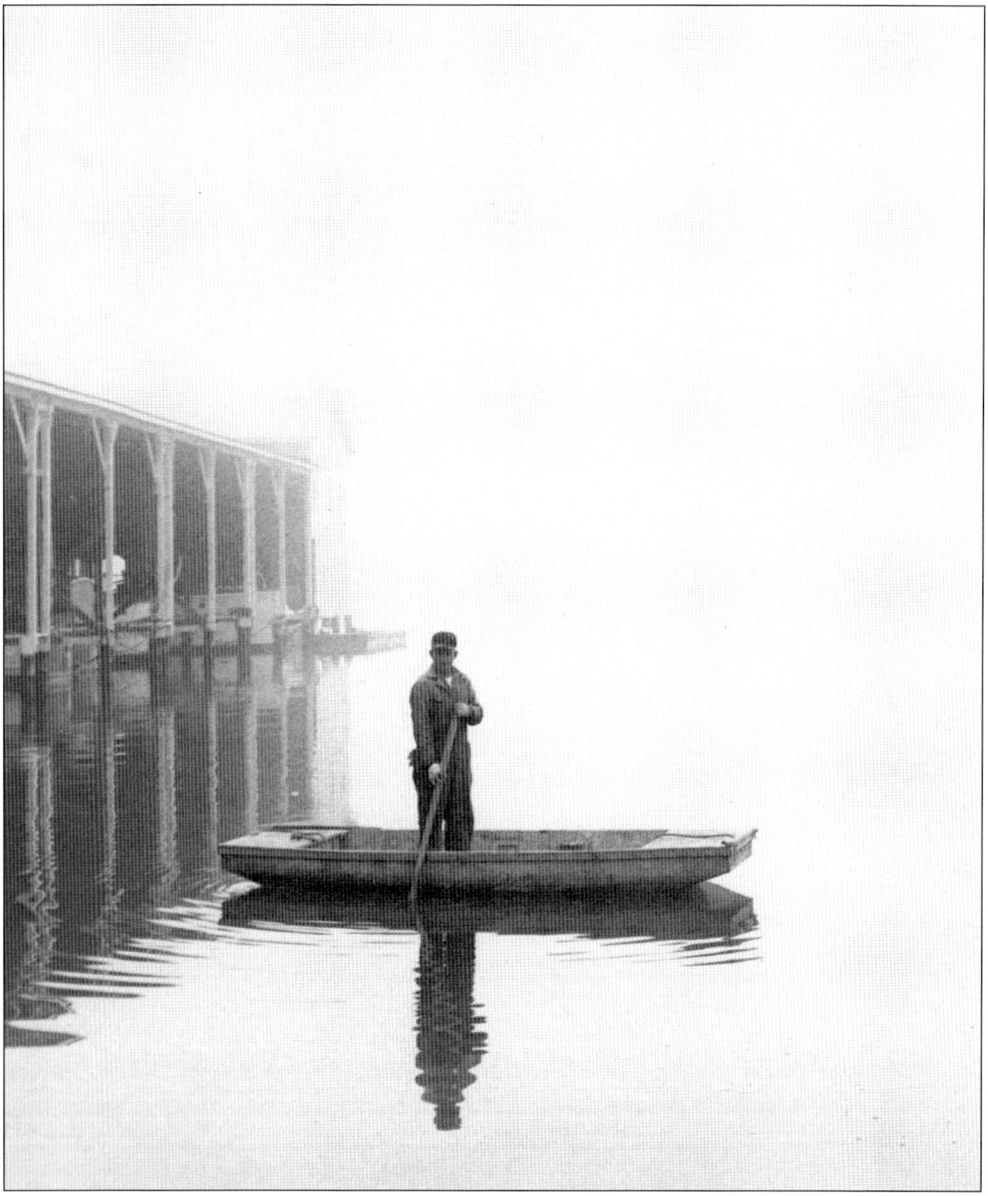

On April 18, 1955, W.E. Norton, president of the Deltaville Improvement Association, was quoted in the *Richmond Times Dispatch* as saying that, in Deltaville, "there are nine marine railways, seven of those have been built since World War II—evidence of a boating boom." The rise of marinas in Deltaville and Urbanna brought newfound prosperity to some in the county. The railway punt was a small craft used to work on boats from the water. Their trademark was a rainbow of paint colors scattered fore and aft, dropped by workers standing inside the punt while painting boats from the water. (C.C. Chowning collection.)

Four

Steamboats

In 1821, the first commercial passenger steamboats, named *Petersburg* and *Albermarle*, arrived on the Rappahannock River, ushering in the steamboat era that lasted until 1937, when the last steamboat, *Anne Arundel*, came from Baltimore on a final trip.

George Weems of Baltimore started the first commercial steamboat route on the Rappahannock River in 1828. The 123-foot *Patuxent* was used on the route, and Urbanna was one of its main stops. In 1830, Weems sent *Patuxent* into the Piankatank River to probe the commerce on that river, but it was discontinued when it proved unprofitable.

Through the Antebellum period, steamboats became more prevalent on the Rappahannock. In 1830, the Baltimore and Rappahannock Steam Packet Company started sending the steamboat *Rappahannock* to the river.

Although there was some steamboat traffic on the Piankatank before the Civil War, commerce got a boost there in 1872 when the Maryland Steamboat Company opened up a new route on the river with the vessel *Massachusetts*.

Most of the early steamboat landings had been public or private landings leftover from colonial days when English ships arrived in March with boatloads of goods for settlers and to haul hogsheads of tobacco back across the ocean.

The Piankatank had three such landings: Kemps (later known as Conrad's Wharf), Stampers, and Fairfield landings. These landings served Middlesex residents living in the eastern end of the county. The Piankatank service was greatly expanded in 1885 when Tom and Mark Hewitt built Jackson Creek Wharf, and the steamboat arrived every Sunday and Wednesday, weather and tide permitting. The steamboat also landed at Ruark on Fishing Bay.

On the Rappahannock, a series of long river wharves were built in the late 1880s by the Baltimore and Susquehanna Steamboat Company. They were North End or Grinels Wharf at Amburg, Mill Creek at Wake, Burhans at Locust Hill, West Urbanna just outside of Urbanna, and Water View Wharf.

For some time thereafter, commerce grew around these wharves and affected everyone living in the neighborhood. However, improved automobile and truck transportation along with better roads contributed to declining profits for steamboat companies. The August storm of 1933 destroyed most of the Rappahannock River wharves and brought finality to steamboats arriving in Middlesex.

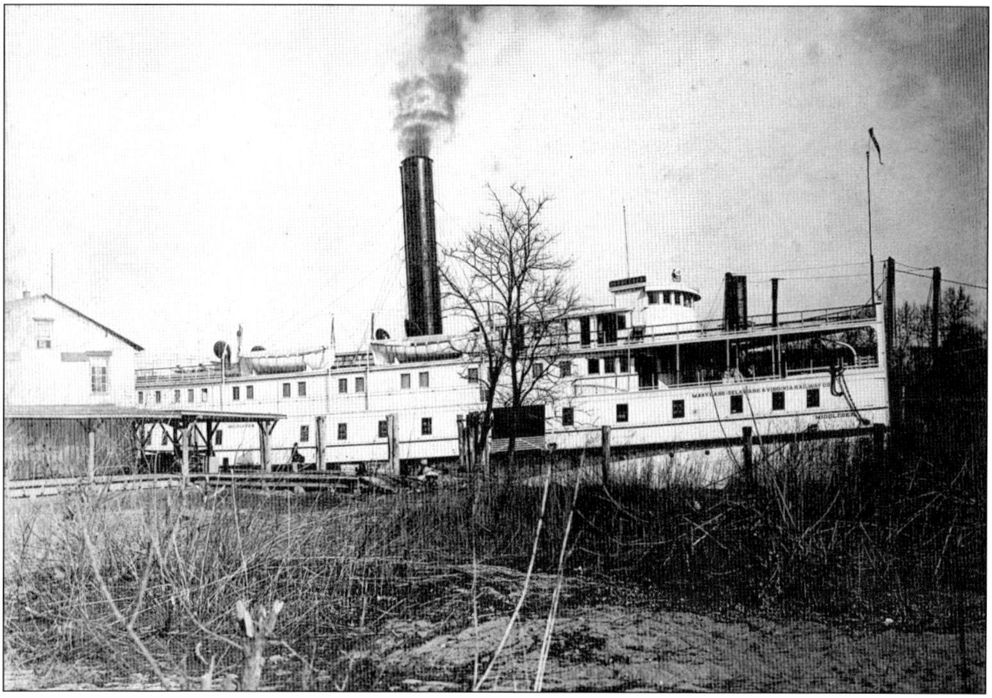

The steamboat *Middlesex* was built in 1902 and named after Middlesex County. Communities up and down the county were tied to the city of Baltimore, Maryland, by the steamboat. Dorothy Norris, 90 years old in 1994, recalled that the daily newspaper in her childhood home was the *Baltimore Sun*. The *Sun* arrived by steamboat to North End Wharf and was delivered to Sandy Bottom Post Office by a man in a horse-drawn two-wheel sulky, always a few days late. (Courtesy of Emily Chowning.)

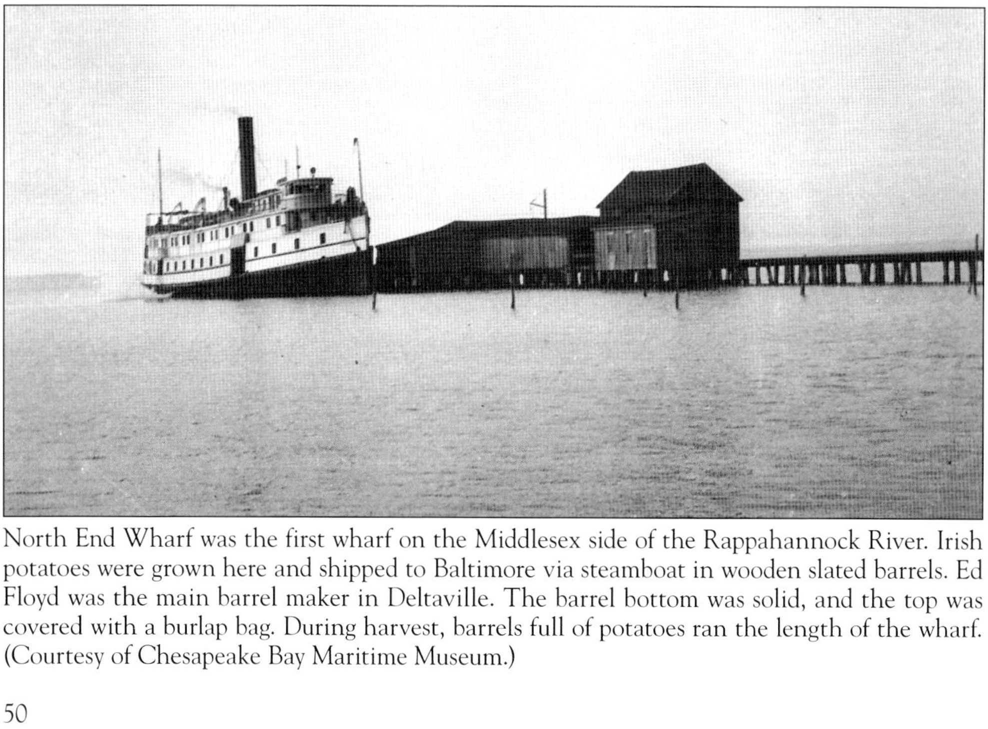

North End Wharf was the first wharf on the Middlesex side of the Rappahannock River. Irish potatoes were grown here and shipped to Baltimore via steamboat in wooden slated barrels. Ed Floyd was the main barrel maker in Deltaville. The barrel bottom was solid, and the top was covered with a burlap bag. During harvest, barrels full of potatoes ran the length of the wharf. (Courtesy of Chesapeake Bay Maritime Museum.)

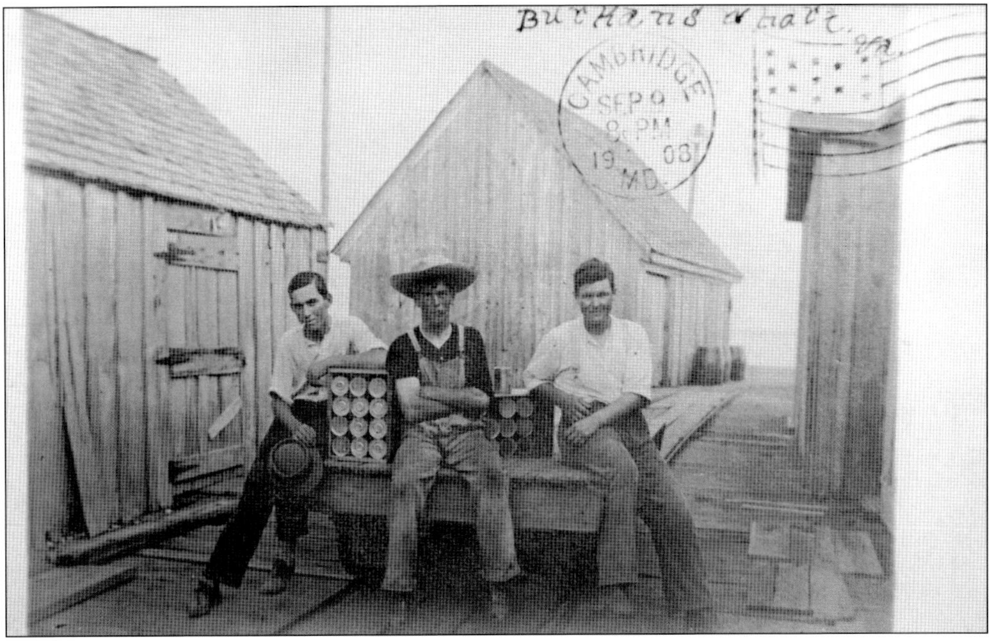

Burhans Steamboat Wharf was between Christ Church and Locust Hill and had a post office there named Cooper. A pickle factory was located on shore where local farmers sold cucumbers and were paid for each basket of 100 cucumbers. A rail cart on the wharf deck hauled cans and freight from the end of the wharf to shore. These boys are sitting on the rail cart. The wharf was named after John S. Burhans of New Jersey, who built it in 1887. (Courtesy of Jack Miller.)

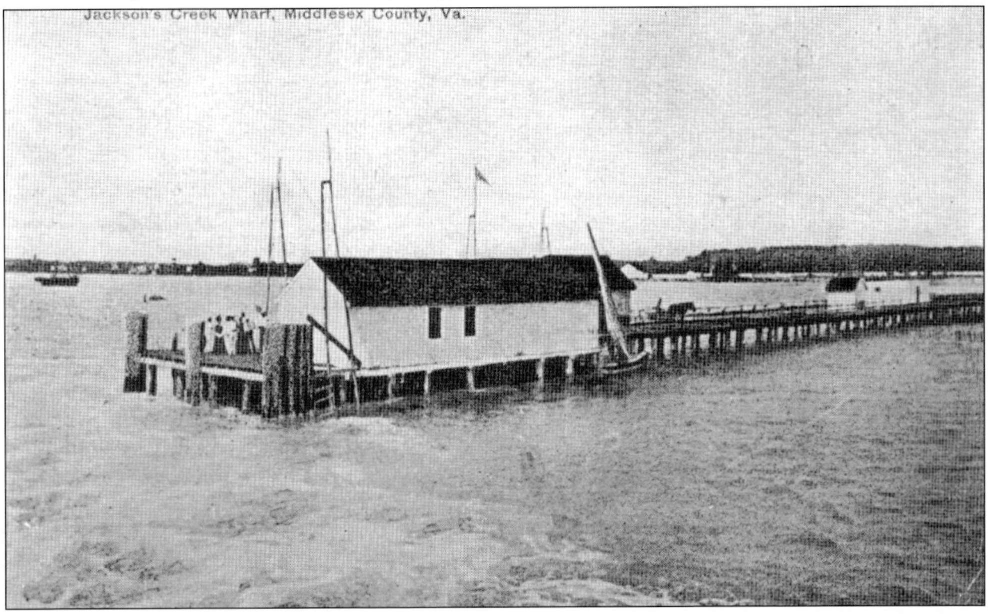

Jackson Creek Wharf was built by Tom and Mark Hewitt in 1885. The area of the wharf was called Enoch, and Enoch Post Office opened on the wharf the same year the wharf was built. The steamboat wharf extended across Jackson Creek's channel and out into the deep water of Chesapeake Bay. This required the wharf to have a unique hand-operated drawbridge to allow boats into Jackson Creek. Steamboats moored at the end of the dock. (Author's collection.)

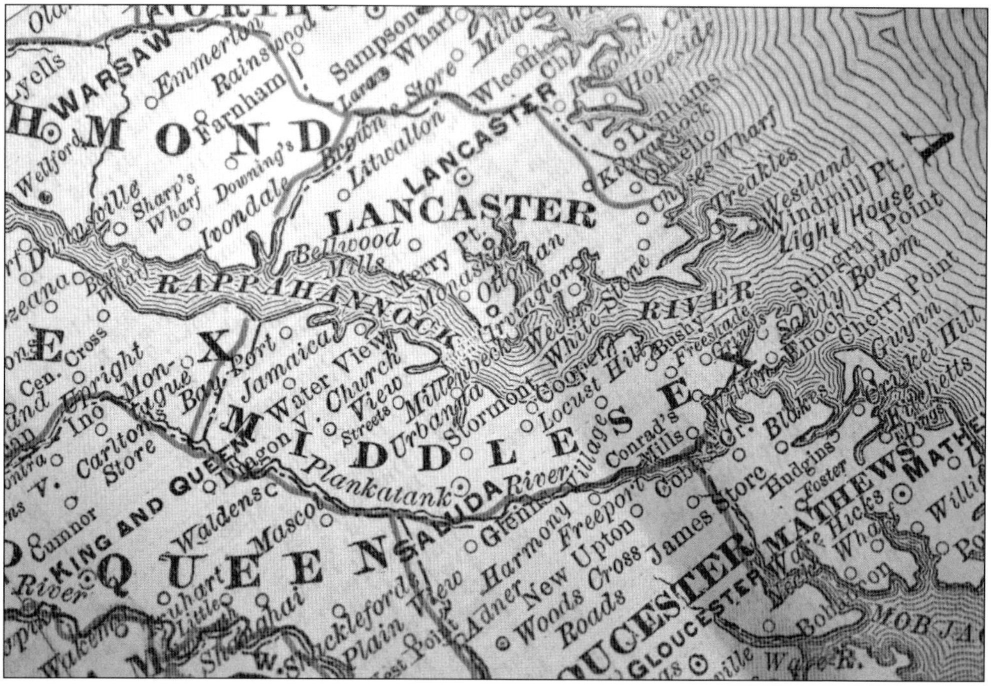

This 1894 map of Middlesex County shows all the steamboat landings and most of the post office communities. At the far western end of the county was Bay Port, and moving east was Jamaica, Water View, Streets, Urbanna, Stormont, Cooper, Harmony Village, Locust Hill, Bushy, Freeshade, Conrad's Mills, Wilton, Grinels, Sandy Bottom, and Enoch. The commercial life on and near these landings was greatly enhanced by the steamboats coming out from Baltimore and Norfolk. When the steamboat stopped, much of the commerce stopped. (Courtesy of Lola Watson.)

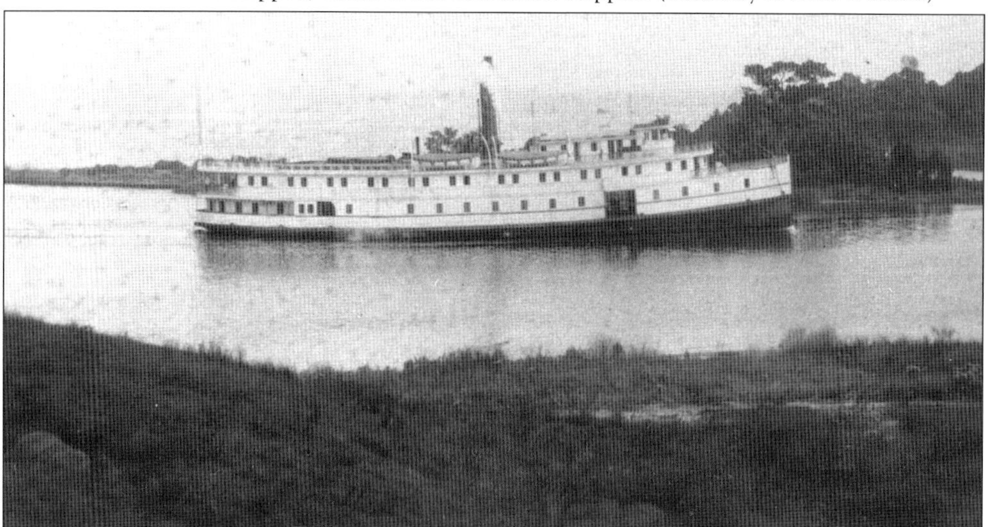

Urbanna had three steamboat wharves in town. Donaldson's, Gressitt's, and Burton's wharves were all regular stops. The steamboat provided city-type amenities for rural life. During the steamboat era, a Sunday church suit could be placed on a steamer on Monday, delivered to a Chinese laundry in Baltimore and cleaned and delivered back to the owner in Urbanna by Friday, well ahead of church on Sunday. (Courtesy of Buddy Davis.)

Mill Creek Wharf on Rappahannock River had buildings on it for storage of cucumbers, watermelons, and other vegetables and fruits to be shipped to Baltimore by steamboat. The oyster shucking houses in this picture have an inverted V–type apparatus over the doors to lift bushels of oysters from tong boats. There was also a general merchandise store on the wharf, operated by E.L. Keiningham, and Bushy Post Office was located in the store. (Courtesy of Al Miller.)

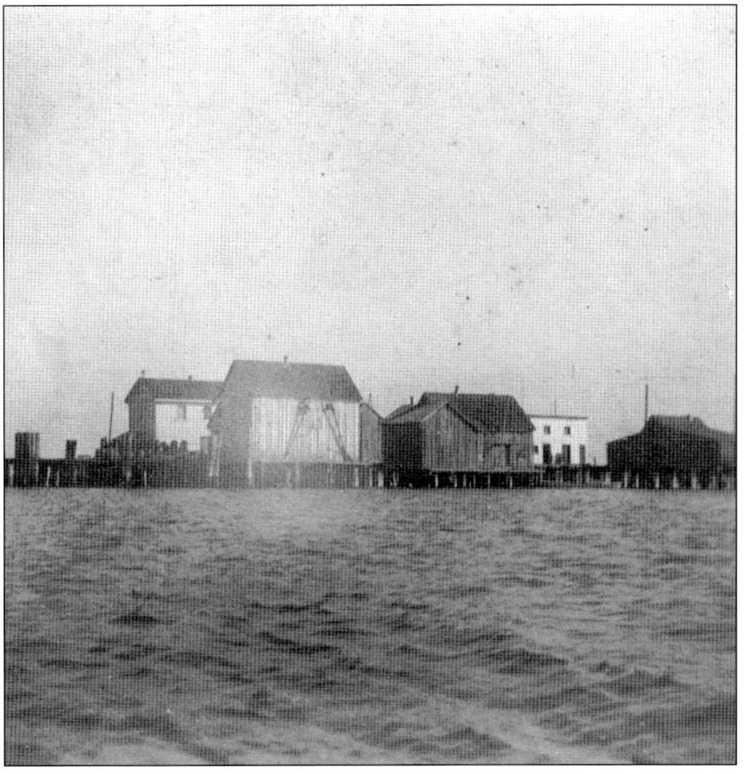

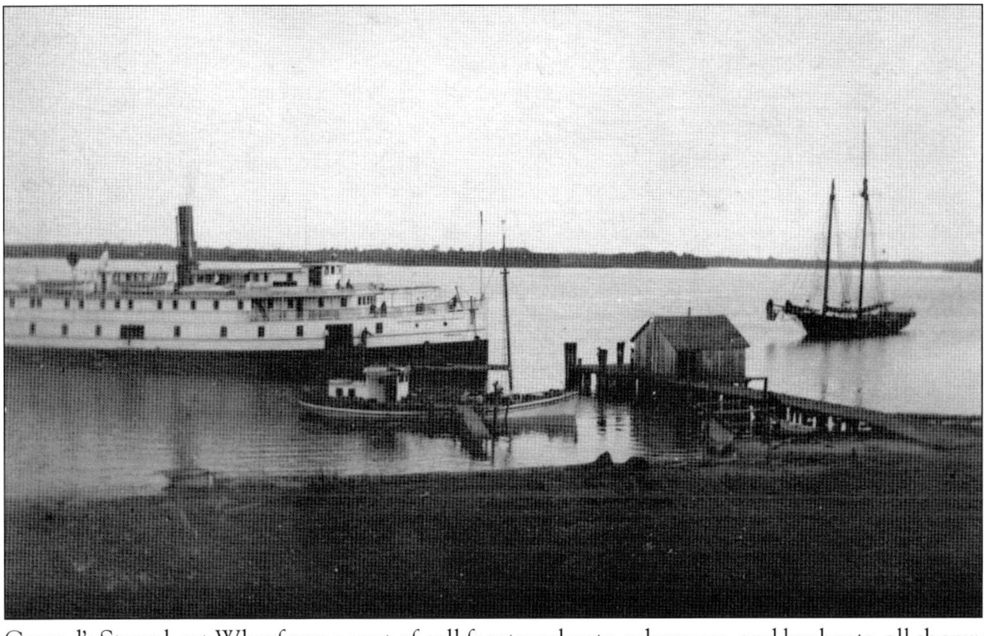

Conrad's Steamboat Wharf was a port of call for steamboats, schooners, and buyboats, all shown in this photograph. The wharf was one of just a few locations on Piankatank River where there is six to eight feet of water up close to shore, making it an ideal commercial boat landing. The buyboat is loaded down with watermelons. The two-masted schooner is most likely waiting for the steamer to move on so it too can pick up a load of melons. (Courtesy of Nola Watson.)

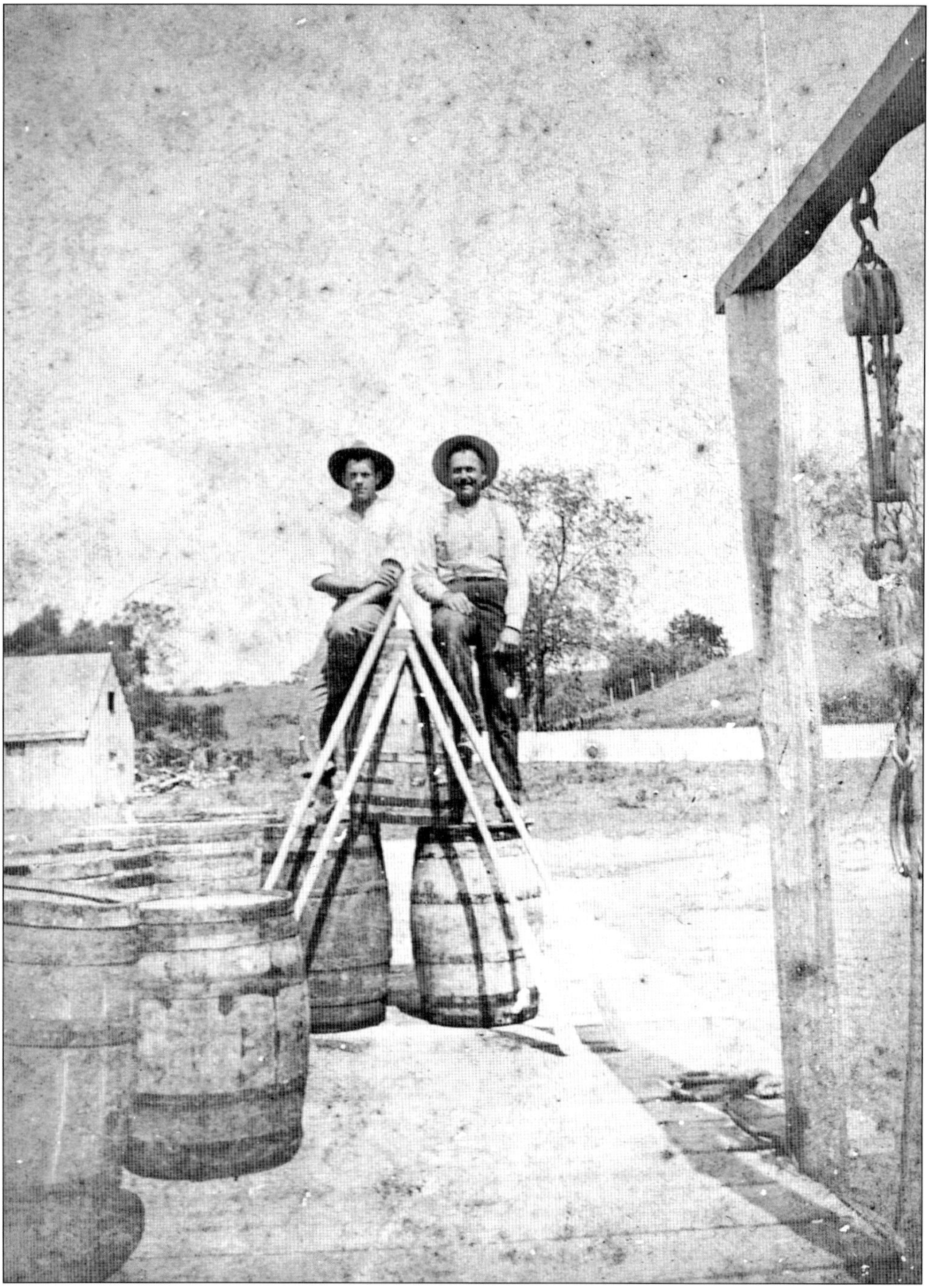

A barrel factory and woodworking shop were located at Conrad's Wharf, where barrels and oars were made. Staves and metal straps for barrels came from Baltimore on the steamboat and were put together at the factory. Barrels were used for carrying everything from potatoes to whiskey. When loaded with potatoes, barrels lined the wharf awaiting the steamboat. When loaded with whiskey, they were padlocked in a secure storage shed. Whiskey thieves were often quite creative in finding ways to bypass the padlock. (Courtesy of Nola Watson.)

Five

EDUCATION

Education in Middlesex County can be broken down into three periods: colonial education, academy schools, and public education. Early colonial education was limited to the sons of the very wealthy, and their schooling took place in England. The agrarian lifestyle, with large plantation tracts and limited transportation, was detrimental to the development of schools. During the colonial era, Ralph Wormeley II was reportedly Middlesex County's first student to graduate from college. Wormeley graduated from Oxford in 1665, and Henry Perrott was the first to matriculate from law school, at Grays Inn in 1674. Throughout the colonial period and beyond, most county residents were illiterate. Women were not encouraged to write, as white males dominated society and signed all documents of value. The mark "X" is more prevalent in Middlesex colonial records than signatures. Starting in the colonial period, some farsighted individuals recognized the value of education for the poor. In 1685, William Gordon of Middlesex gave 100 acres of land for a "free school" on Town Bridge Road near Urbanna. The colonial church sponsored workhouses for poor that taught carding, spinning, and knitting of stockings. Toward the end of the colonial era through the antebellum period and into the 20th century, there was an evolution of private sponsored academies, where a wealthy landowner in the neighborhood built a school, and middle-class parents helped pay for tutors. Academies lasted until about 1920. Public education evolved from the state's concern for the education of the poor. In 1810, the Virginia General Assembly established a literacy fund to establish schools specifically for the poor, and in 1845 adopted a "fee school system," allowing counties to levy a school tax to subsidize the cost of all white students. Public education for the masses came on July 11, 1870, as a mandate by the Virginia General Assembly to create separate public schools for blacks and whites. The Civil Rights Act of 1964 forced desegregation of Virginia public schools under a freedom of choice policy, where parents had a choice to either send their children to all-black schools or to all white schools. In the 1963–1964 school year, 13 black children integrated Middlesex's white public schools. In 1969, a federal order mandated total integration of Middlesex County schools.

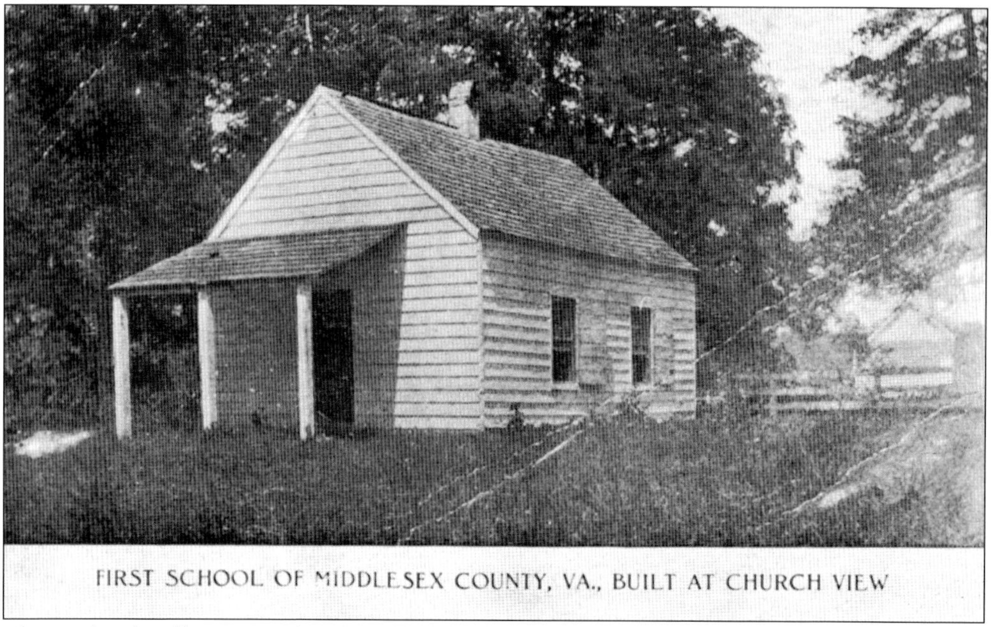

This early schoolhouse in Church View was typical of the style of school buildings erected just before and after the Civil War in Middlesex County. Before consolidation of elementary schools, one- and two-room schoolhouses for whites and blacks were scattered throughout Middlesex. Right after the Civil War, the Virginia General Assembly required the county to build new one-room log schools throughout Middlesex for children of former slaves. (Author's collection.)

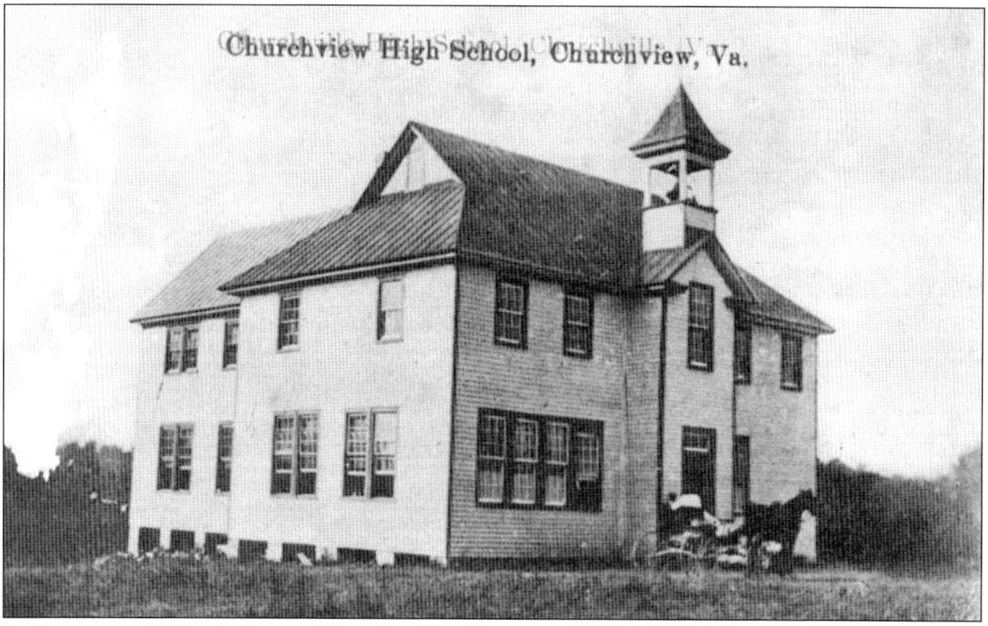

Built prior to 1880, the first public school building in Middlesex was a one-room school located near where Hermitage Baptist Church cemetery is today. The school pictured was built in 1907 just down the road as a high school and was accredited in 1915–1916. The elementary school near Hermitage burned in 1923, and it was decided to tear down this structure and erect a new building to house both primary and secondary students. (Courtesy of George Northam.)

Delta Academy was a private academy in Sandy Bottom. Schools built from the antebellum period into the early 20th century were named academies. They were privately funded and were usually just for white students. Sandy Bottom was renamed Deltaville in 1907, which leads to speculation that it may have derived its name from Delta Academy. (Courtesy of Nola Watson.)

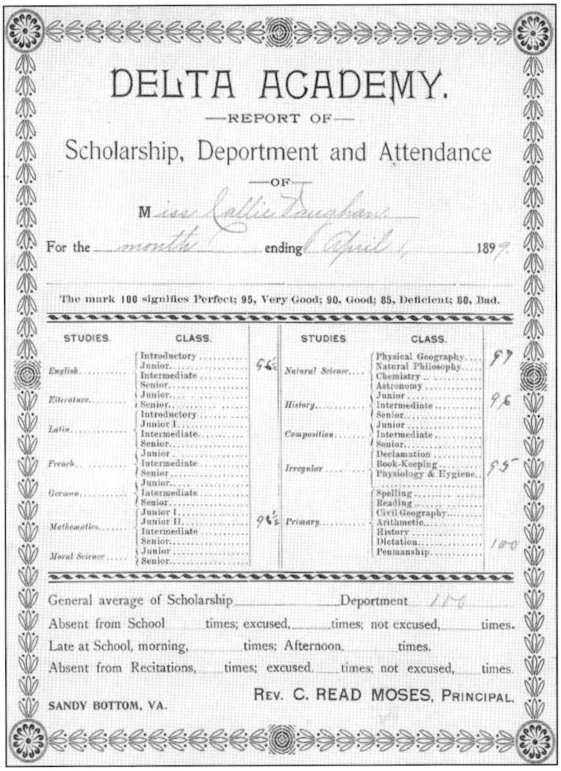

DELTA ACADEMY.

—REPORT OF—

Scholarship, Department and Attendance

—OF—

Miss Callie Vaughan

For the month ending April 1, 1899.

The mark 100 signifies Perfect; 95, Very Good; 90, Good; 85, Deficient; 80, Bad.

STUDIES.	CLASS.		STUDIES.	CLASS.	
English	Introductory, Junior, Intermediate, Senior	96½	Natural Science	Physical Geography, Natural Philosophy, Chemistry, Astronomy	97
Literature	Junior, Senior		History	Junior, Intermediate, Senior	96
Latin	Introductory, Junior I, Intermediate, Senior		Composition	Junior, Intermediate, Senior	
French	Junior, Intermediate, Senior		Irregular	Declamation, Book-Keeping, Physiology & Hygiene	95
German	Junior, Intermediate, Senior				
Mathematics	Junior I, Junior II, Intermediate, Senior	96½	Primary	Spelling, Reading, Civil Geography, Arithmetic, History, Dictation, Penmanship	100
Moral Science	Junior, Senior				

General average of Scholarship ______ Deportment 100

Absent from School ______ times; excused, ______ times; not excused, ______ times.

Late at School, morning, ______ times; Afternoon, ______ times.

Absent from Recitations, ______ times; excused, ______ times; not excused, ______ times.

SANDY BOTTOM, VA. REV. C. READ MOSES, PRINCIPAL.

Deltaville Graded School was located at the far eastern end of Middlesex in Deltaville. The first secondary public high school in the county was Unionville High School, the forerunner of this school. The county consolidated elementary schools in 1962, closing all the white and black community schools in the county. A separate lunchroom and auditorium were built for the school in 1933 by WPA workers. It still stands today and is the Deltaville Community Center. (Courtesy of Alfred E. Ailsworth Jr.)

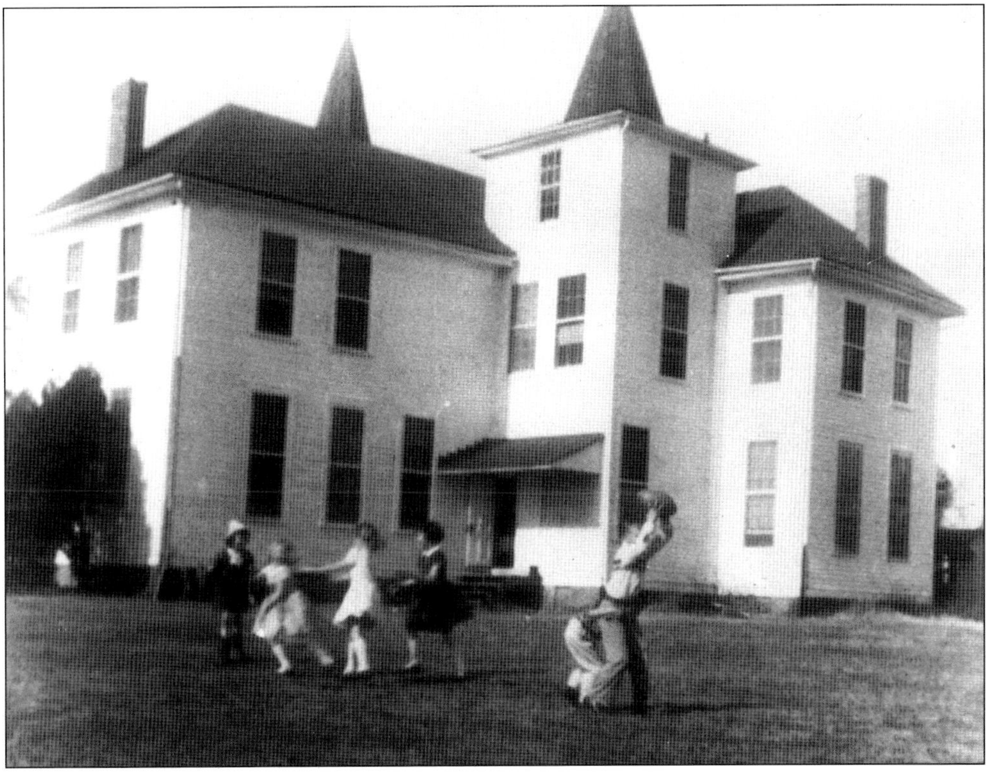

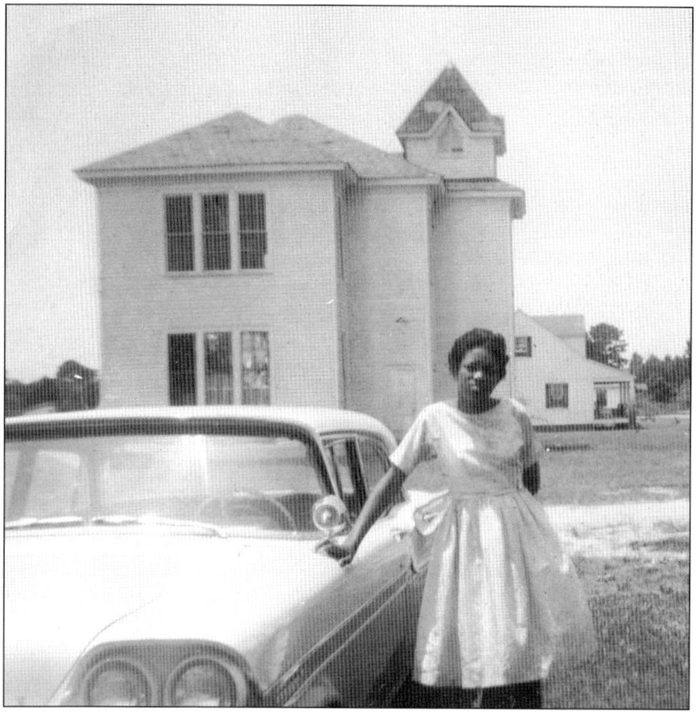

The first one-room Dunbar Graded School for blacks in Amburg was erected in 1886. It was raised to two stories in 1915 through the aid of the all-white congregation of Clarksbury Methodist Church. John Henry St. Clare Walker, a much-admired county black educator, taught at Dunbar for 20 years and was instrumental in making it one of the first black schools in Virginia accredited by the Virginia Board of Education. (Courtesy of Edmonia Scott.)

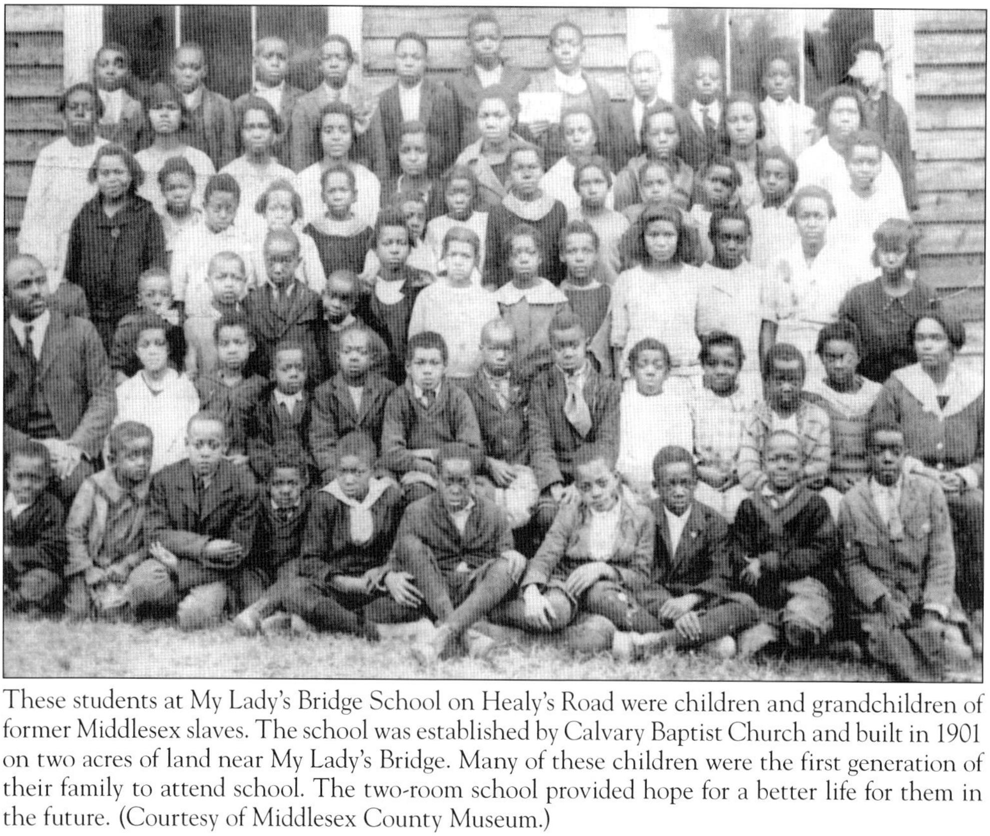

These students at My Lady's Bridge School on Healy's Road were children and grandchildren of former Middlesex slaves. The school was established by Calvary Baptist Church and built in 1901 on two acres of land near My Lady's Bridge. Many of these children were the first generation of their family to attend school. The two-room school provided hope for a better life for them in the future. (Courtesy of Middlesex County Museum.)

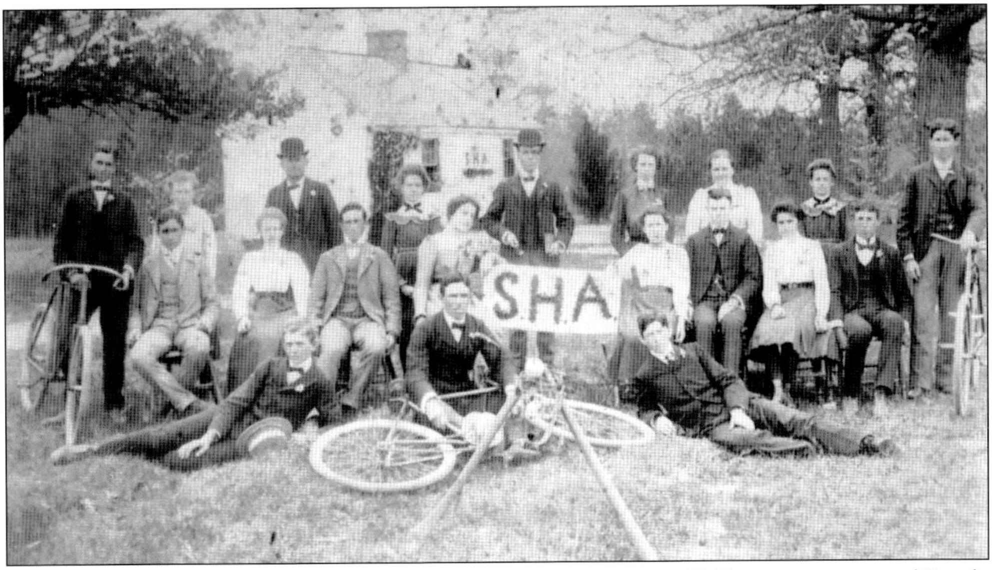

Sandy Hook Academy was located in the Topping area. Prior to 1897, Topping was named Sandy Hook. Warren Topping ran a country store in the community. He applied for a post office inside his store and requested the name of Sandy Hook. The postal service turned down the Sandy Hook name because there was a Sandy Hook Post Office in New York state. Topping then submitted his name, Topping, which was approved. (Courtesy of Jean Holman.)

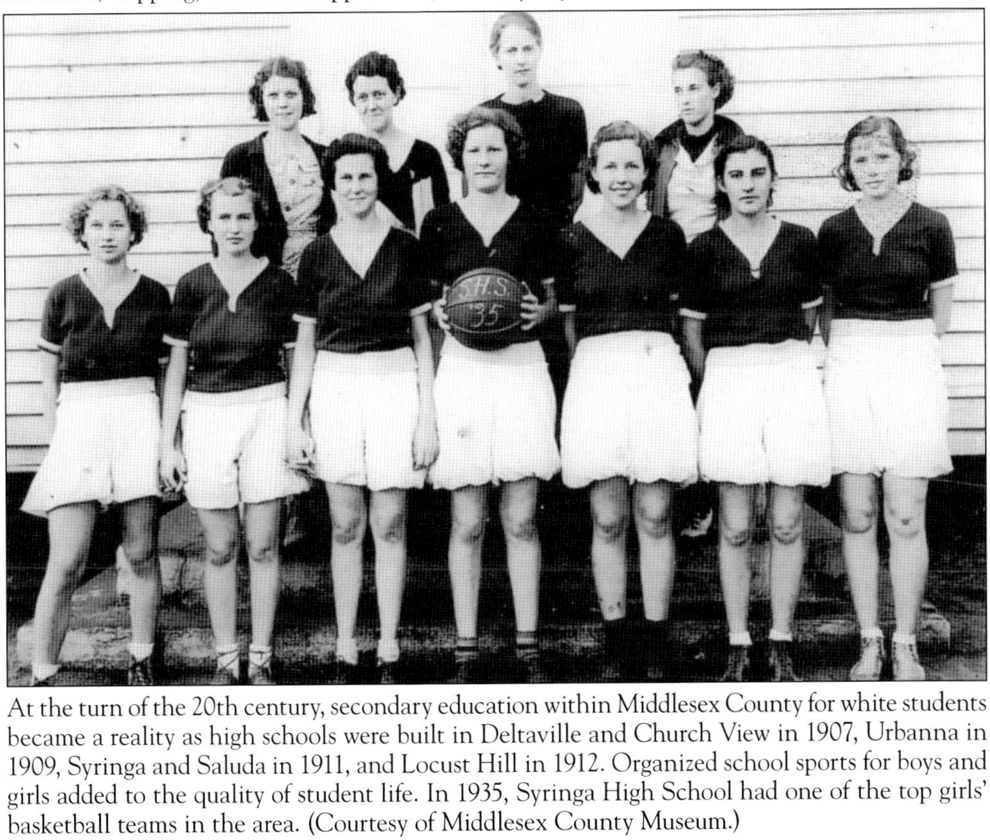

At the turn of the 20th century, secondary education within Middlesex County for white students became a reality as high schools were built in Deltaville and Church View in 1907, Urbanna in 1909, Syringa and Saluda in 1911, and Locust Hill in 1912. Organized school sports for boys and girls added to the quality of student life. In 1935, Syringa High School had one of the top girls' basketball teams in the area. (Courtesy of Middlesex County Museum.)

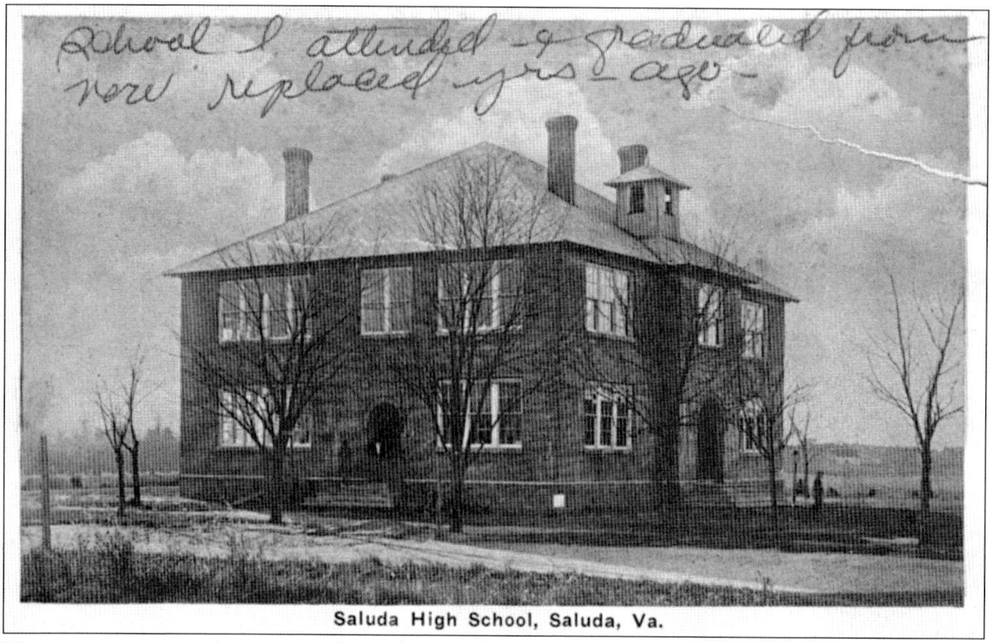

The cornerstone was laid for Saluda High School on April 7, 1911, by members of Urbanna Masonic Lodge No. 83. The school remained an accredited high school until 1949, when consolidation of secondary schools for white students took place. Middlesex High School was built next door to the Saluda High School building, and the old school structure was later razed. (Courtesy of Middlesex County Museum.)

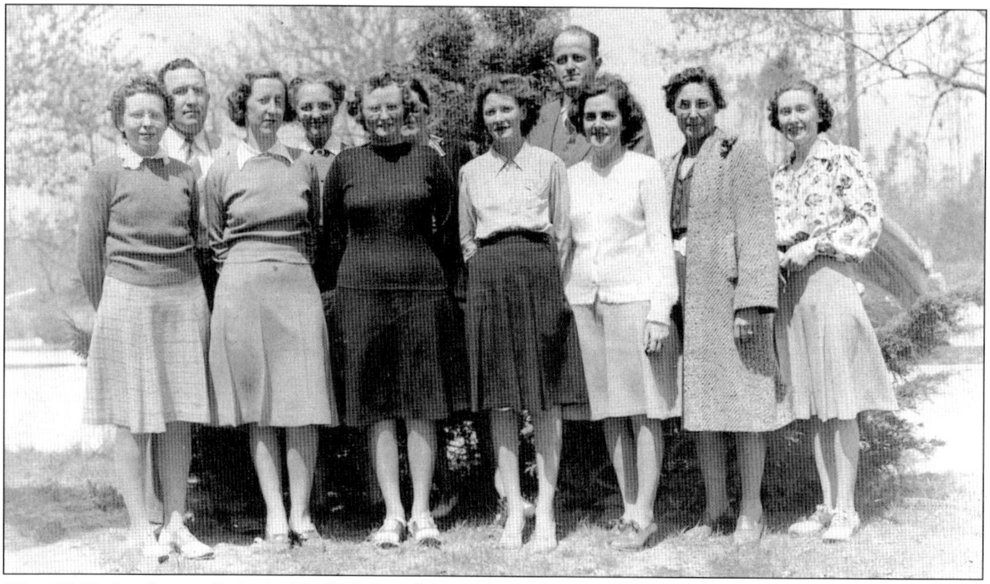

The 1942 faculty at Saluda High School were history and chemistry teacher and principal Mr. Fraley, history and Latin teacher Mrs. Marston, science and math teacher Mary Edna Glenn, English teacher Miss Pittman, commercial teacher Mae Butler Pierce, home economics teacher Miss Vince, agriculture/shop work teacher Mr. Sedivy, seventh-grade teacher Bessie Mae Brown, fifth- and sixth-grade teacher Mrs. Bourne, third- and fourth-grade teacher Miss Spencer, and first- and second grade-teacher Miss Lincoln. (Courtesy of Emily Chowning.)

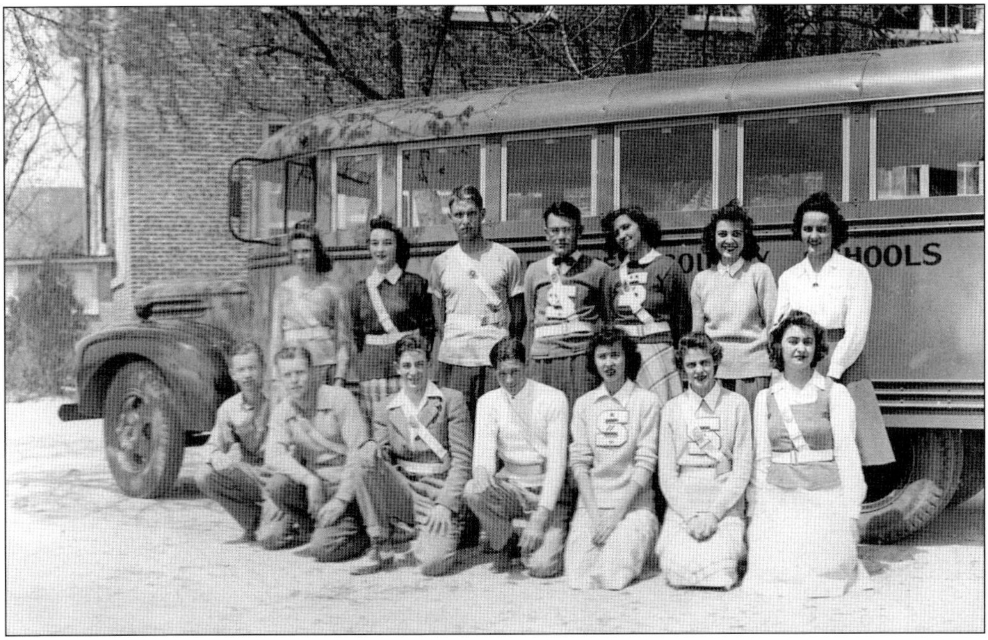

The 1942 Saluda High School safety patrol was composed of two teams. The first team included Billy Wagenen, Mae Derieux, Lena Prince, Thomas Greggs, Dolores Mills, George Daniel, and Garyland Haynes. The second team was made up of Anne Joyce Jordan, Gayle Chowning, Lena Mae Abbott, Marie Major, and Cary Lawson. Joe Green was captain. (Courtesy of Emily Chowning.)

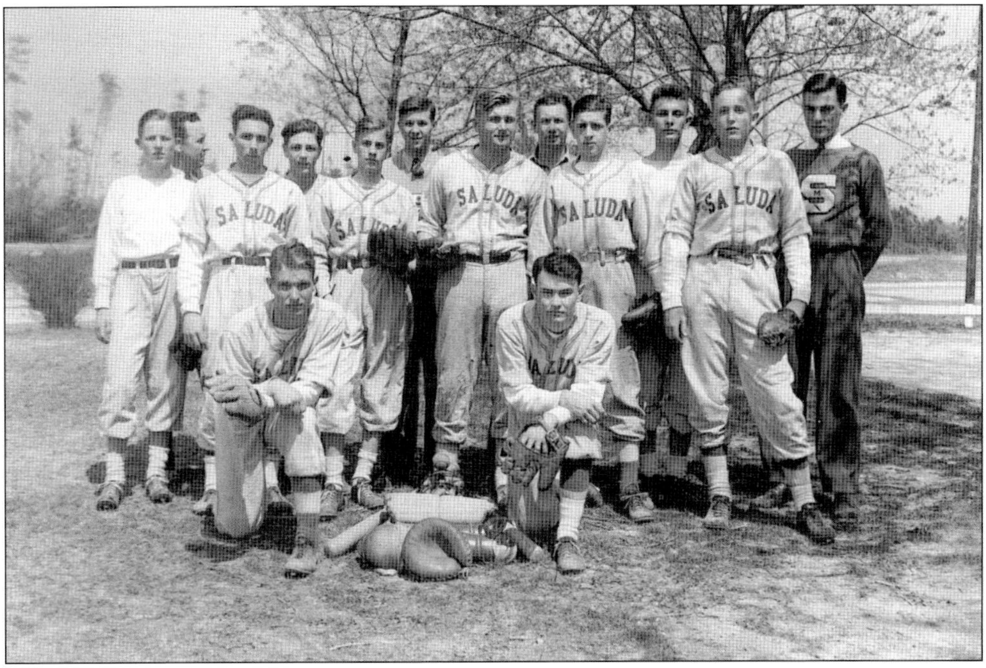

The 1942 Saluda High School baseball team had seniors Billy Wagenen (kneeling at left) and Joe Green (kneeling at right) as co-captains. Several players on the team went on to play for Urbanna, a semipro baseball team. Until about 1948, Urbanna sponsored a semipro team that often paid major league "barnstorming" players to play on the team. (Courtesy of Emily Chowning.)

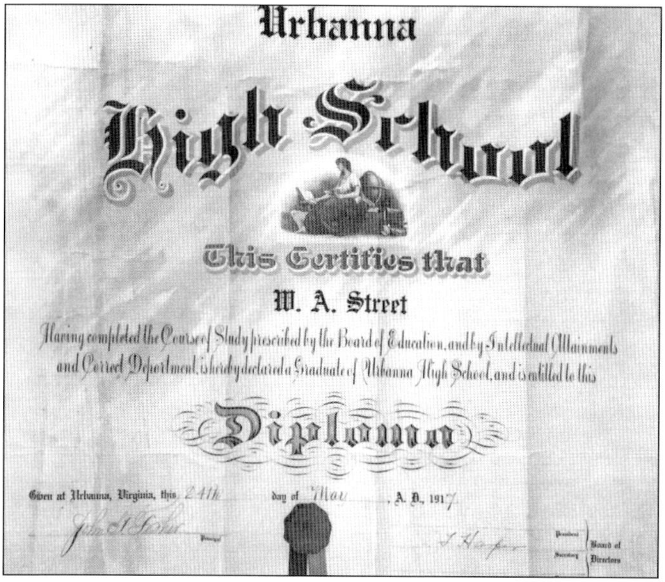
Urbanna

High School

This Certifies that

W. A. Street

Having completed the Course of Study prescribed by the Board of Education, and by Intellectual Attainments and Correct Deportment, is hereby declared a Graduate of Urbanna High School, and is entitled to this

Diploma

Given at Urbanna, Virginia, this 24th day of May, A. D., 1917

The cornerstone was laid for Urbanna High School on June 24, 1909. The school was built as a countywide move to upgrade school buildings and have neighborhood high schools for whites throughout the county. Unionville in Deltaville, Church View, Saluda, and Syringa High Schools all received accreditation. When Saluda became accredited, Urbanna High School closed in 1922 but remained open as an elementary school until 1962. (Author's collection.)

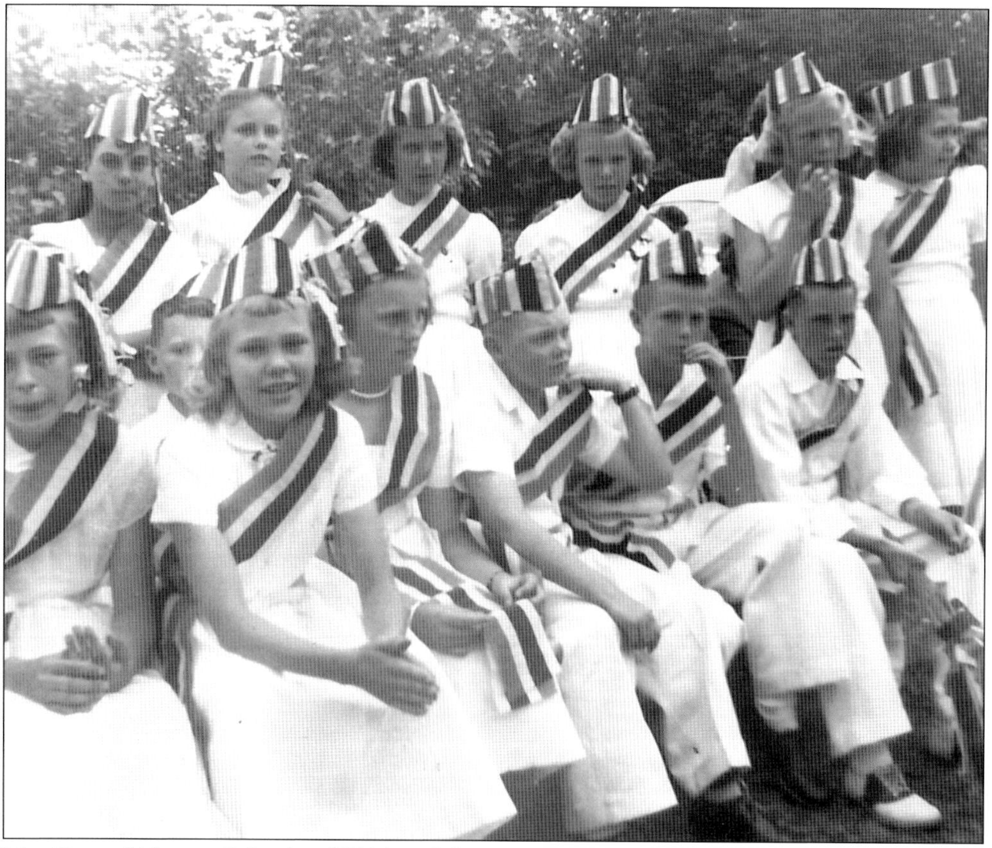

May Day at Urbanna School in 1954 found these youngsters awaiting their turn to dance around the maypole. Younger students longed for the day they would be in the sixth grade and could have their turn to weave back and forth around the maypole. It was seen as a coming of age for these youngsters, as their time was coming soon. (Courtesy of Eva Ann Long.)

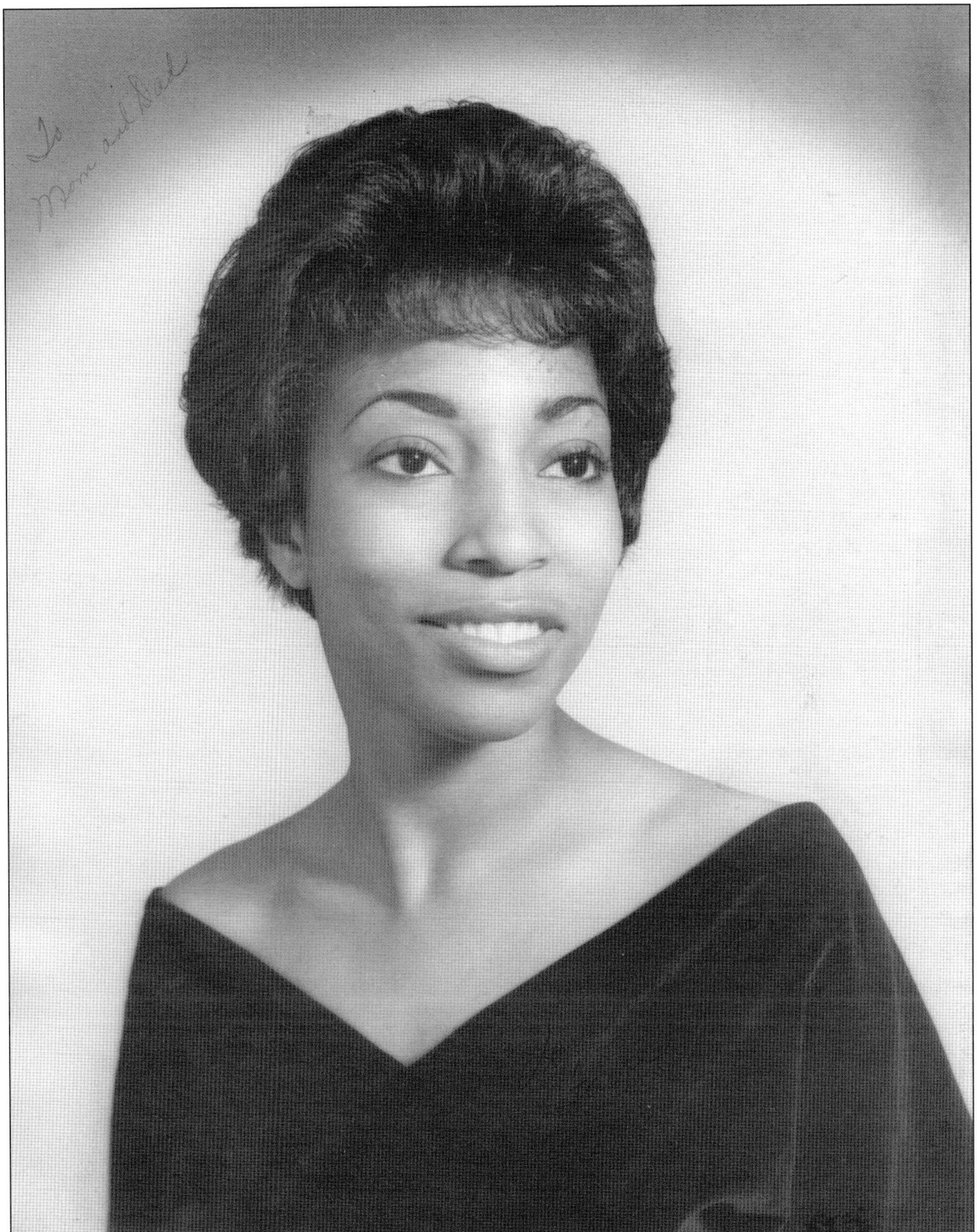

The "Mom and Dad" written in the top left corner of this photograph are Rev. John J. Lewis and his wife, Pearl Ramona Jeter Lewis. Faye Lewis was one of 13 black students to integrate the all-white county schools in 1963 under the freedom of choice plan. The others were Jackie, Jeffrey, Jonathan, and Judith Johnson; Hollis Jordan; Norman Robinson; Violet, Sadie, and George Hodges; Sandra Scott; Paulette Curtis; and Nathaniel Taylor. (Courtesy of Chriscia White.)

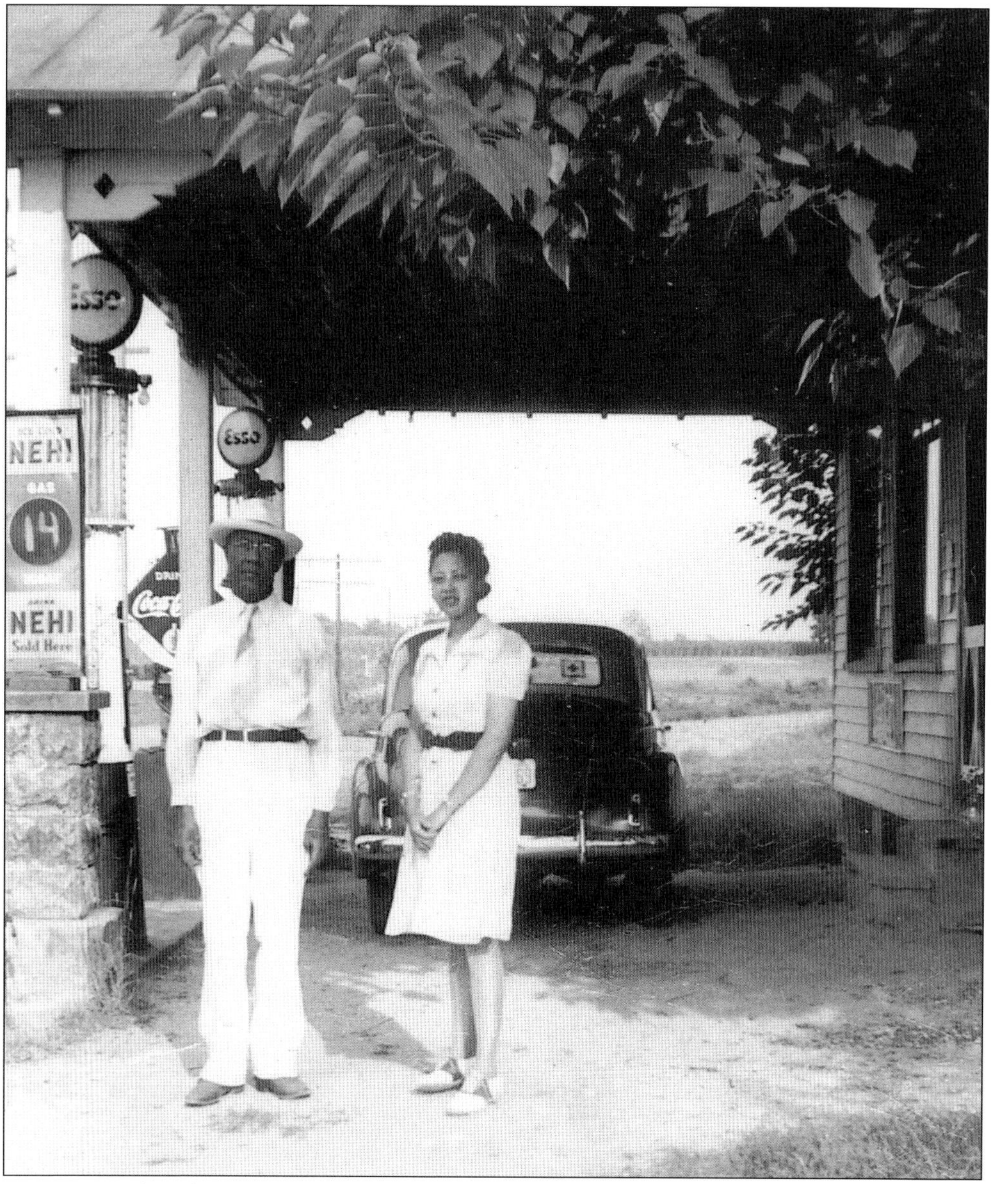

Rev. James Edward Wright (left) was a black leader in the county who owned a country store at Christ Church. Wright was minister at Calvary Baptist, First Baptist of Amburg and Grafton Baptist, and taught at Middlesex Training School before becoming principal of the all-black Middlesex High School. With his own funds, he purchased two school buses to transport black students to and from school. This photograph was taken October 16, 1942, as he was standing by the store. (Courtesy of Ric Davila.)

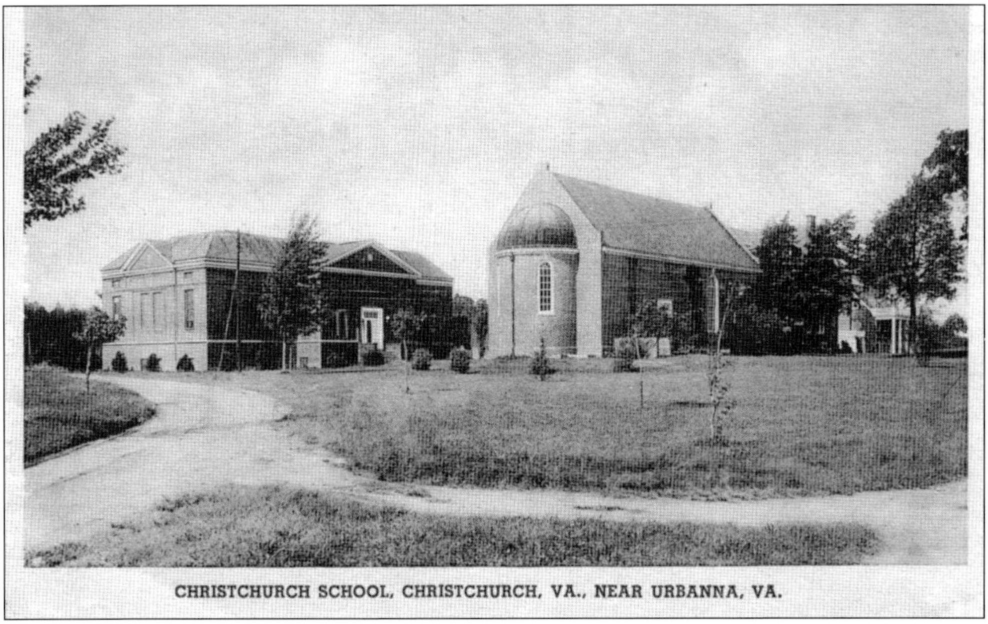

Christchurch School, a private secondary school originally founded for boys, was established by the Episcopal Diocese of Virginia in 1921. At the time, Rev. F. Ernest Warren, the Episcopal rector at the colonial Christ Church, spearheaded a very aggressive and successful campaign to have a church school located in Middlesex. This early postcard shows the gymnasium, chapel, dormitory, and headmaster's home shortly after being built. (Courtesy of Emily Chowning.)

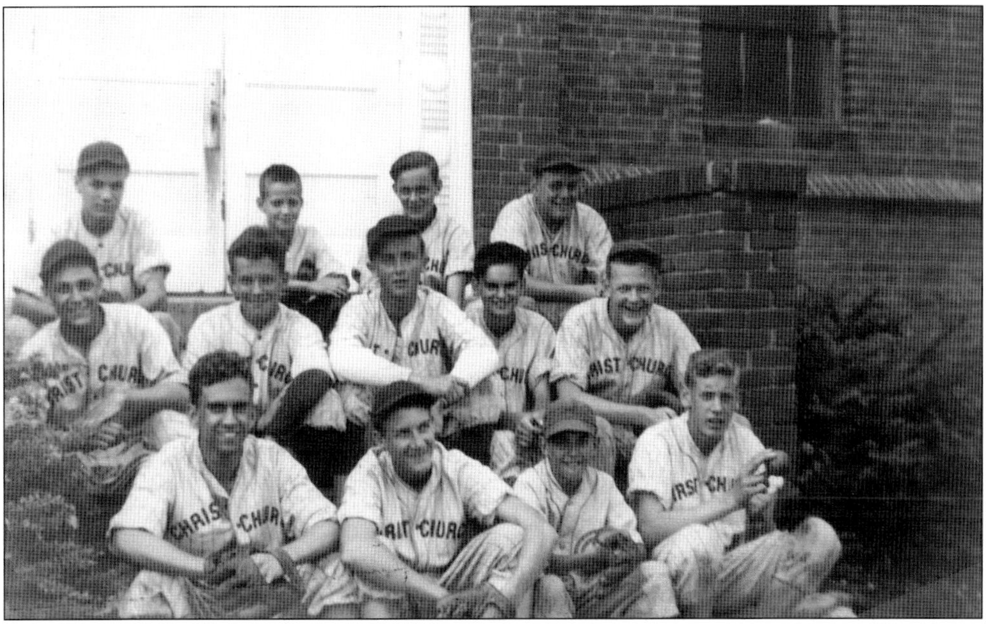

This photograph of the Christchurch baseball team was taken in the early 1940s. Richard Marshall of Urbanna attended as a day student and is second from right in the second row. Prior to 1949, secondary schools in the county stopped at the 11th grade. Some parents sent their sons to Christchurch for a 12th year of school to strengthen their academics for college. (Courtesy of Pat Marshall.)

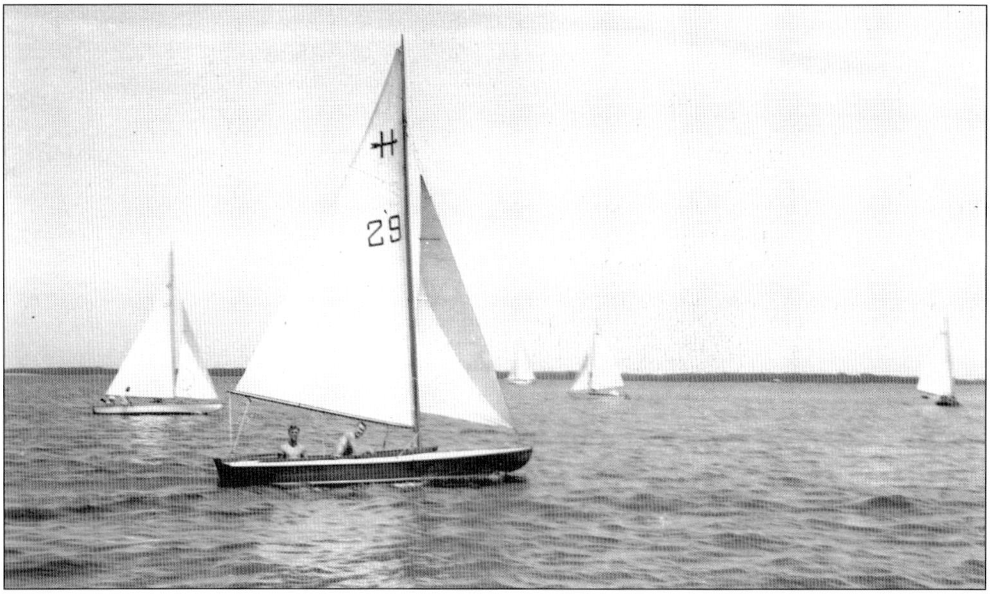

As part of their studies, Christchurch boys learned to sail Hampton One Design sailboats and competed in races on Urbanna Creek and the Rappahannock River sponsored by the Urbanna Yacht Club. The club, founded in 1939, hosted the Hampton One Design national championship in 1948. Club member Lloyd Emory had won the trophy the year before, which brought the championships to Urbanna. The club moved in 1949 and was renamed Fishing Bay Yacht Club. (C.C. Chowning collection.)

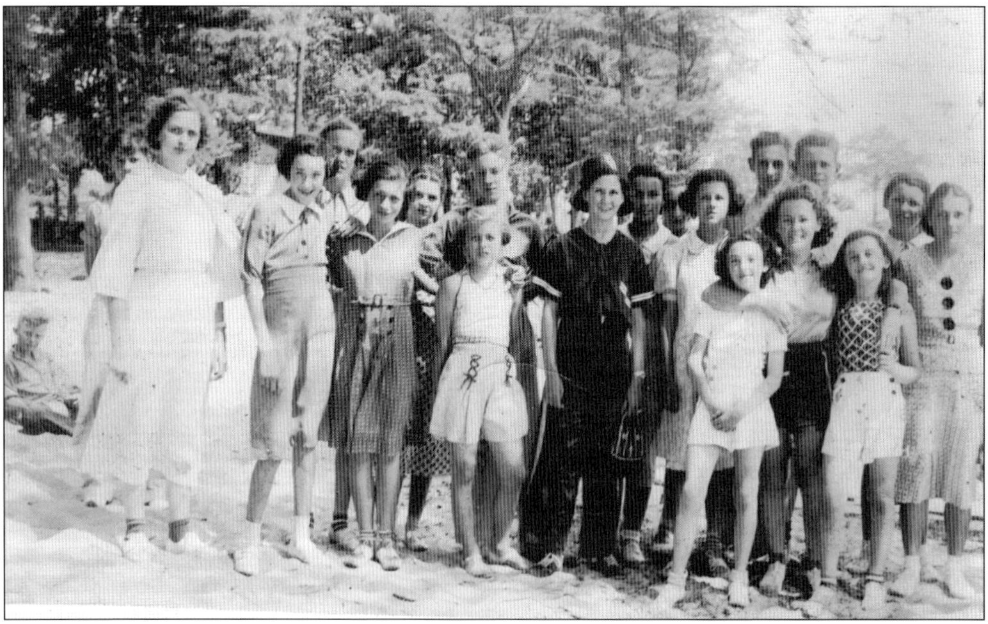

This group of happy Saluda campers are on their way to the Jamestown 4-H camp. The Hs in the 4-H motto stand for head, heart, hands, and health. When this group of Middlesex children were on their way to camp in the mid-1930s, the national motto for 4-H was not yet 10 years old, as it was officially adopted in 1927. Middlesex County has been engaging youth in the 4-H program for over 80 years. (Courtesy of Jean Holman.)

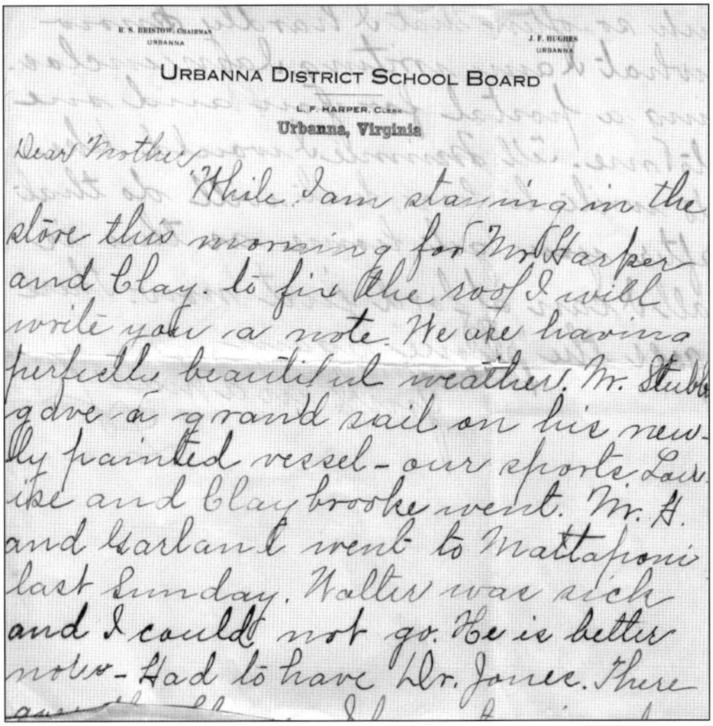

R. S. BRISTOW, CHAIRMAN
URBANNA

J. F. HUGHES
URBANNA

URBANNA DISTRICT SCHOOL BOARD

L. F. HARPER, CLERK

Urbanna, Virginia

Dear Mother,
While I am staying in the store this morning for Mr Harper and Clay to fix the roof I will write you a note. We are having perfectly beautiful weather. Mr. Stubbs gave a grand sail on his newly painted vessel – our sports Lawrie and Claybrooke went. Mr. H. and Garland went to Mattaponi last Sunday. Walter was sick and I could not go. He is better now – Had to have Dr. Jones. There

At the turn of the 20th century, public schools in the county were divided into school districts, and each district had its own school board. R.S. Bristow, chairman; L.F. Harper, clerk; and J.F. Hughes were Urbanna District school board members. Storekeepers were prominent civic leaders in those times, as Bristow and Harper owned general merchandise stores in Urbanna and Hughes was a storekeeper at Streets. (C.C. Chowning collection.)

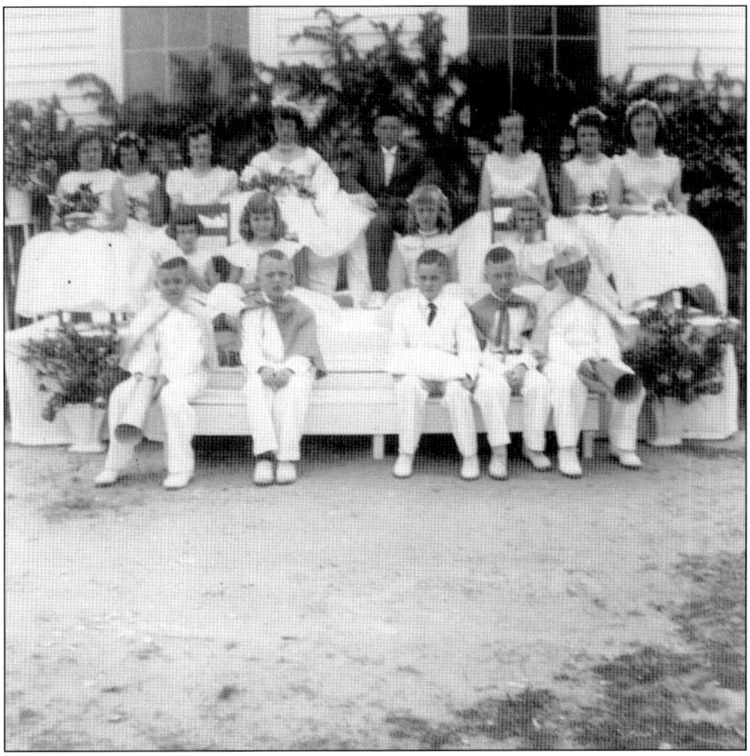

May Day was an annual celebration at schools throughout the county. The crowning of the king and queen of May Day and the dance around the maypole was a life memory for students who attended the neighborhood schools of those times. This photograph is of a May Day court at Deltaville Elementary School. (Courtesy of Garland Robins.)

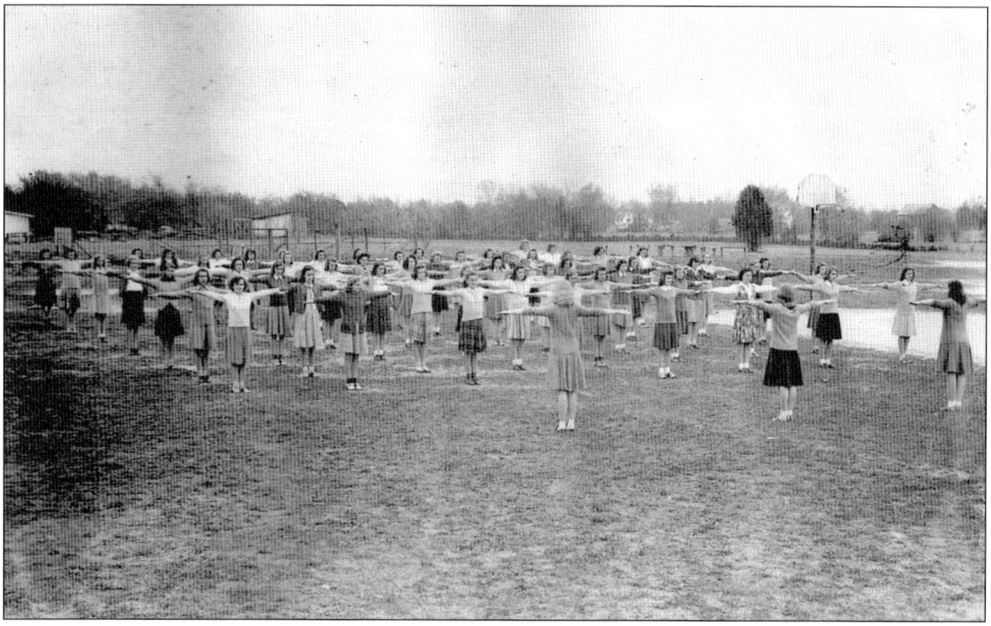

Girls at Saluda High School in 1943 played no varsity sports that year as part of a World War II effort to conserve gasoline. Instead, they played intramural sports, which consisted of basketball, softball, volleyball, and a calisthenics program, as seen here. The outside basketball court and goal, shown on the right, consisted of a tree pole, backboard, and hoop, but no net. (Courtesy of Emily Chowning.)

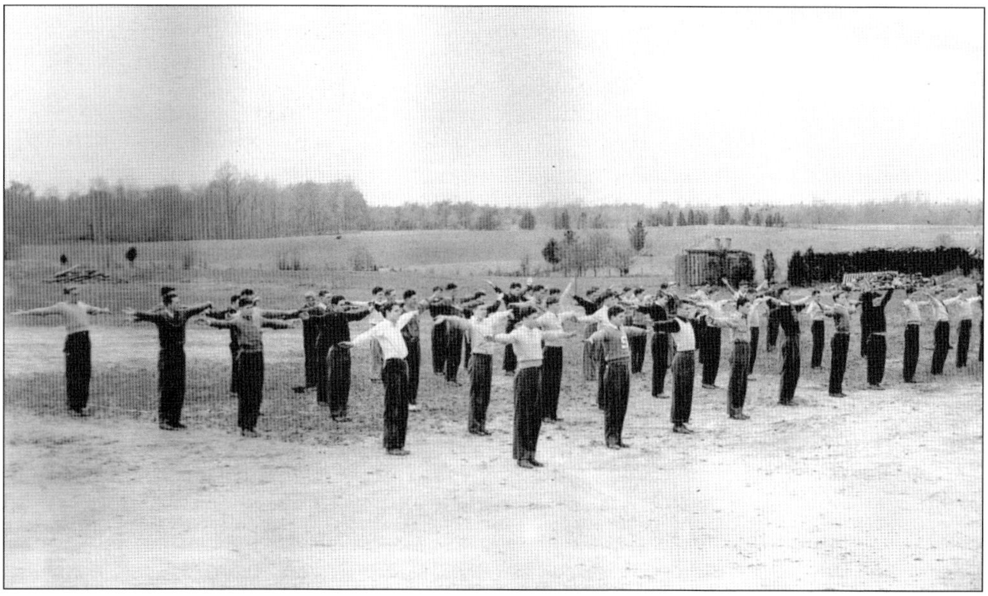

Many of these boys at Saluda High School in 1943 were just months away from enlisting in the armed forces to go off and fight in World War II. Travel was suspended for sporting activities during the school year of 1942–1943 due to the nationwide rationing of gasoline to support the war effort. Christchurch School and Saluda, just down the road from each other, played one another in basketball and baseball over and over as all other games were canceled. (Courtesy of Emily Chowning.)

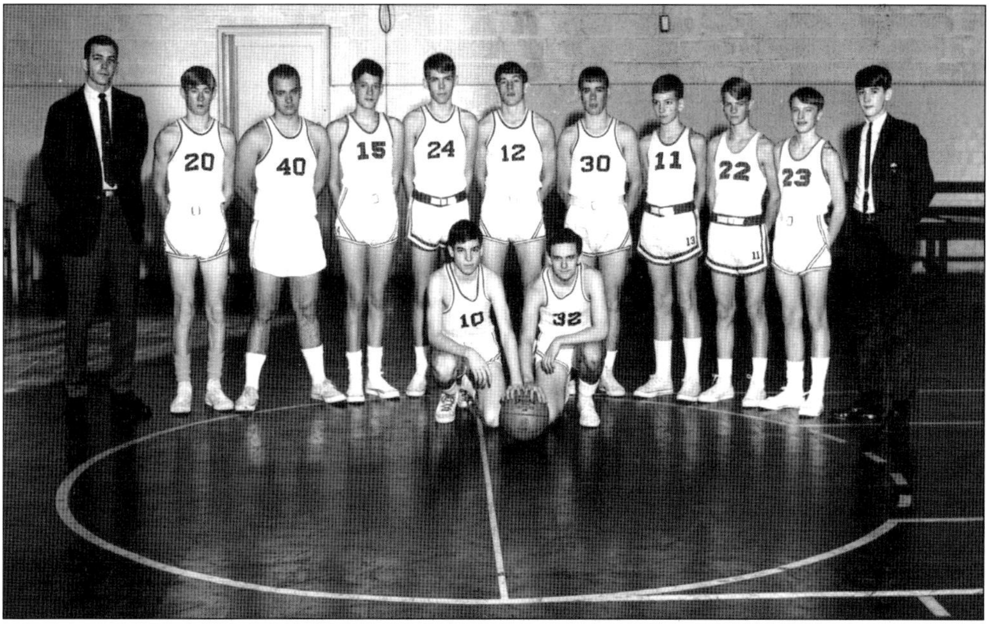

The 1967 Middlesex High School junior varsity basketball team was composed of, from left to right, (first row) co-captains Ray Rodgers and Everette Wright; (standing) coach Bob Johnson, Eddie Payne, Richard Wright, David Barrick, Danny Staples, David Hooks, Donny Walton, Bill Davies, Roy Jackson, George Daniel, and manager Richard Haynes. Desegregation of Middlesex County schools came at the start of the 1969–1970 school year. (Courtesy of the *Southside Sentinel*.)

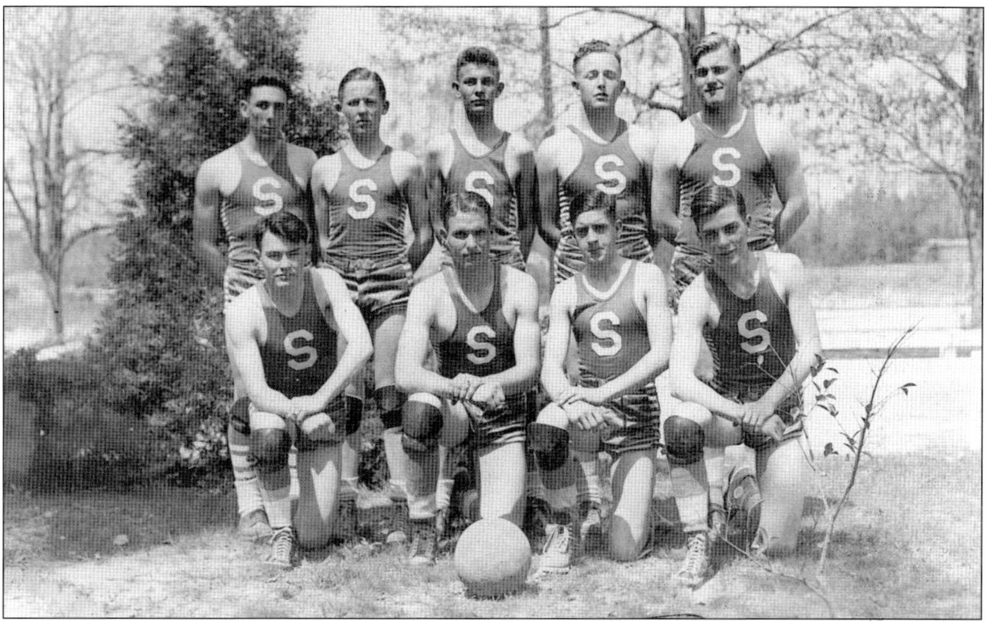

During the 1941–1942 season, the Saluda boys' basketball team was 10-3. Colonial Beach won the Class D championship, but Saluda held the champs to a 28-28 tie in regulation time only to lose the championship in overtime, 30-28. Tyler Thrift and Glenn Williams were co-captains. Other members were Joe Green, Billy and Ben Wagenen, Guy Williams, Andrew Davis, Lee Bristow, Tommy Marshall, and Walter Boyd Hurley. (Courtesy of Emily Chowning.)

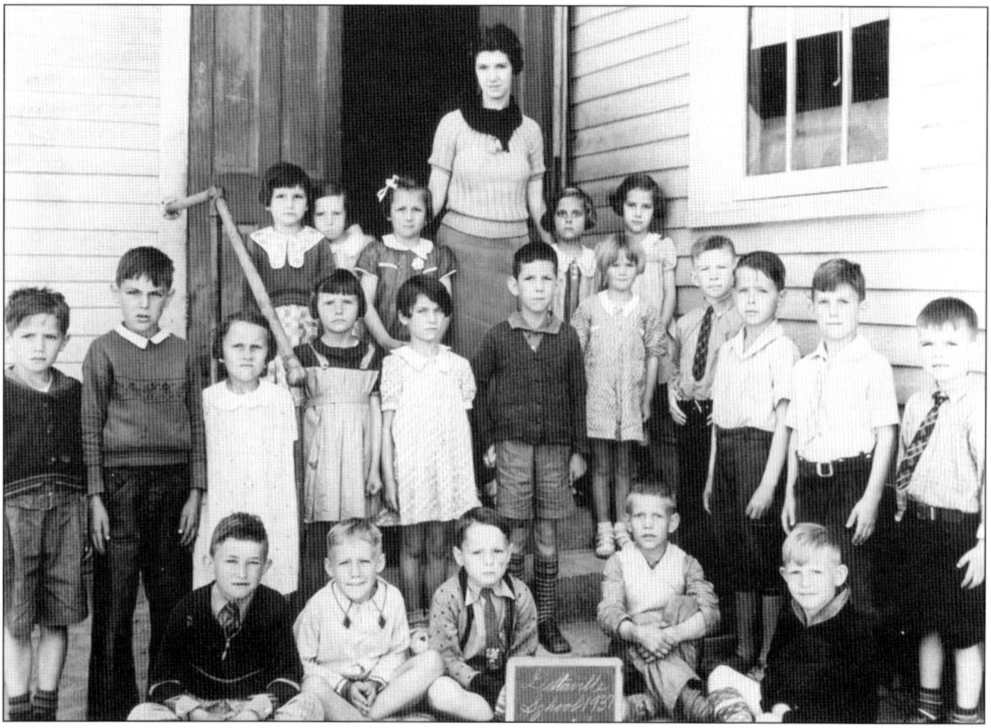

Deltaville Elementary School operated from 1924 to 1962 when the eastern end of Middlesex County consolidated elementary schools in what became known as Wilton Elementary School. Prior to 1924, Deltaville's school was known as Unionville High School, which included both elementary and secondary classes to the 11th grade. The first grade of 1937 attended Deltaville Elementary School and later went to Syringa High School for secondary training. (Courtesy of Willard and Shirley Norris.)

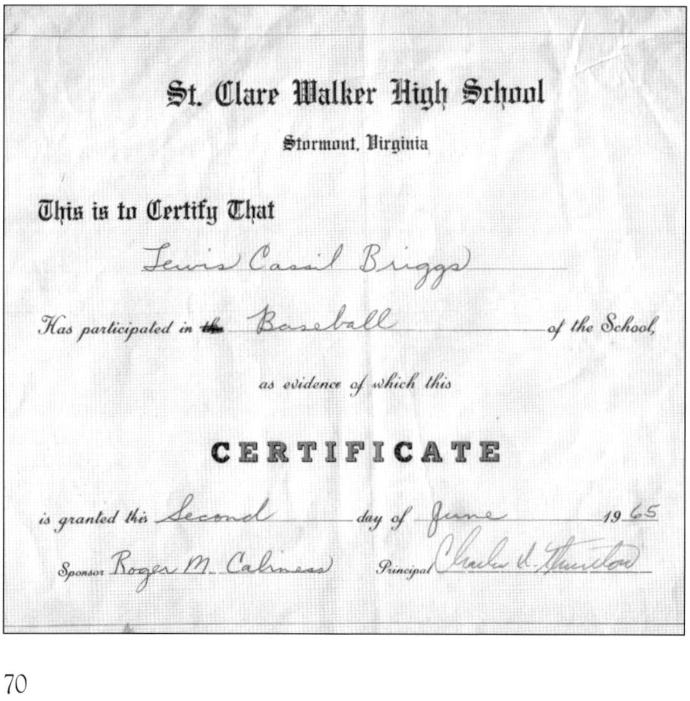

St. Clare Walker High School

Stormont, Virginia

This is to Certify That

Lewis Casil Briggs

Has participated in ~~the~~ Baseball of the School,

as evidence of which this

CERTIFICATE

is granted this Second day of June 1965

Sponsor Roger M. Calmess Principal Charles L. Thurston

Lewis Briggs of Locust Hill attended St. Clare Walker High School, the all-black high school at Stormont. In 1960s, Briggs was a star pitcher on the Wolverine baseball team. In 1965, against Mathews County's all-black Thomas Hunter High School baseball team, Briggs pitched a no-hitter and struck out 20 batters. He was recruited by baseball scout Syd Thrift to play Major League Baseball, but opted to make a career at Newport News Shipbuilding Co. (Courtesy of Lewis Briggs.)

The Saluda High School mascot was the Blue Jay, as seen on the sweatshirt worn by Sara Booth (second from left). Pictured in 1942 are, from left to right, Betty Woodward, Booth, Hannah Bourne, Gayle Chowning, and Glenn Williams. The team name changed to the Middle Saxons in the 1950s, when the all-white high schools in the county were consolidated to form Middlesex High School. With integration, the name changed to the Chargers in the 1969–1970 school year. (C.C. Chowning collection.)

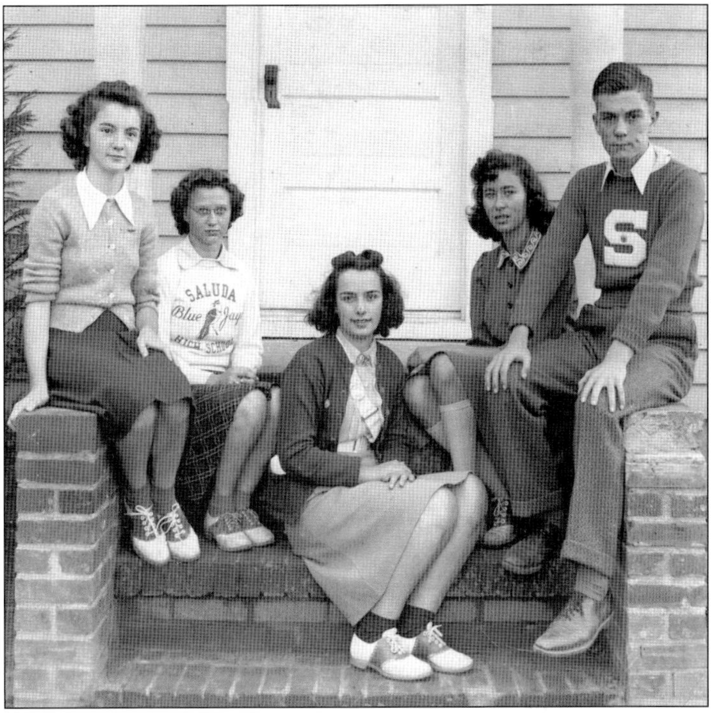

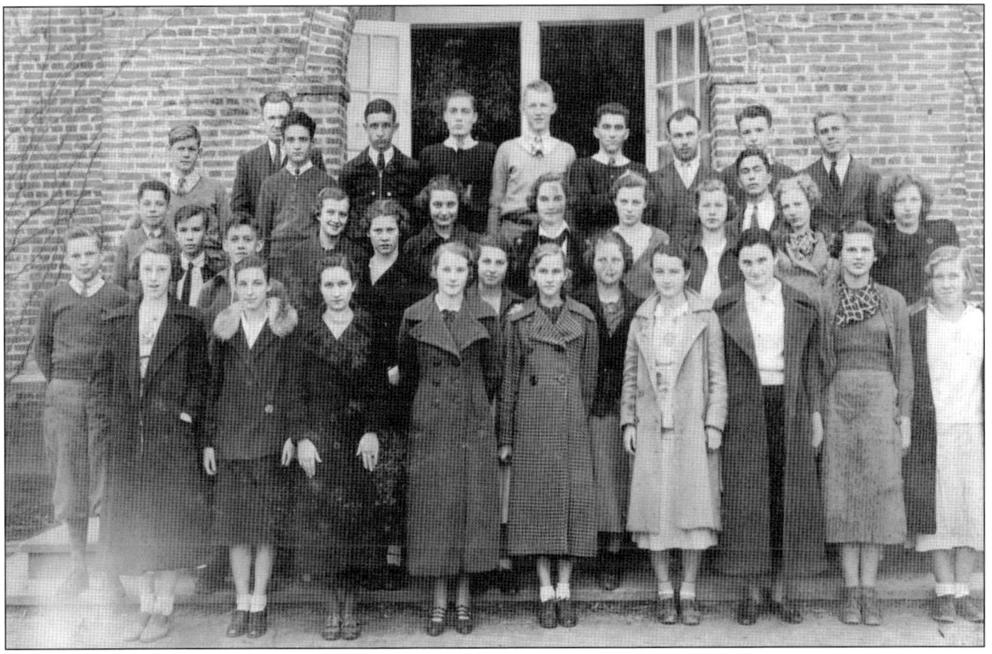

Several members of this Saluda High School group took part in the water strike of 1937. In 1934, running water and indoor plumbing was installed in the school. The well that served the school went dry in December 1936, and there was no water by February 1937. A group of students refused to attend until it was fixed. The strike gained statewide attention and prompted General Assembly legislation that mandated drinking water and sanitary toilets inside all public schools. (Courtesy of Louise Gray.)

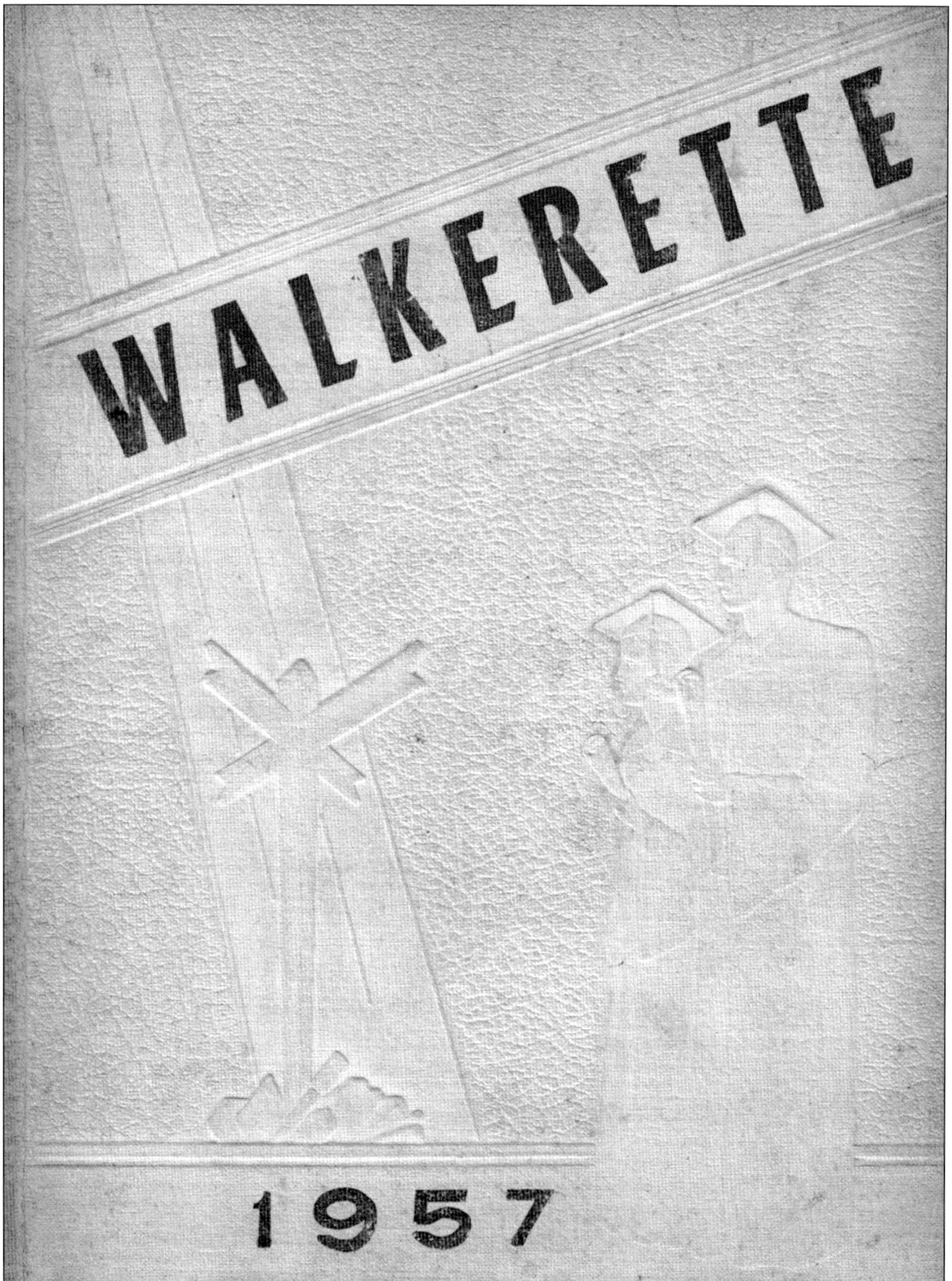

John Henry St. Clare Walker was an African American educator who had a major impact on education of African Americans in Middlesex. The all-black St. Clare Walker High School was named in his honor. When school desegregation came in 1969, the high school closed. Today, the county's St. Clare Walker Middle School is named in his honor. In 1957, the high school annual was named *Walkerette*, another acknowledgment of St. Clare Walker's legacy on education in Middlesex. (Courtesy of Lewis Briggs.)

Six

RELIGION IN MIDDLESEX

When the first Englishmen settled Middlesex, the established church of the Virginia colony was the Church of England, also known as the Anglican Church. The church, with its regular weekly service, occupied a much larger place in the social life of the colonial community. There was a time set during the service for the reading of official notices, governor's proclamations, and new laws required to be brought to the attention of the people.

When Middlesex was part of Lancaster County, there were two church parishes, Lancaster and Peanckatanck, both established in 1657. Churches were built in these two parishes. Christ Church Parish, which would include both Lancaster and Peanckatanck Parishes, was created in 1666 and became the county's "mother church." The upper and lower churches became "chapels of ease," and all three churches remained active until the end of the American Revolution, when the Anglicans fell from grace.

Shortly before the Revolutionary War, Baptists and Methodists came to the county, spreading a new style of religion. As early as 1763, Methodist reverend George Whitefield spent time in Urbanna, and two decades later in 1785, Methodist bishop Francis Asbury came to the county. In 1829, Methodists began to have regular worship services in an area known as the Forest. Forest Chapel, the mother church of all county Methodist churches, was built in 1840, and from that, six other Methodist churches were founded in the county.

When the Baptist movement came to the county, it spread like wildfire. Baptist minister John Waller came in 1772, and along with several Middlesex residents, was thrown into prison by the Anglican authority for preaching without a license. This fueled a fire of religious change and contributed to a strong and determined Baptist movement. The Baptist Church has remained the most active denomination in Middlesex. During slavery, the Baptist churches integrated as white slave owners allowed slaves to attend church, with whites downstairs and blacks in the balcony. Shortly after freedom came, former slaves in the 1860s founded Antioch, Grafton, and Metropolitan Baptist Churches. The white and black churches have remained segregated, and today there are 13 black Baptist churches in the county.

By the mid-1800s, Old Christ Church, abandoned by the Anglicans and in ruin, was given new life by Episcopalians, and it stands today as a place of worship and a tribute to a long religious heritage.

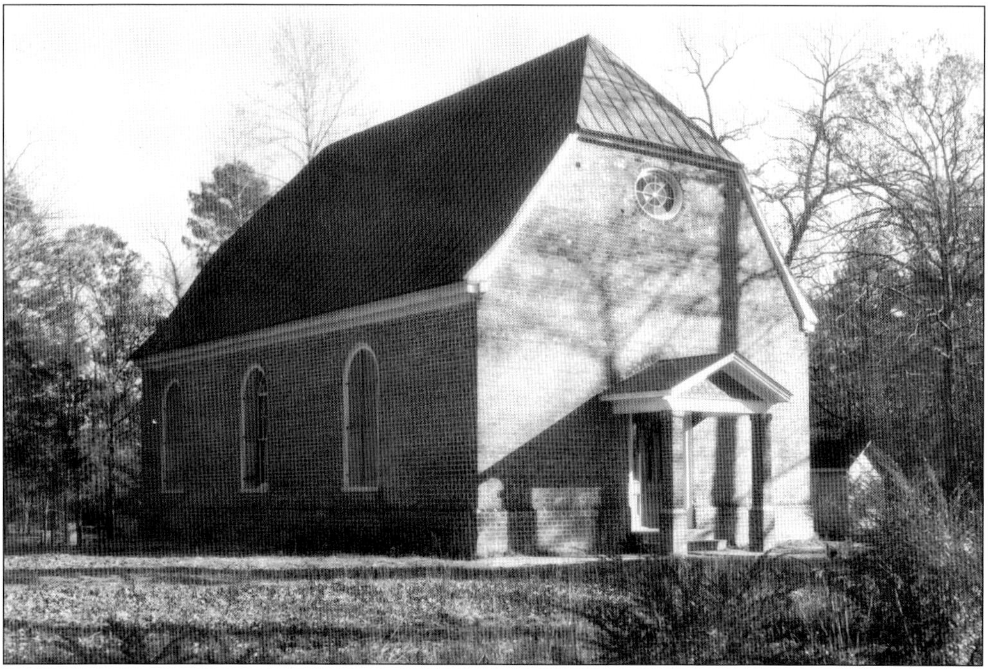

Edmund Kemp and others in the lower end of Middlesex (then Lancaster) County formed Lower Church in 1657. The church was used as an Anglican chapel until after the Revolutionary War. A date of "17A15" is carved in a brick at the entrance. The A is likely for Henry Armistead, who was in charge of construction. Methodist Robert Healy purchased the church from the Protestant Episcopal Church for $300 in 1857, and it is today Lower United Methodist Church. (C.C. Chowning collection.)

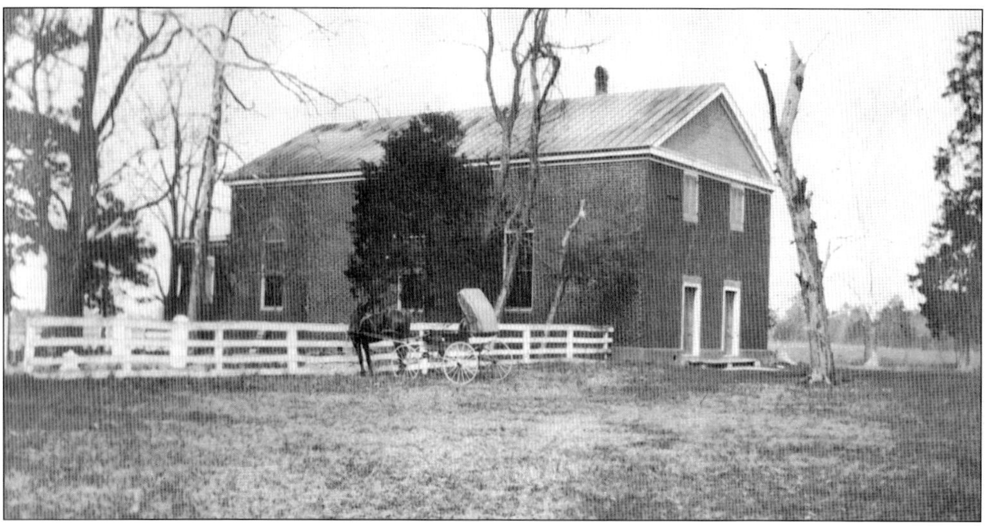

The Upper Chapel of Ease, built in 1773, was a relatively new structure when the Anglican congregation abandoned the building shortly after the Revolutionary War, and Hermitage Baptists started using it as a chapel in 1827. It was the third Upper Anglican Chapel structure, and replaced the second chapel that had been located on the same site since 1712. The 1773 church building burned in 1948 and was replaced on the same site with a new Hermitage Baptist Church building. (Courtesy of Jean Holman.)

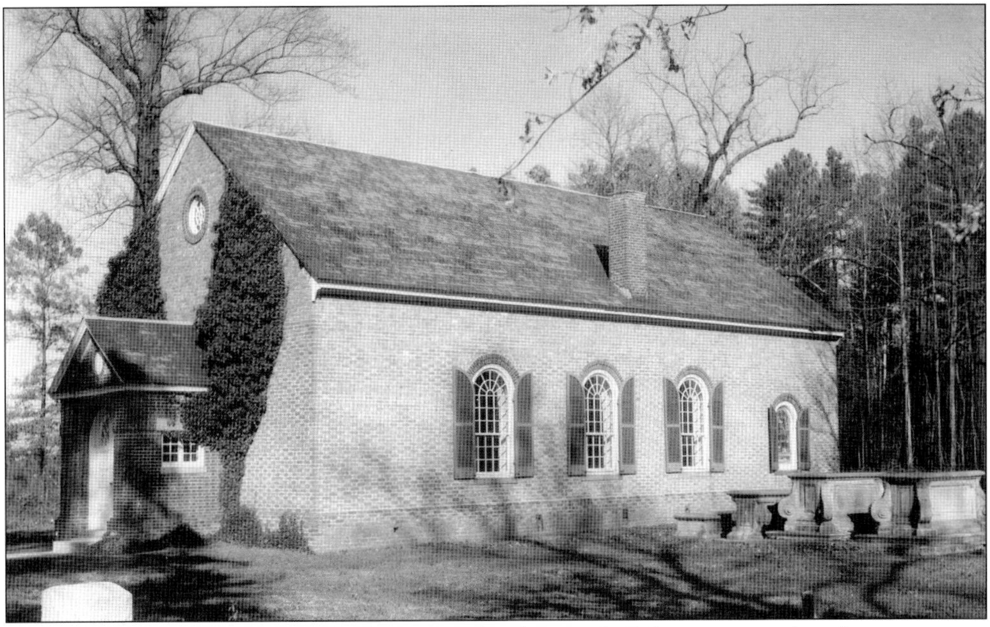

Christ Church is believed to have been completed around 1714, two years after the vestry gave orders for a new brick church to be built on the site of the first structure. Christ Church became the mother church in 1666, when Lancaster and Peanckatanck Parishes merged to become Christ Church Parish with the upper and lower churches becoming chapels of ease. (C.C. Chowning collection.)

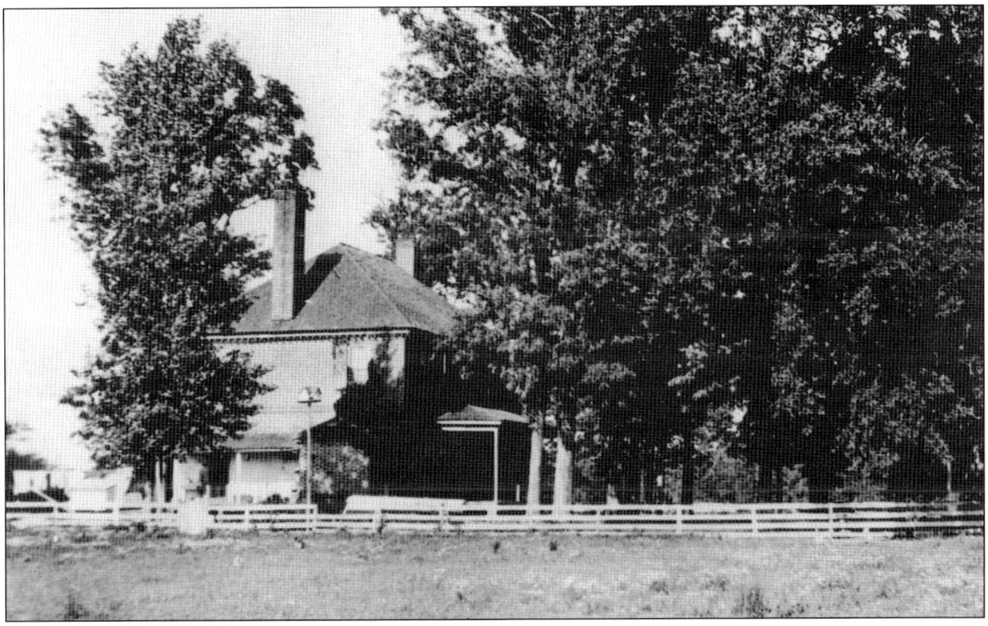

The Glebe, on Town Bridge Road between Saluda and Urbanna, was the residence of ministers of the Anglican Christ Church Parish from its beginning in 1666 until the disestablishment of the church following the revolution. An earlier Glebe home was torn down, and this building was erected around 1757, along with a new free-standing kitchen and dairy. The old home burned to the ground in 1913. (C.C. Chowning collection.)

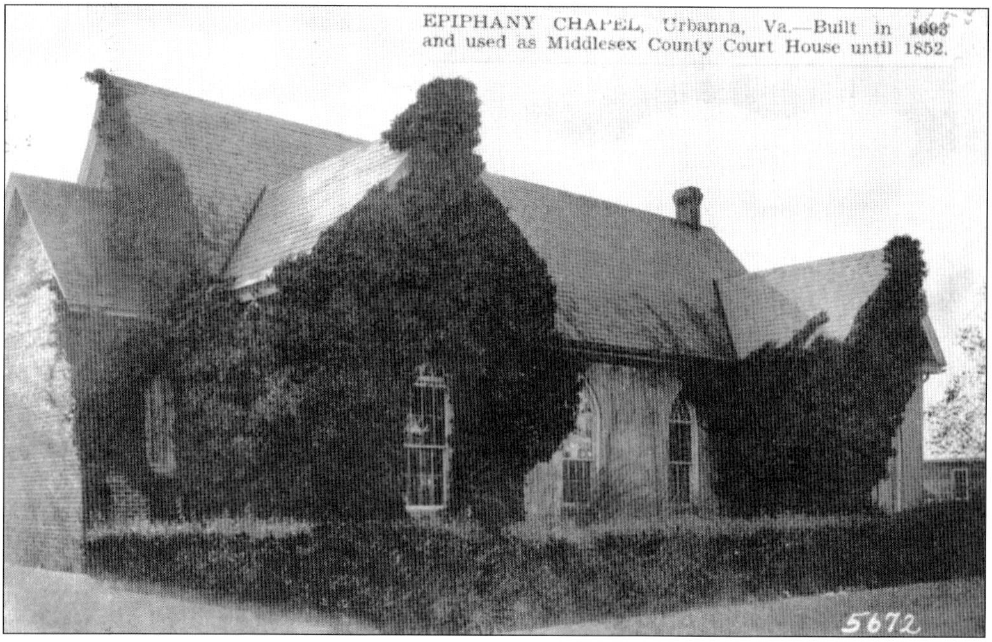

Built in 1748, this building in Urbanna was used as the county courthouse of Middlesex County for 104 years. It was in this structure that Baptist minister John Waller was put on trial by Anglican authority for "carrying on a meeting against the authority of the land" and "preaching without a license" in 1771. Waller was jailed and preached from the jailhouse window to large crowds of people, soon to be Baptists. (Courtesy of Emily Chowning.)

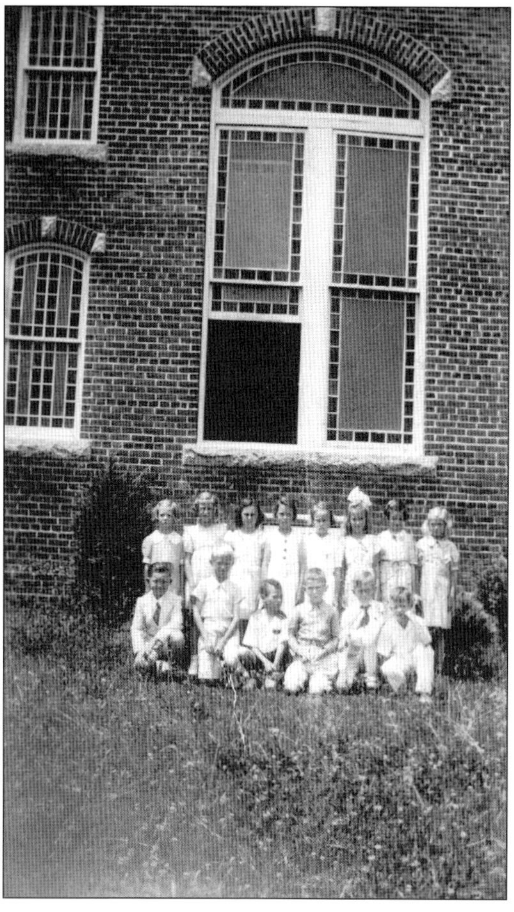

Sunday school was where children were taught the spiritual lessons and golden rules of life found in the Bible. This photograph of the five- to eight-year-old Sunday school class at Harmony Grove Baptist Church was taken in front of the church around 1935. Emily Blake Chowning is standing at far right and Bankie Stiff Benton has a bow in her hair. Between 1838 and 1847, Zoar Baptist Church released 58 whites and 66 blacks to found Harmony Grove Baptist Church. (Courtesy of Emily Chowning.)

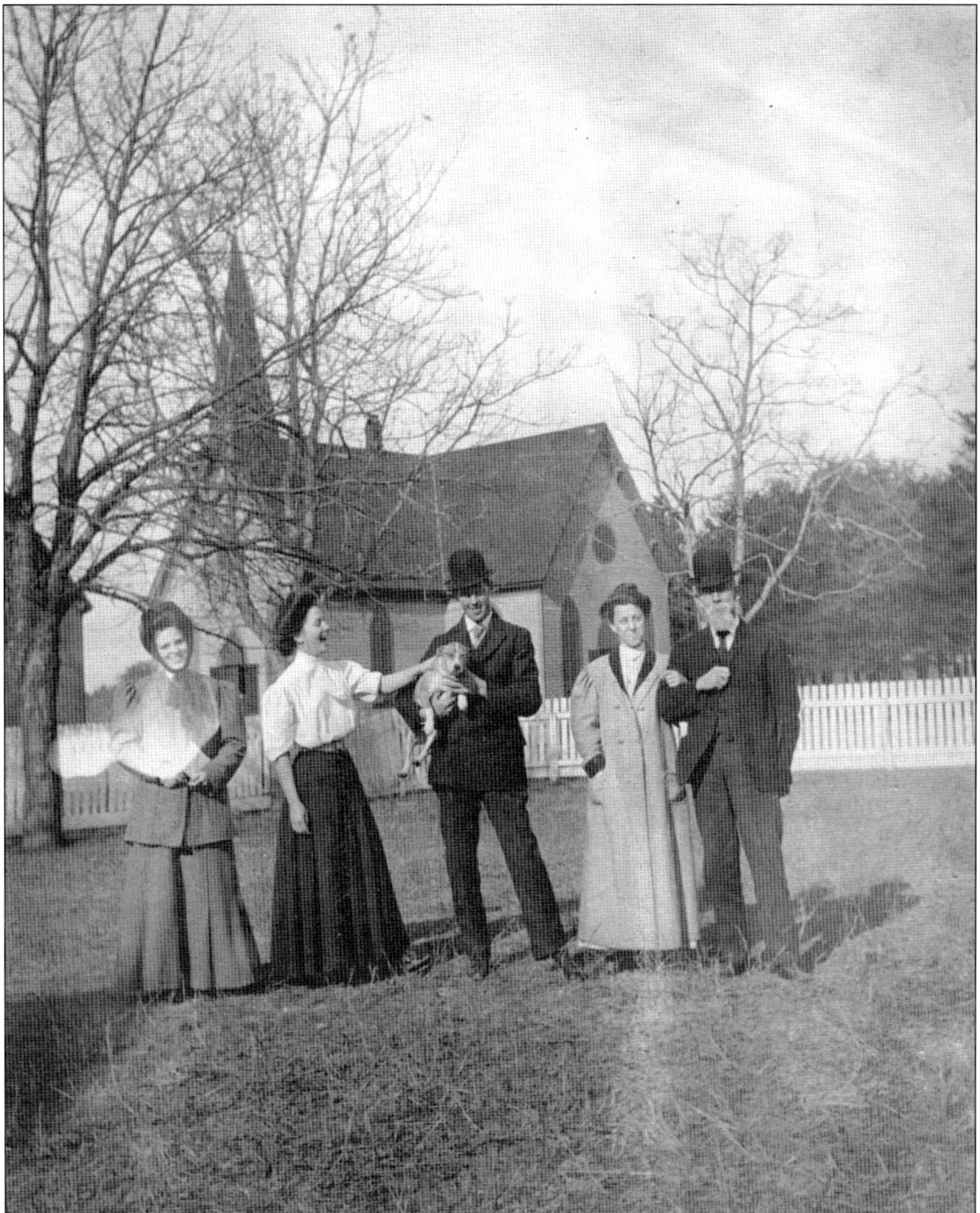

Zoar Baptist Church, seen in the background, was founded in 1808. Zoar is the daughter church of Hermitage Baptist Church and granddaughter of Glebe Landing Baptist Church. It was founded during the religious integration period of Middlesex County Baptist churches, when blacks and whites worshiped together. On November 4, 1808, about 100 members were dismissed from Hermitage to organize a meeting place in lower Middlesex. Twenty white and eighty black members left to create Zoar Baptist. (Courtesy of Nola Watson.)

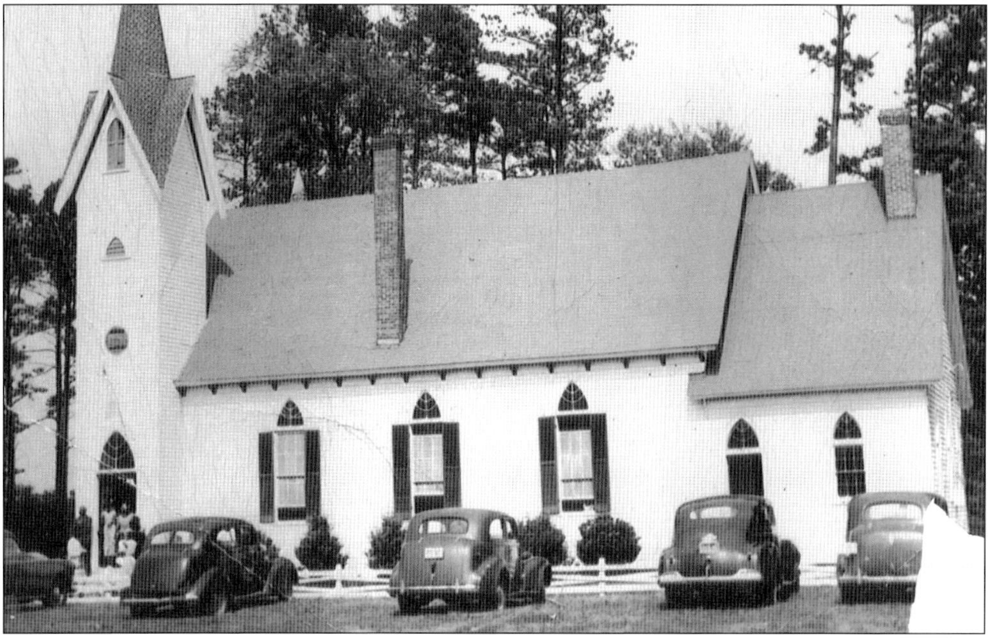

First Baptist Church of Amburg was originally part of Zoar Baptist Church. After the Civil War in 1867, Zoar's black members decided to organize their own church, and First Baptist of Amburg was formed. This photograph is of the structure that stands today and was built in 1901 after the original church building burned in 1895. (Courtesy of First Baptist of Amburg.)

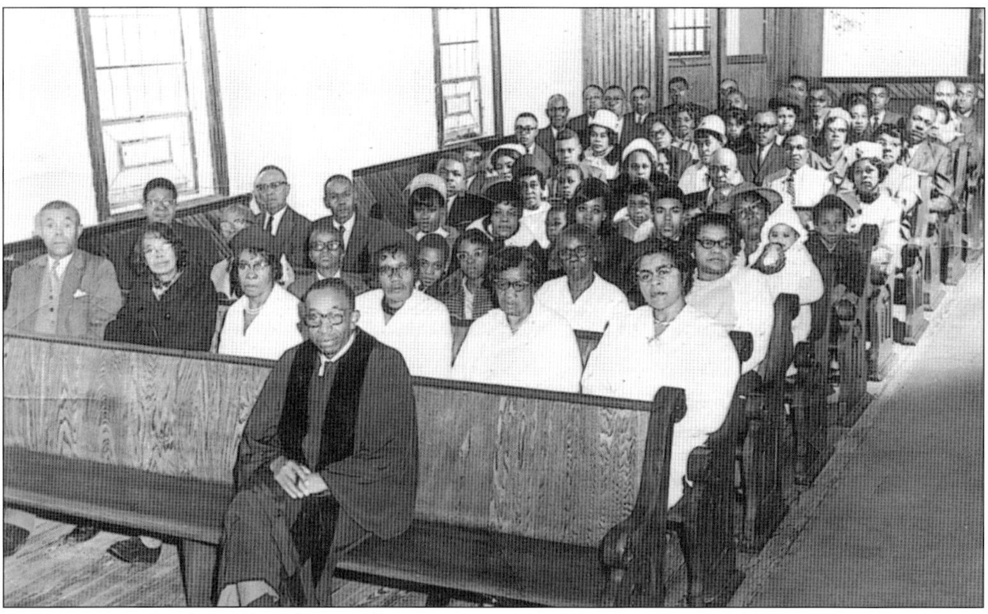

Rev. W.E. Payne (seated in first row) was pastor of First Baptist of Amburg for 45 years. Right after and during slavery, blacks worshiped in white churches but under rules and stipulations of white authority. Blacks were often encouraged to hold services and church meetings at different times than whites. There was probably mutual encouragement from both races when blacks from Zoar Baptist Church left the congregation in 1867 to form First Baptist of Amburg. (Courtesy of First Baptist of Amburg.)

Rev. James Kinner was a pioneer in bringing religion and education to former slaves of Middlesex. Kinner was born September 19, 1821, a slave to Warner Lewis of Essex County. After slavery, he went to Washington, DC, to attend Wayland Seminary and became a Baptist minister. About 1870, he was called to pastor at Antioch Baptist Church in Saluda (founded 1866) and Grafton Baptist Church near Hartfield (founded 1867). (Courtesy of James Conway and Otelia Arugunes.)

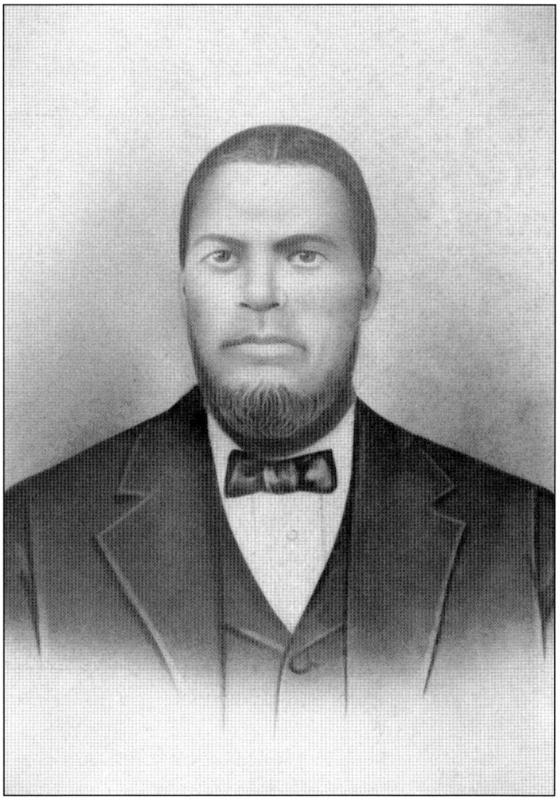

During slavery, many Middlesex African Americans were denied the opportunity to worship. When freedom came, they organized and built their own churches. In the 1980s, these children of Grafton Baptist Church in Hartfield anxiously await their turn at being baptized in the Rappahannock River. Grafton is one of the few churches that still carry on the tradition of holding baptism down by the river. (Author's collection.)

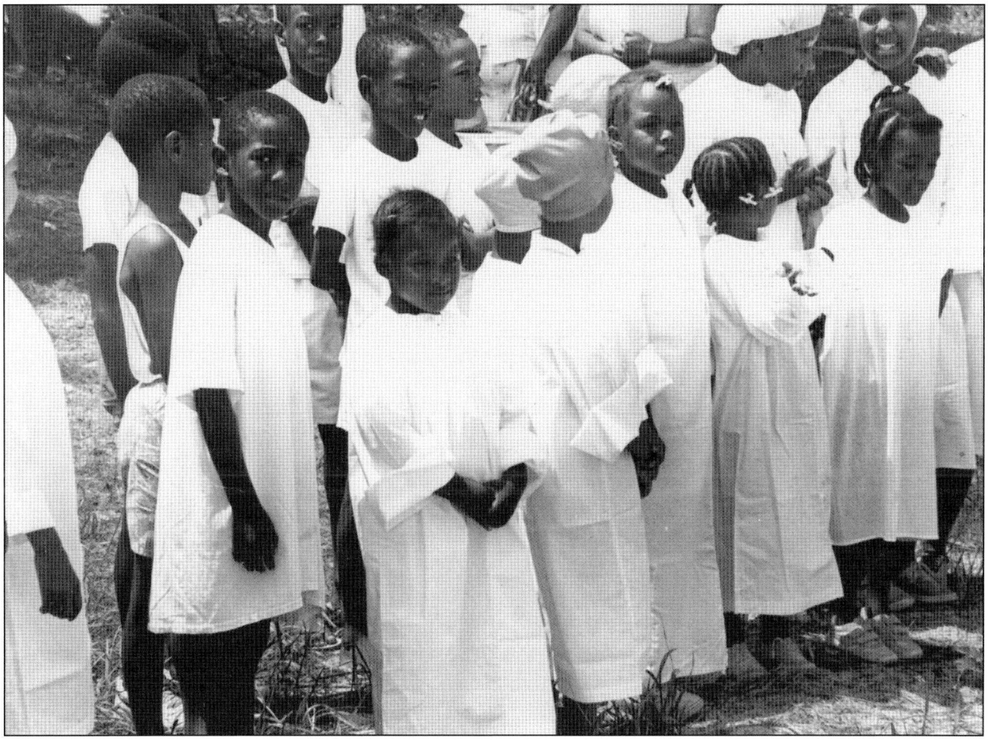

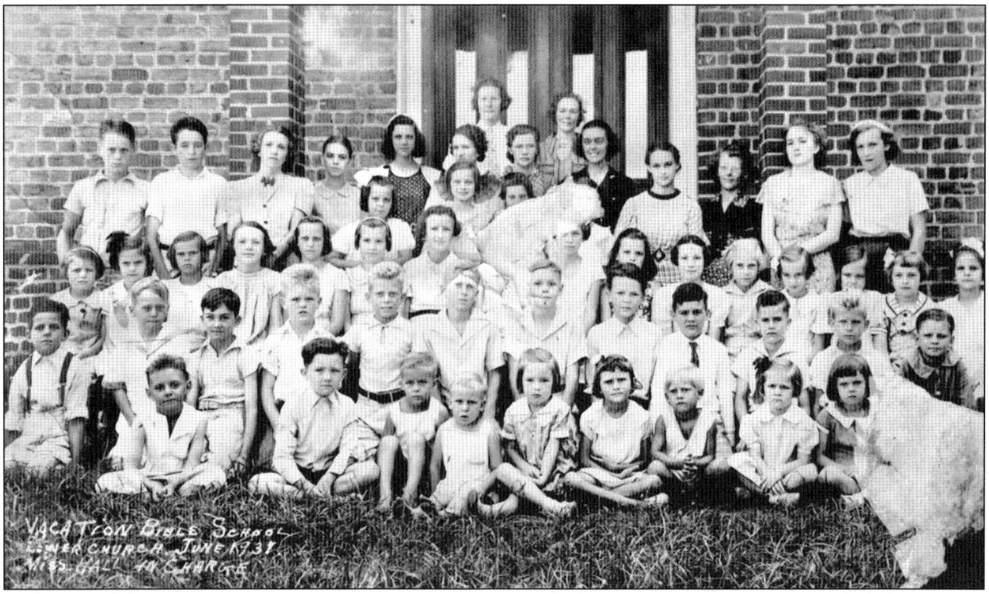

This 1937 Lower Methodist Church Vacation Bible School group are posed in front of the front door of the 1714 former Anglican Lower Chapel near Hartfield. Vacation Bible schools were held throughout the county in the summertime to provide children with additional religious training. Bible school provided a week of worship, exercise, crafting, and fellowship. If their Bible school did not fall on the same week, children often attended Bible classes of other denominations. (Courtesy of Frances Johnston.)

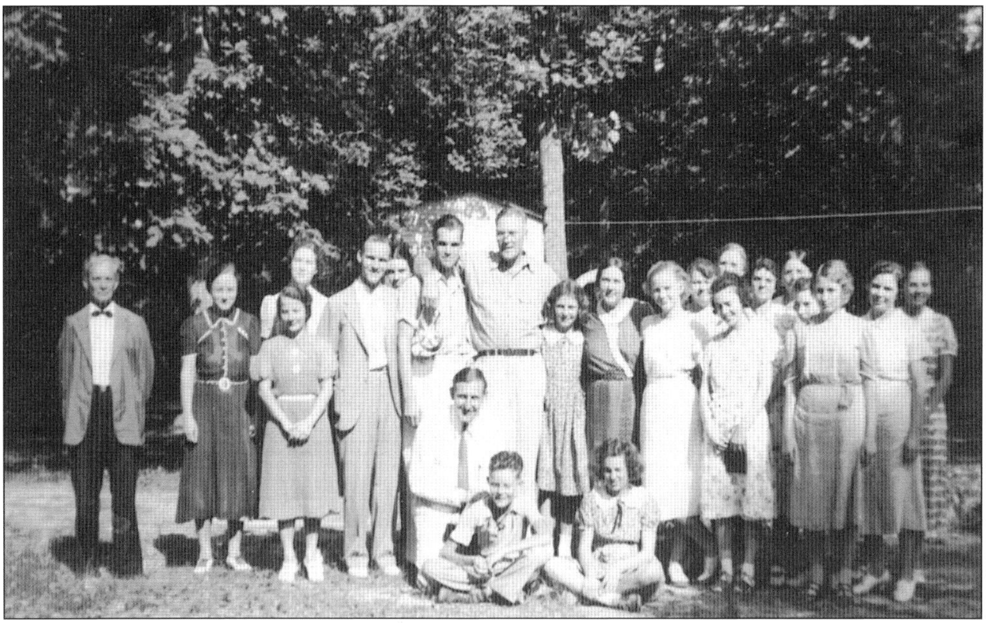

The Middlesex Holiness Association was officially organized on November 27, 1909, and was led by Rev. Edwin J. Moffitt of Deltaville. Moffitt, J.H. Norton, K.C. Yates, George Kellum, and E.D. Moore founded the association and built an outdoor tabernacle. Holiness camp meetings were held regularly there, and as one attendee said, "You could get saved in the sawdust. Salvation was instant." Reverend Moffatt (left) and camp members are pictured here. (Courtesy of Garland Robins.)

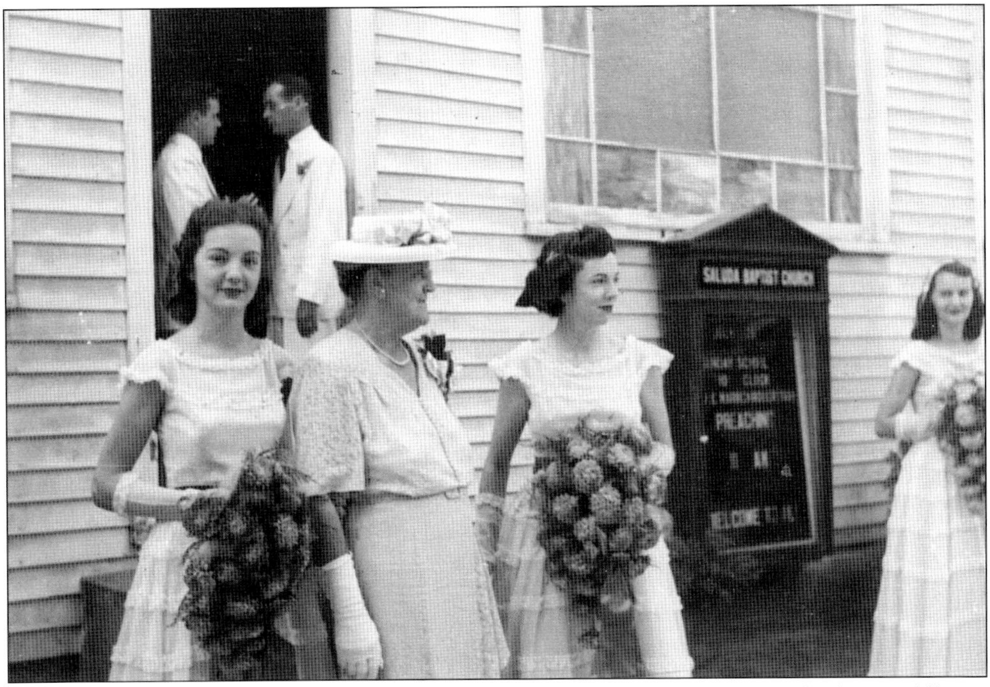

Church weddings have been a part of county culture since the first churches were built in Middlesex. Tommy and Roberta Marshall were married at Saluda Baptist Church in 1949. Roberta's mother, Lucy Boxley Woodward, with her splendid hat and white gloves, and her sisters await the arrival of the bride. The Woodward family of Plan View Farm held the wedding reception at their home, outside of Saluda. (Courtesy of Pat Marshall.)

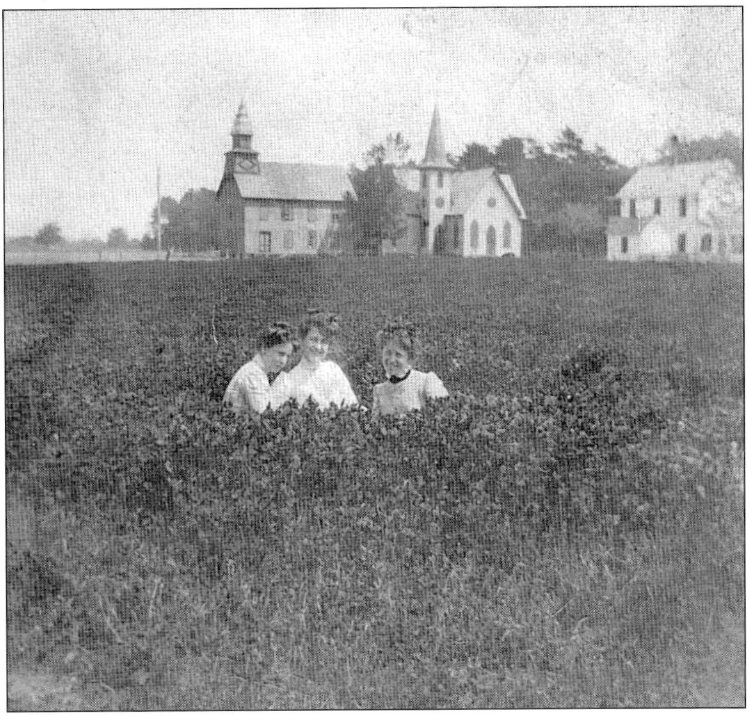

After church, the Vaughan family sisters of Sandy Bottom sit in a bean field on a warm Sunday. Zoar Baptist Church and Bay View Masonic Lodge can be seen in the background. The lodge and church were closely tied in that members stood for Christian ethics and a charge to make the community a better place. (Courtesy of Nola Watson.)

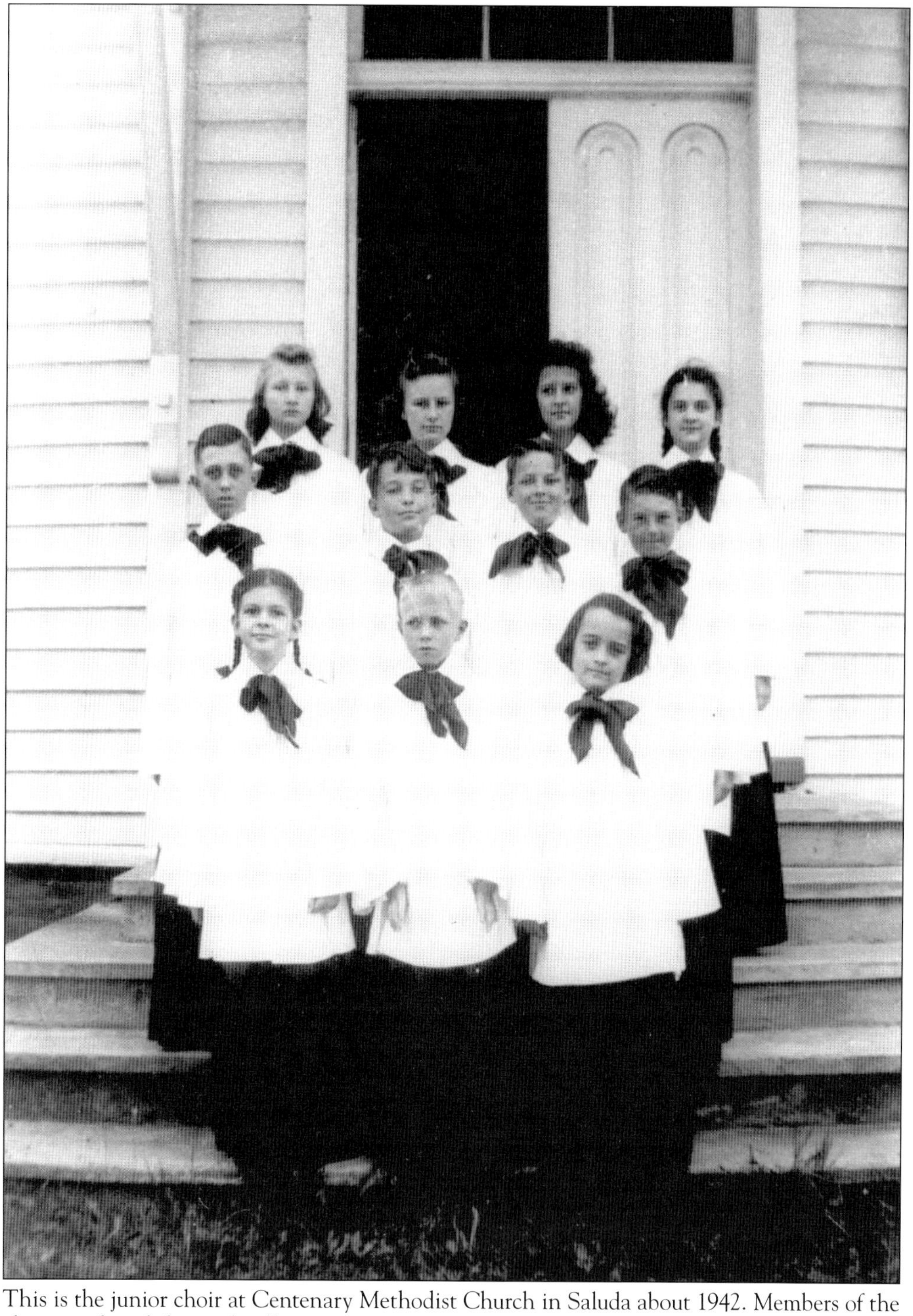

This is the junior choir at Centenary Methodist Church in Saluda about 1942. Members of the choir are, from left to right, (first row) Betsy James Simmons, Merrill Barton, and Kathryn Kipps Fitchett; (second row) William Wood, Granville Kipps, Bobby Moody, and Tom Moody; (third row) Anne St. John Ward, Helen Moody Healy, Nancy Dunn Speas, and Carolyn Gray. (Courtesy of Betsy Simmons.)

Seven

Making a Living in Middlesex

The county's colonial commerce was closely tied to Great Britain's international tobacco trade. Tobacco was grown commercially in the county until 1810.

During the antebellum period, New England oystermen came south to the Rappahannock River to harvest oysters to supply a large and established oyster industry in New York and Connecticut. These Northern oyster growers provided knowledge of the business that would lead to oysters becoming the county's next great commercial commodity. After the Civil War, oystering and oyster packinghouses provided work for poorer whites and former black slaves and helped boost the overall local economy.

The steamboat out of Baltimore and Norfolk provided an avenue for Middlesex farmers to sell their produce to a larger, steady marketplace. Middlesex-grown watermelons, Irish and sweet potatoes, string and lima beans, green peas, cucumbers, and tomatoes were often found on dining room tables of Baltimore families. Growing, picking, pickling, and canning of county-grown produce provided jobs for many in the county. The county's timber industry grew as housing and boatbuilding markets created demand for Middlesex lumber. Sailing schooners manned by Middlesex men hauled to lumber to market.

Steamboats provided an avenue for generations of city families to come to Middlesex to relax and enjoy the attributes of being near the water. Hotels and boardinghouses had been built near steamboat landings and provided treasured, weeklong vacations for generations of city families. The steamboat stopped in 1937, slowing down commercial activities at river and creek landings. However, the State of Virginia took over the maintenance and building of roads in 1932 under the Byrd Road Act. Concrete bridges were built in the 1950s across the Piankatank and Rappahannock Rivers, eliminating slow ferry rides. As land transportation improved, people came by land to the river. This all contributed to a waterfront land rush in the 1970s–1990s that brought people from all over buying land on the water and building large homes.

The early 19th and 20th century tourist trade and a backyard wooden boatbuilding culture in Deltaville and throughout the county paved the way for a large commercial boating industry involving maintenance and mooring of boats at railways and marinas. Deltaville is known today as the "Boating Capital of Chesapeake Bay."

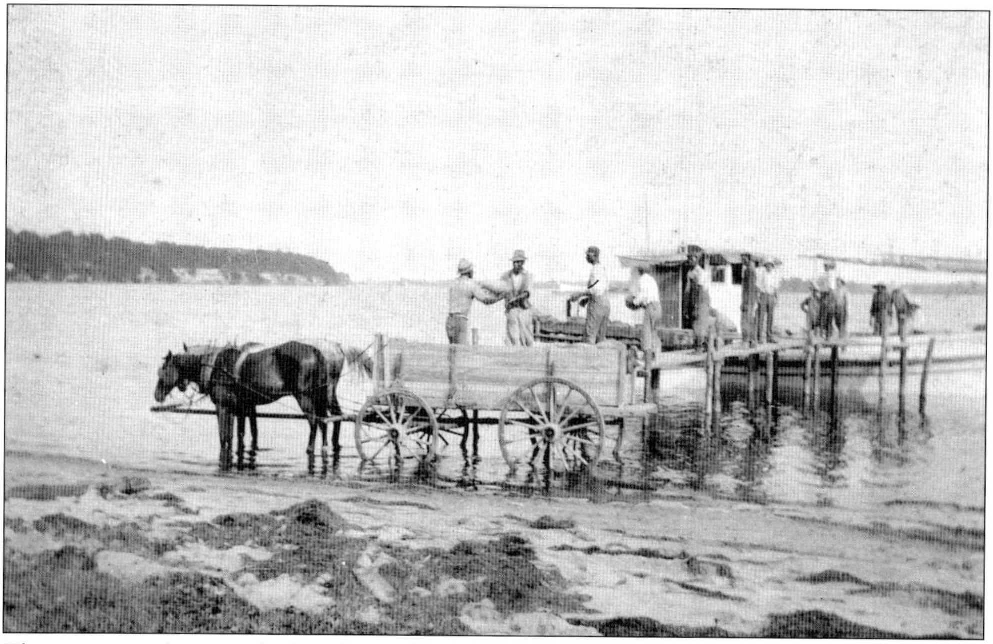

This is a rare photograph that shows the way watermelons were loaded onto freight boats at Conrads Wharf on the Piankatank River. The dock was built specifically for the loading process, out far enough into deep water for the boat to float and close enough inshore for the wagon to be offloaded. Although seasonal, watermelons sold in Baltimore and Washington, DC, provided an annual income that farmers could count on. (Courtesy of Nola Watson.)

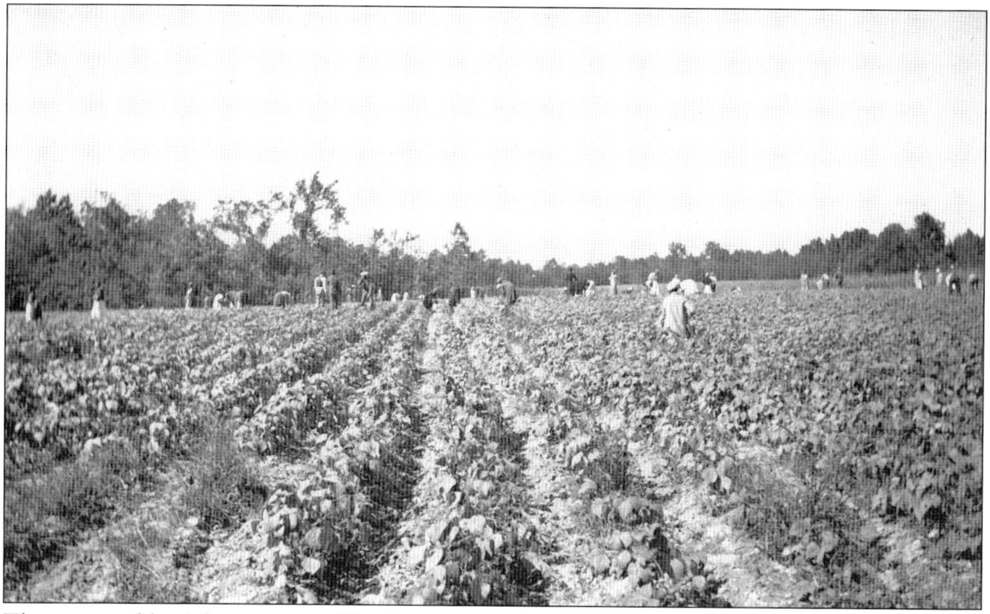

These vegetable pickers were paid by the amount of product they could pick in a day. During the 1920s and 1930s, tomato and vegetable packing businesses thrived in Middlesex. Just in the Wake area, Chowning Stiff, Parker Grinels, A.B. Stiff, and Bee Fleet all had canning factories. John Grinels had a plant at North End Wharf; J.C. Payne's was at Wilton, B.L. Wood's was at Lot (Hartfield), and George W. and Henry Daniels's were at Amburg. (Courtesy of Anne Wheeley.)

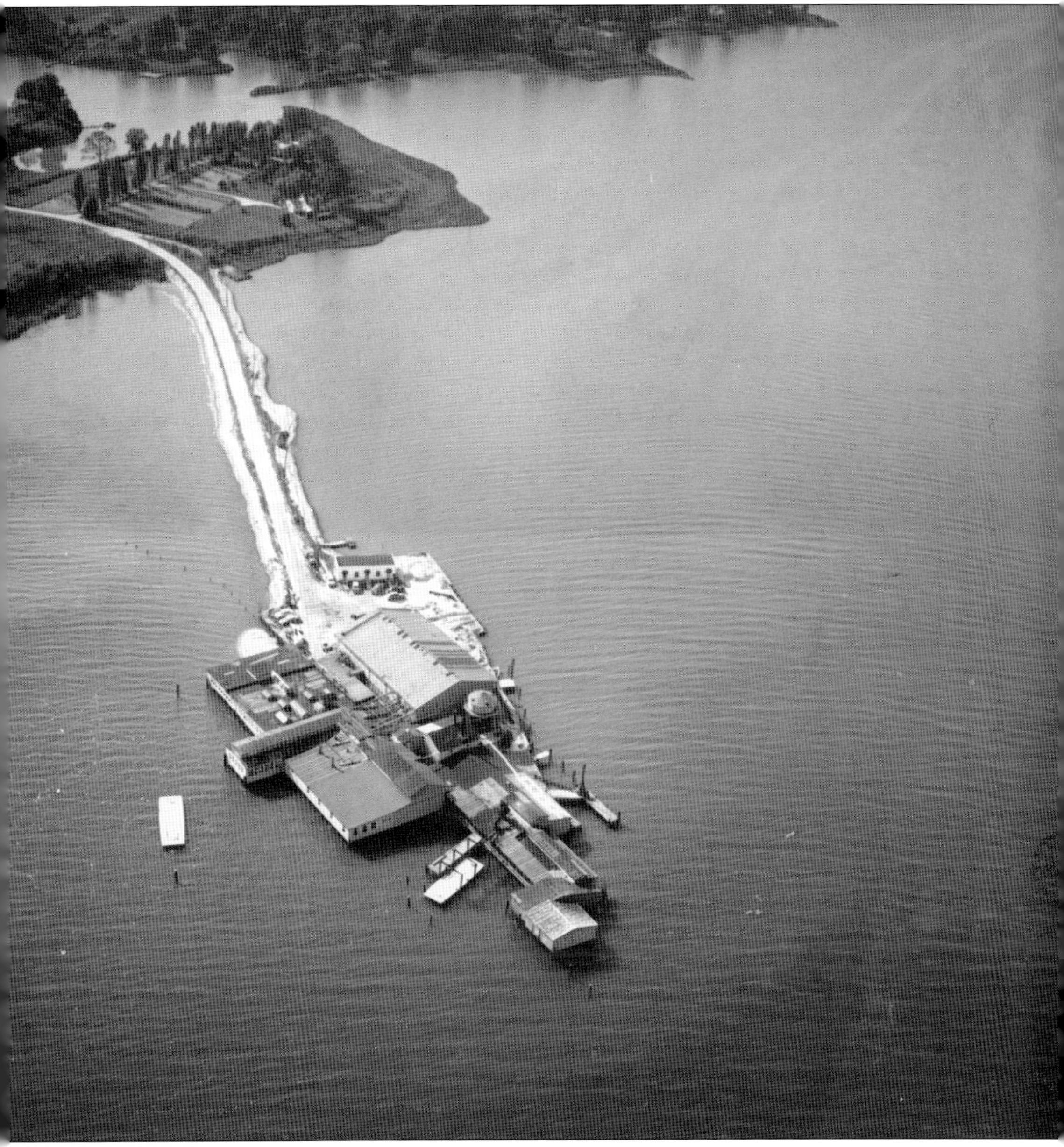

When this photograph was taken in the 1960s, Lord Mott Canning factory was operating under the ownership of the Duffy-Mott Company. The plant was located at the mouth of Robinson Creek. It started as West Urbanna Wharf in 1871. Steamboats stopped frequenting the wharf in 1933. By then, Lord Mott Corp. of Baltimore had a thriving vegetable canning factory. The cannery closed in 1976, marking an end to the 100-year-old vegetable-canning industry in the county. (Courtesy of the *Southside Sentinel*.)

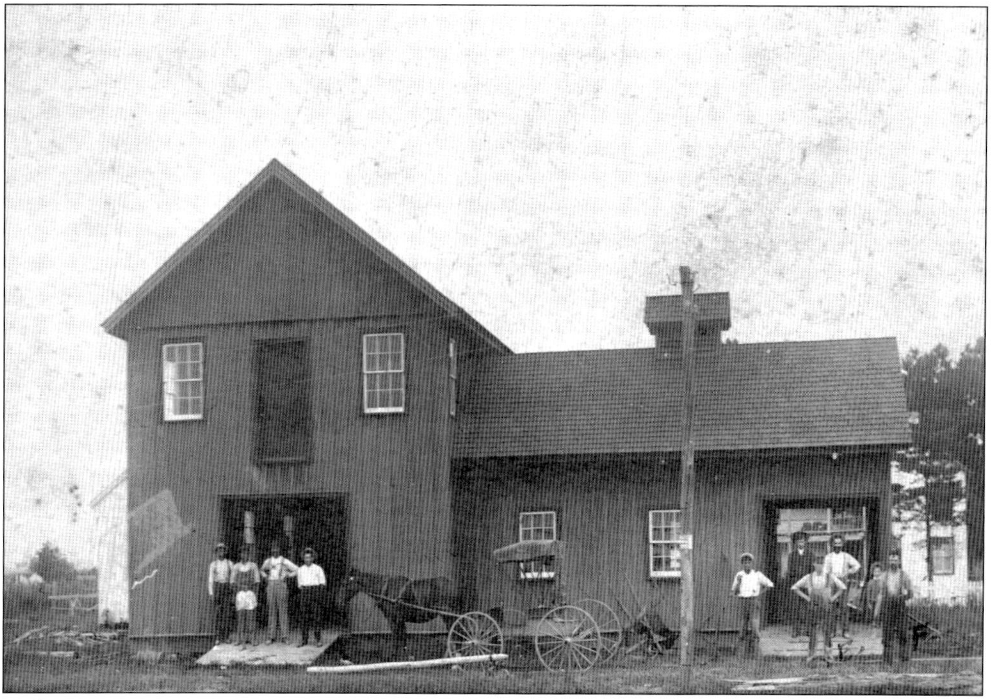

A farrier was an important person in neighborhoods throughout Middlesex. The forging of horseshoes was just part of the blacksmith's job, as many county smithies made more profit making oyster shaft tong heads and building wooden caskets. The upstairs in this blacksmith shop in Sandy Bottom was used to store caskets. The back of this photograph states, "Mr. Earnest Fox and Roland Evans at blacksmith shop." (Courtesy of Hugh and Dorothy Norris.)

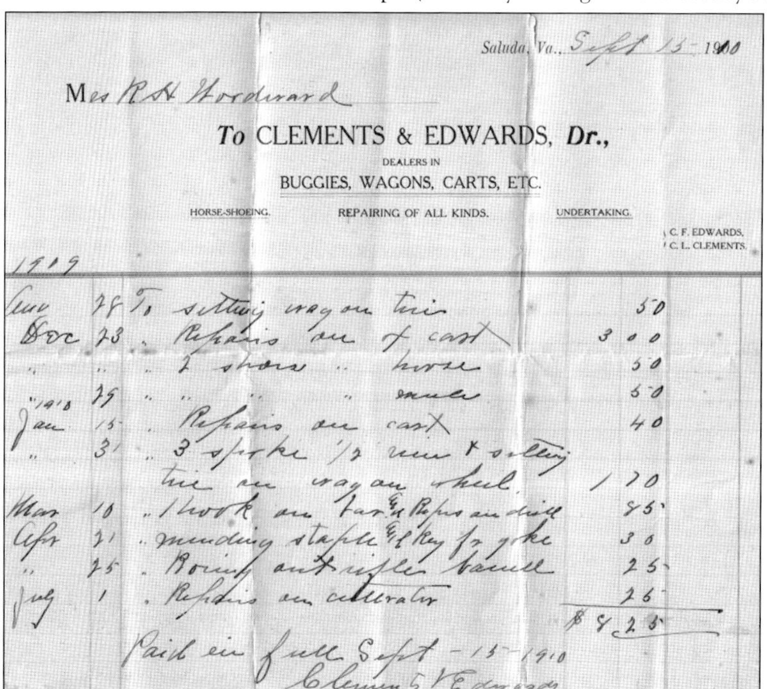

Saluda, Va., Sept 15 1910

Mes R.H. Woodward

To CLEMENTS & EDWARDS, **Dr.**,

DEALERS IN

BUGGIES, WAGONS, CARTS, ETC.

HORSE-SHOEING. REPAIRING OF ALL KINDS. UNDERTAKING.

C. F. EDWARDS,
C. L. CLEMENTS.

1909

Nov	28	To setting wagon tire	50
Dec	23	" Repairs on cart	3 00
"	"	" 2 shoes " horse	50
"	29	" " " mule	50
1910 Jan	15	" Repairs on cart	40
"	31	" 3 spoke 1/2 rim & setting tire on wagon wheel	1 70
Mar	10	" 1 hook on bar & Repairs on drill	85
Apr	21	" mending staple & Key for yoke	30
"	25	" Boring out rifle barrel	25
July	1	" Repairs on cultivator	26
			$8 23

Paid in full Sept - 15 - 1910
Clements & Edwards

C.F. Edwards and C.L. Clements ran the blacksmith shop in Saluda in 1909. The firm sold horse-drawn buggies, wagons, and carts and was the town undertaker. R.H. Woodward of Walboro, just outside of Saluda, paid 50¢ for two shoes on a horse, 25¢ for boring out a rifle barrel, and $1.70 for fixing a tire on a wagon wheel. (Courtesy of Bettie James.)

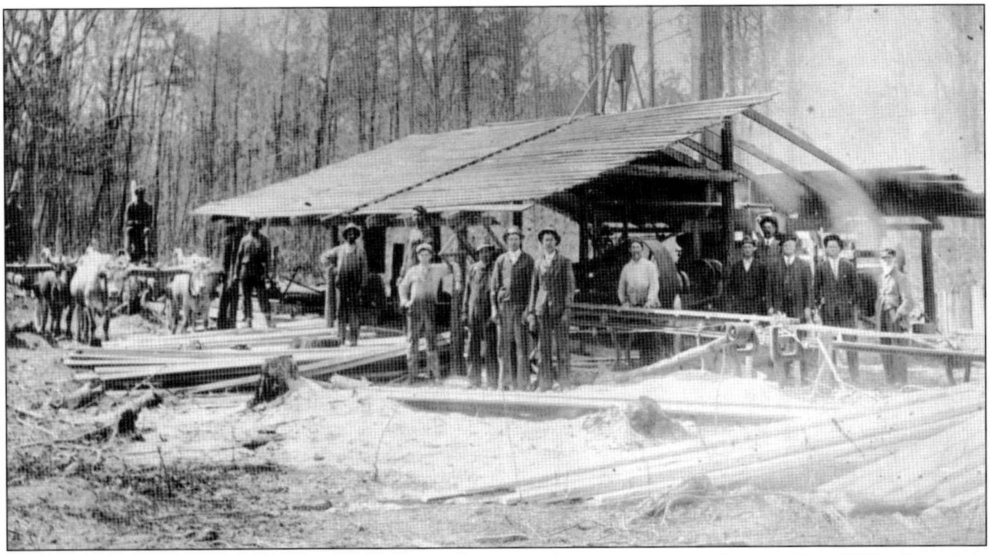

Bernard L. Wood of Lot, today called Hartfield, operated a steam-powered sawmill in 1913 when this photograph was taken. Later known as Wood Brothers, the mill became a significant part of the area's backyard boatbuilding industry. It specialized in cutting boat lumber, particularly 38-foot-long keel logs used to build deadrise wooden boats. Accessibility of good boat lumber gave Middlesex boatbuilders an advantage over those in other communities. (Courtesy of Helen Hatton Collison.)

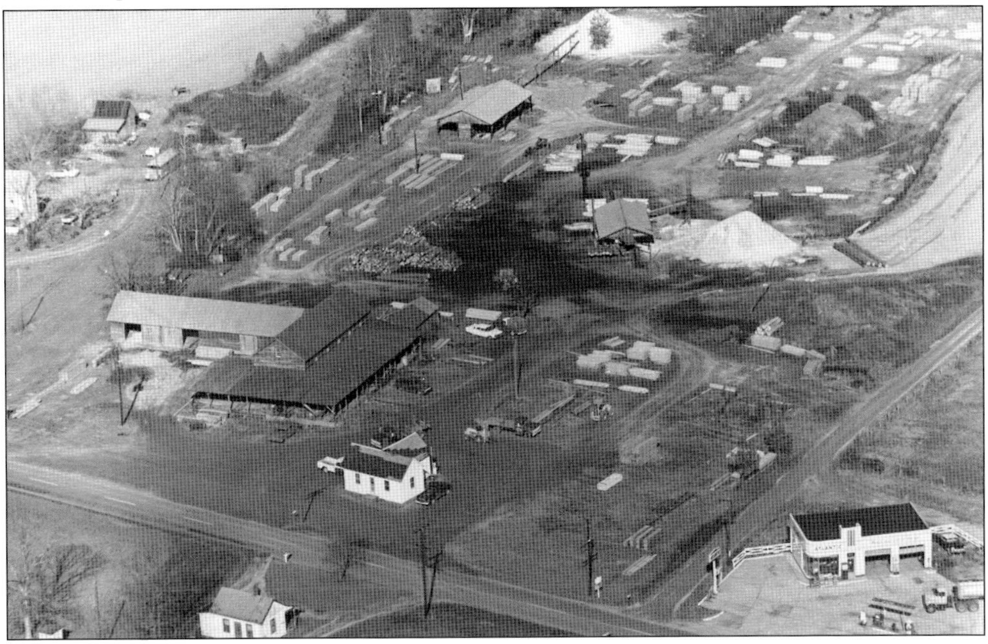

Wood Brothers sawmill in Hartfield, just a few miles down the road from Deltaville, played a key role in the success of that community's boatbuilding heritage. When a boatbuilder needed a 12-inch-by-12-inch-by-42-foot-long keel in a hurry, Wood Brothers already had them cut and cured and would deliver the timbers to the backyard boatbuilders in Deltaville. Over time, Deltaville gained a competitive edge over other areas because the mill was close and able to produce high-quality boat lumber. This aerial photograph shows the mill and a sign of more modern times coming, as a new Atlantic service station had recently been built. (Courtesy of the *Southside Sentinel*.)

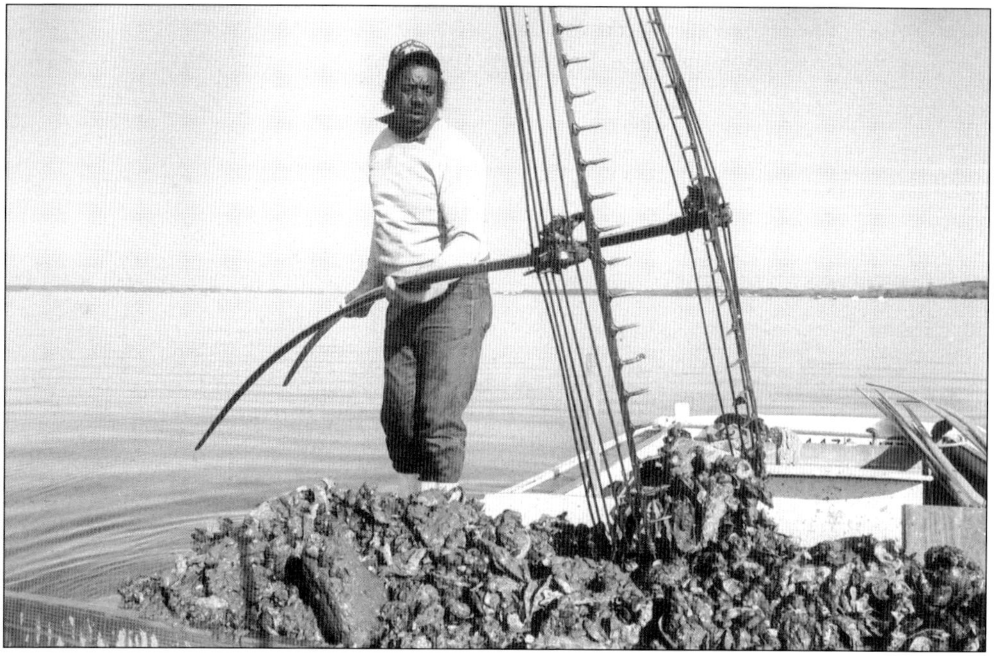

Roosevelt Wingfield was born in 1932 in Middlesex County. He hand tonged for oysters in the winter and fall and milked cows at Frank Moore's dairy farm at Stormont in the spring and summer. When he was young, he went to work as a cork man on a menhaden fish boat. For several years, he worked in menhaden fisheries on the Chesapeake Bay and the Gulf of Mexico. The oyster and menhaden fisheries provided jobs for many county workers. (Author's collection.)

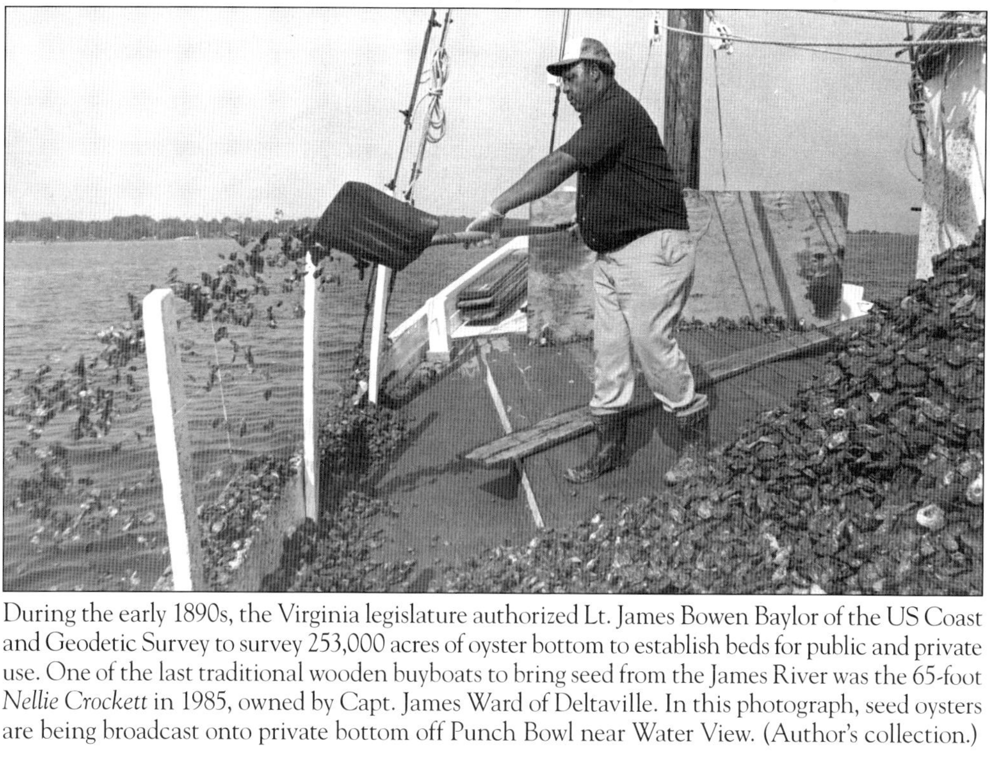

During the early 1890s, the Virginia legislature authorized Lt. James Bowen Baylor of the US Coast and Geodetic Survey to survey 253,000 acres of oyster bottom to establish beds for public and private use. One of the last traditional wooden buyboats to bring seed from the James River was the 65-foot *Nellie Crockett* in 1985, owned by Capt. James Ward of Deltaville. In this photograph, seed oysters are being broadcast onto private bottom off Punch Bowl near Water View. (Author's collection.)

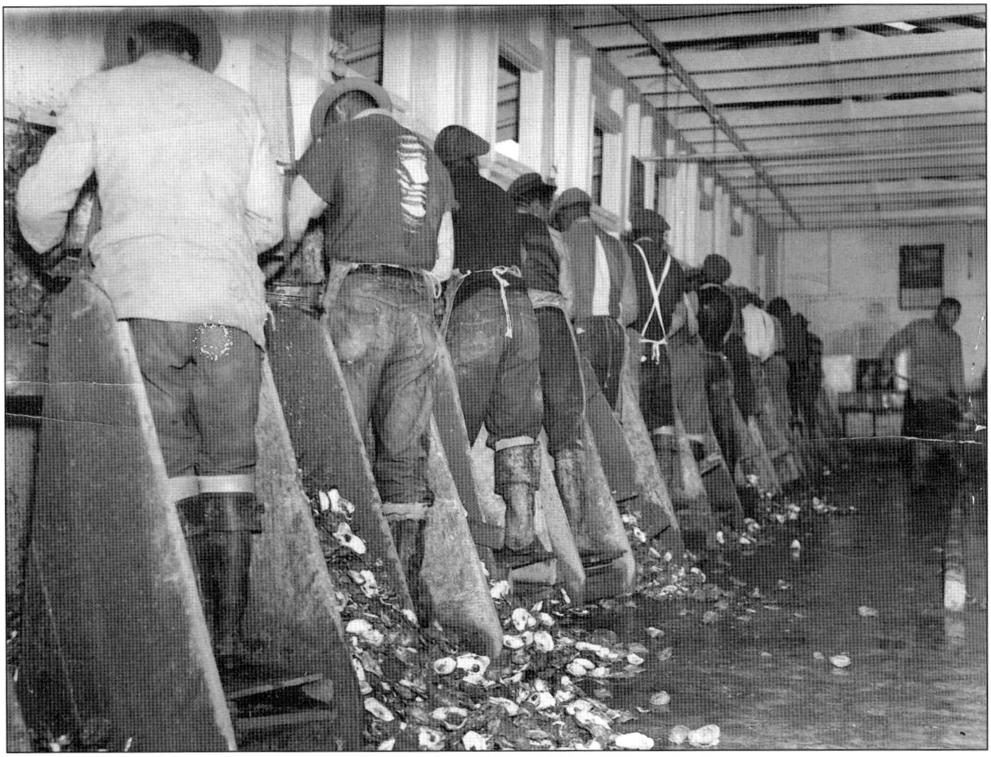

Inside an oyster house, shuckers stand in their stalls and shuck oysters. The men were paid piecemeal for the amount of oysters they shucked. The faster they shucked, the more money they earned. Oyster shuckers worked long hours. While working, shuckers often broke out in song to pass the time and keep from thinking about the hard work ahead of them. (Courtesy of Jonesey Payne.)

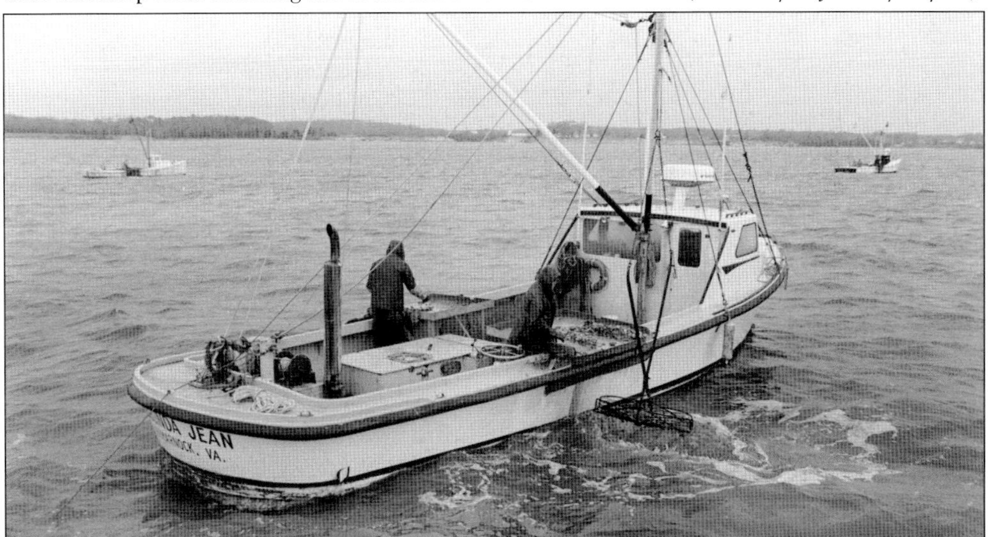

In 1890, this Virginia style of patent tongs was invented by Joseph Allen Bristow of Stormont and William M. Dixon of Mathews County. Patent oyster tongs were mechanically operated and allowed watermen to work on deep-water oyster beds, where shafts on hand tongs were not long enough to reach the bottom. (Author's collection.)

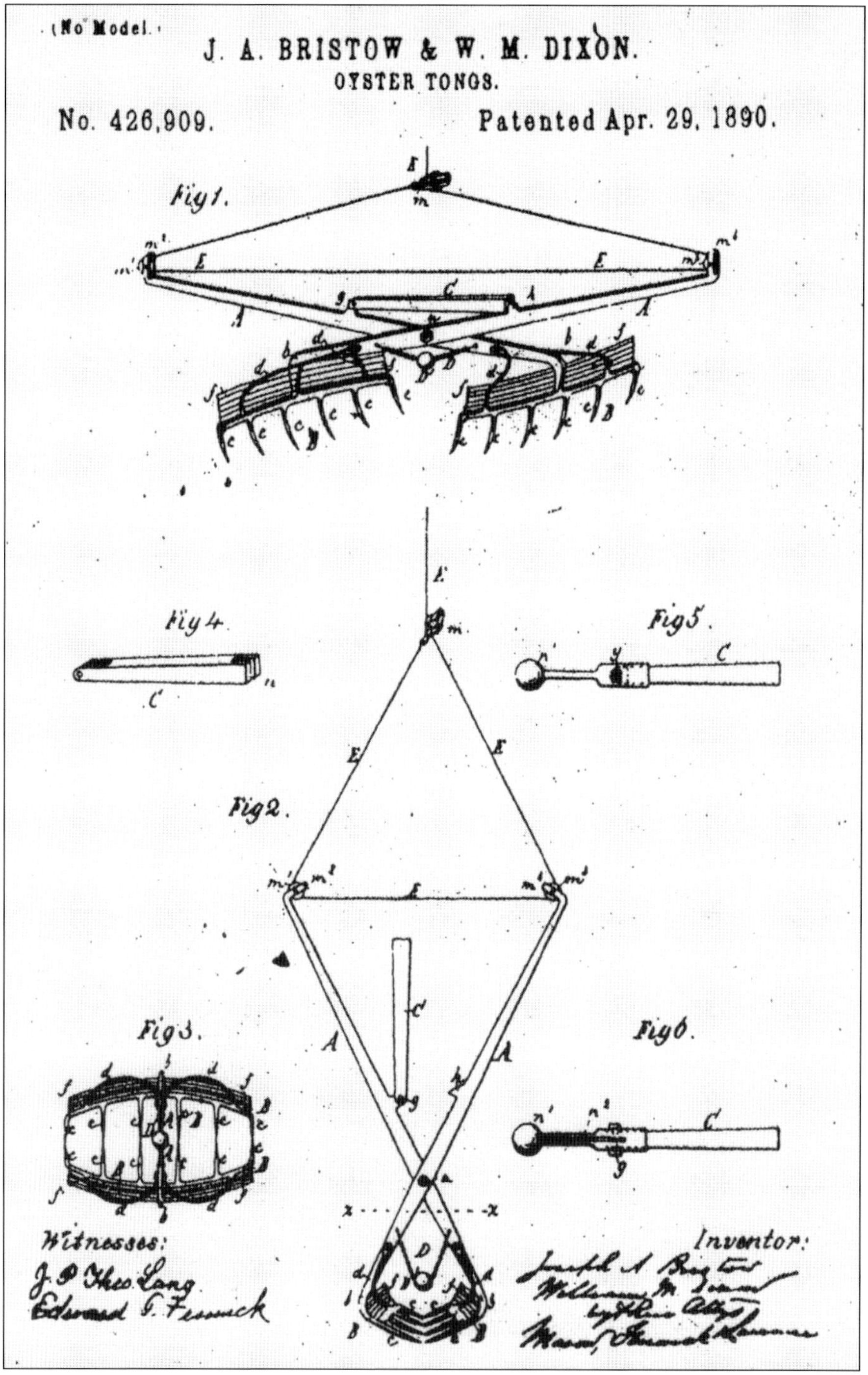

Country store owner and local politician Joseph Allen Bristow and blacksmith William M. Dixon invented and patented a Virginia style of deep water tong that become known as patent tongs. The inventors received a patent on April 29, 1890. The two men and their invention gained international fame in 1893 when the tongs won a blue ribbon at the World's Fair in Chicago. (Courtesy of John M. "Buddy" Moore.)

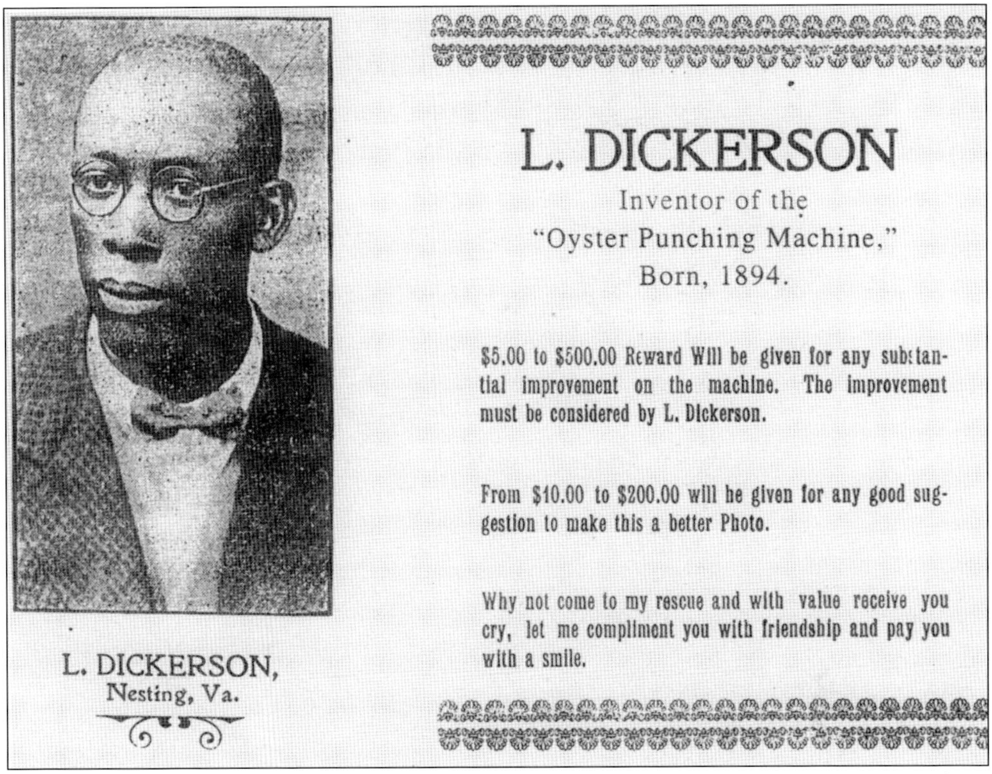

Leary Dickerson of Nesting spent a lifetime trying to improve on the oyster-punching machine that he invented. The machine punched a hole in the beak of an oyster, allowing a shucker to shove the oyster knife inside. He traveled up and down the Chesapeake Bay region trying to sell his invention, but in the end, a good shucker was able to open an oyster faster on their own than with Dickerson's oyster punch. (Courtesy of William Dickerson.)

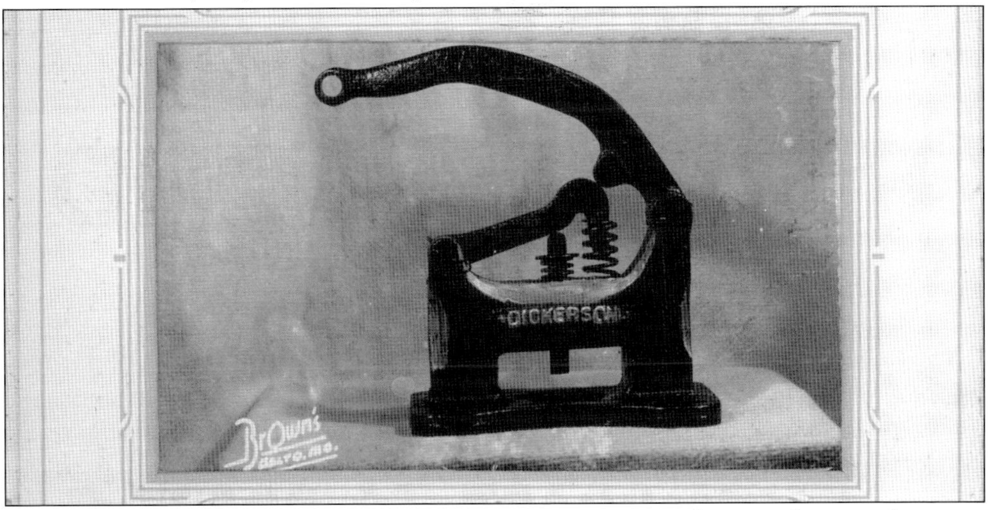

Leary Dickerson of Nesting held several patents on an oyster-punching machine used in some oyster-shucking houses to aid oyster shuckers in opening oysters. His first patent was issued September 30, 1924. He received a second patent on the machine October 20, 1942, and a third was issued July 6, 1948. (Courtesy of William Dickerson.)

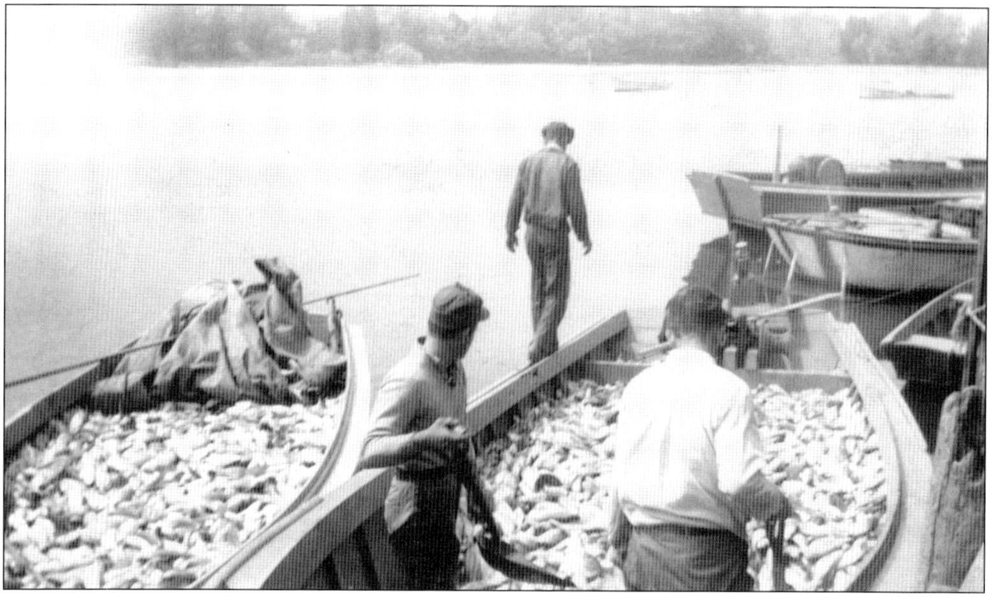

During the 1940s, the Rappahannock River haul seine harvests made some county watermen wealthy overnight. The haul seine is an ancient net gear brought to Virginia from England. Modern improvements enabled watermen to harvest thousands of pounds of fish in a haul and brought paychecks of upwards of $10,000 a night. Pictured are two skiffs loaded down with croakers on Parrott's Creek at Water View. (Courtesy of Middlesex County Museum.)

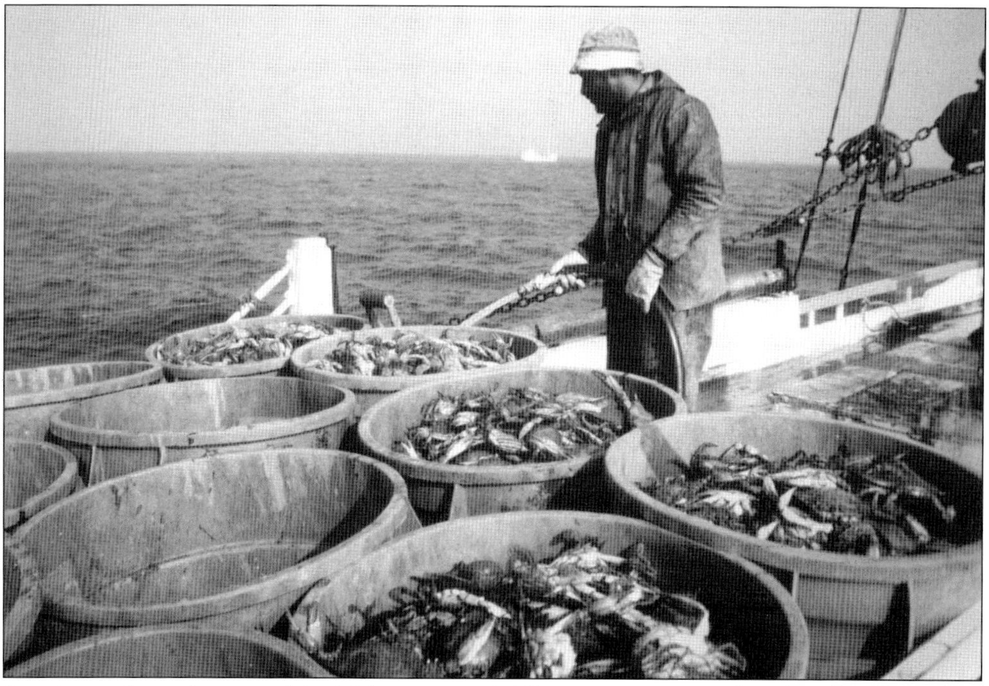

Starting at about the turn of the 20th century, Middlesex men were employed in the Chesapeake Bay wintertime crab dredge fishery. In 2008, the Virginia Marine Resources Commission banned dredging of crabs for conservation reasons. This photograph was taken in 1985 aboard the deadrise deck boat *Iva W.*, owned by the late Capt. Johnny Ward of Deltaville. (Author's collection.)

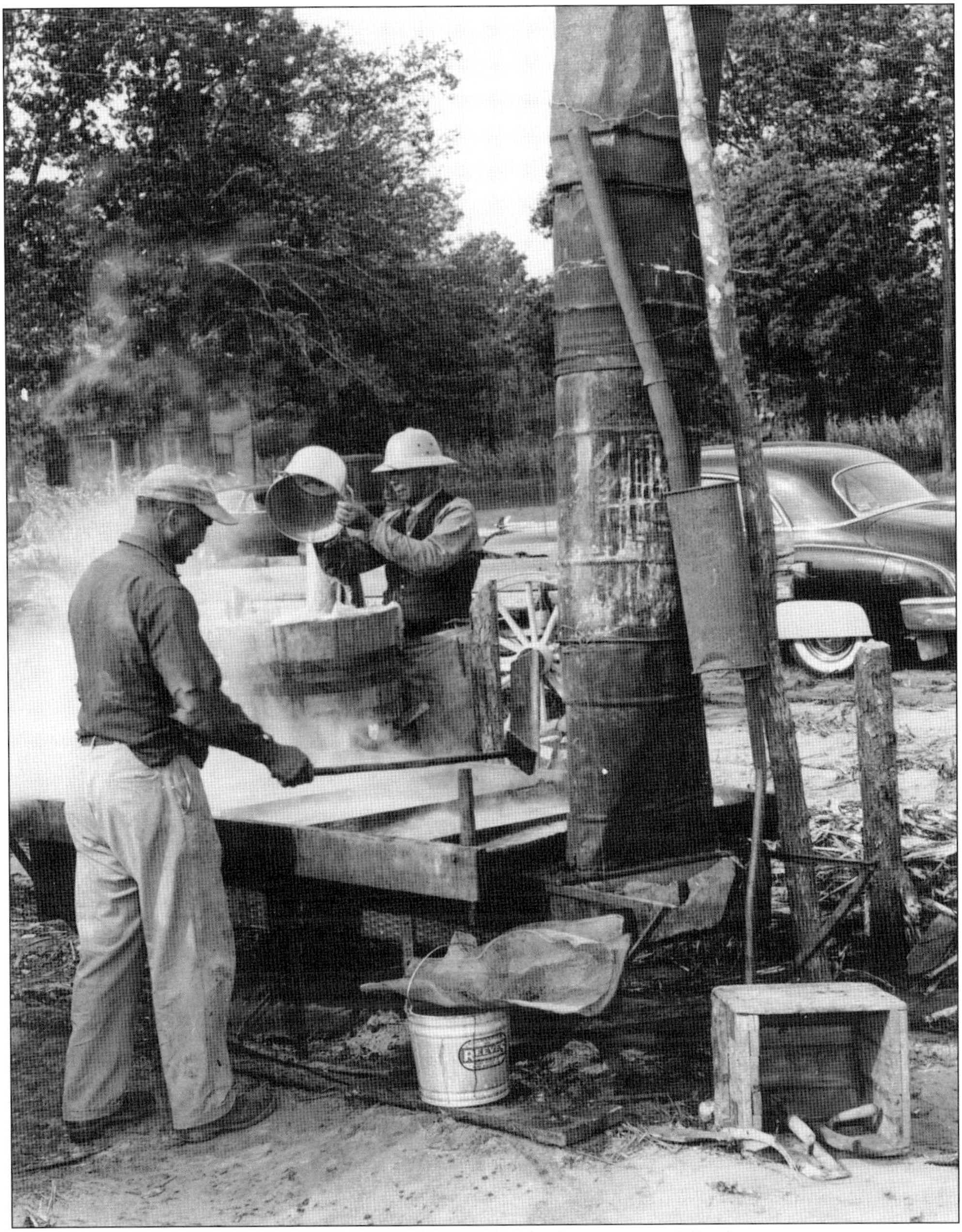

The mingled scent of hickory wood and corn shucks burning and boiling cane syrup was an autumn moment for many in the county when molasses was being made. A portable cooker was constructed near the sorghum field for making molasses. This 1952 photograph shows syrup being made in Essex County, the adjoining county to Middlesex. Many farmers in Middlesex had one field where they annually grew sorghum and paid a miller to make enough molasses to last the year. (Courtesy of Richmond County Museum-Patton Collection.)

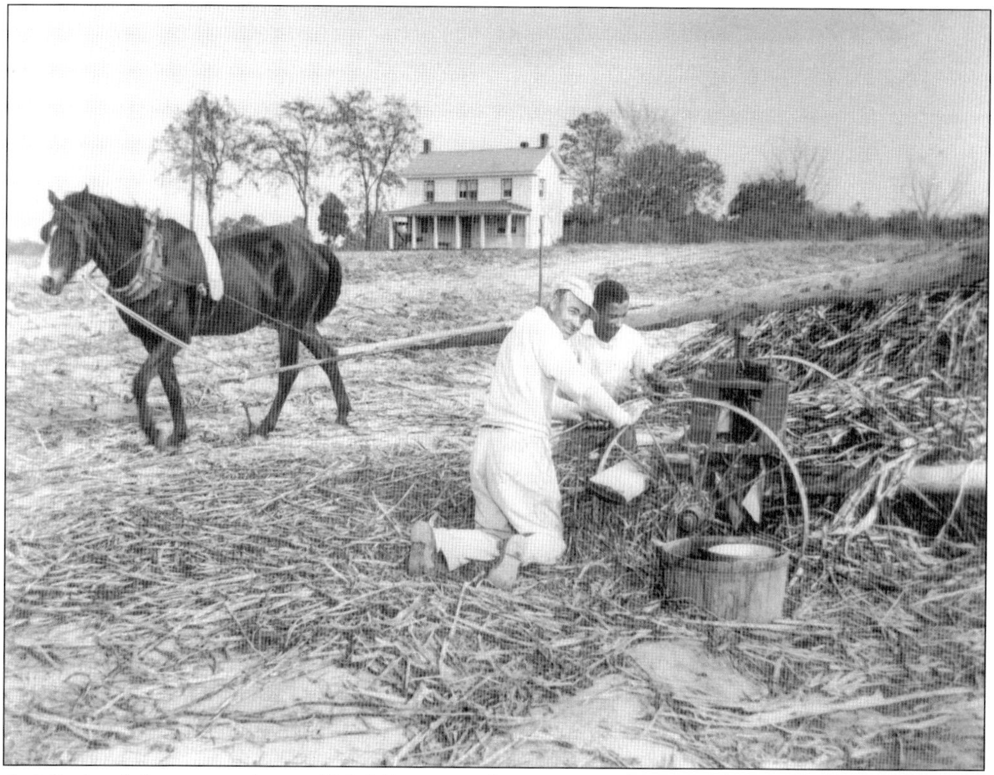

A fall ritual for generations of Middlesex residents was making sorghum molasses. Sorghum, harvested just before frost, was grown for the juice extracted from stalks. A sorghum mill owner traveled with horse and mill to grind stalks and cook the syrup for a toll of the crop. Molasses was a stable condiment used as a topping on biscuits and bread and a sweetener for cookies, gingerbread, and molasses pudding. A year's supply of molasses was stored in most farm households. (Courtesy of Richmond County Museum-Patton Collection.)

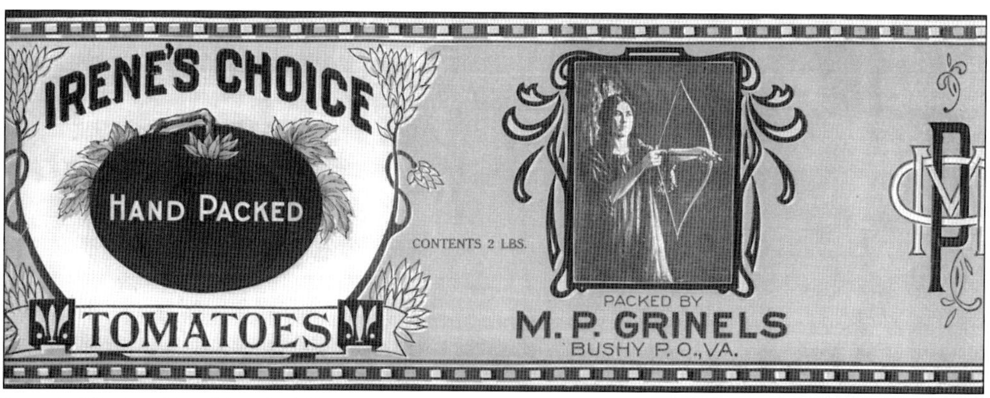

Irene's Choice Hand Packed Tomatoes were processed at a vegetable canning factory on Mill Creek, owned by Maj. Parker Grinels of Bushy. The brand was named for his wife, Irene, and the Indian girl on the label was his daughter Marion. Grinels also canned potatoes, peas, and berries. These products reached the Baltimore market by way of local freight boats, either sail or motorized deck boats. (Courtesy of Emily Chowning.)

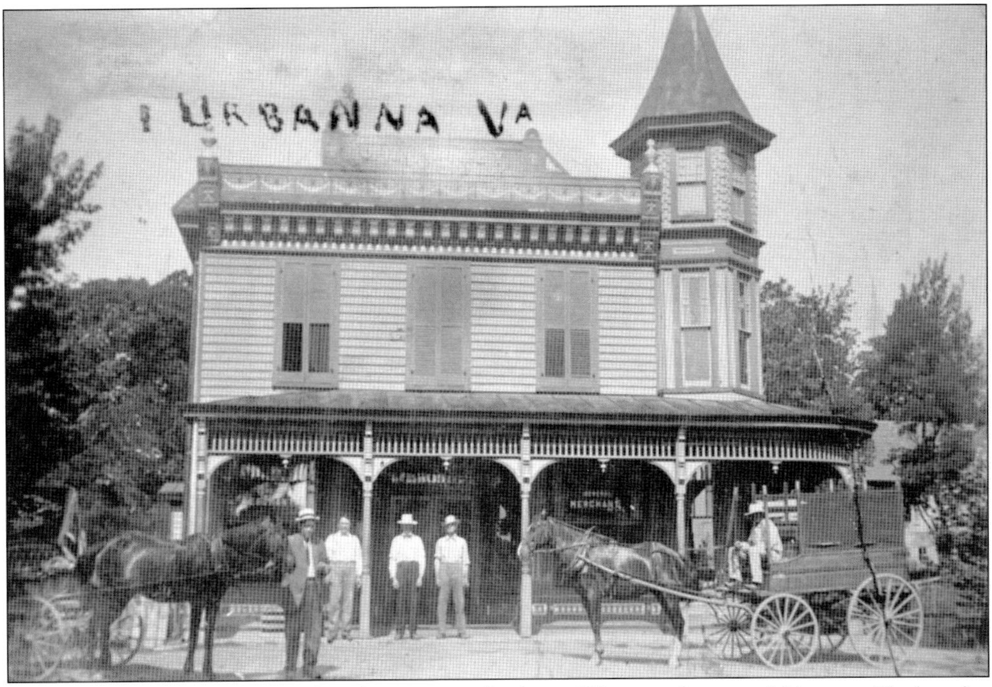

J.W. Hurley ran a general merchandise store at the foot of Virginia Street in Urbanna. Hurley also had an oyster-shucking house, and at its peak, had over 100 oyster shuckers working there. Some years later, J.W. and his son Boyd moved the building across the street facing Urbanna Creek and converted it into a hotel and restaurant. The general merchandise store was moved into the front portion of the oyster-shucking house. (Courtesy of Mary and Danny Loving.)

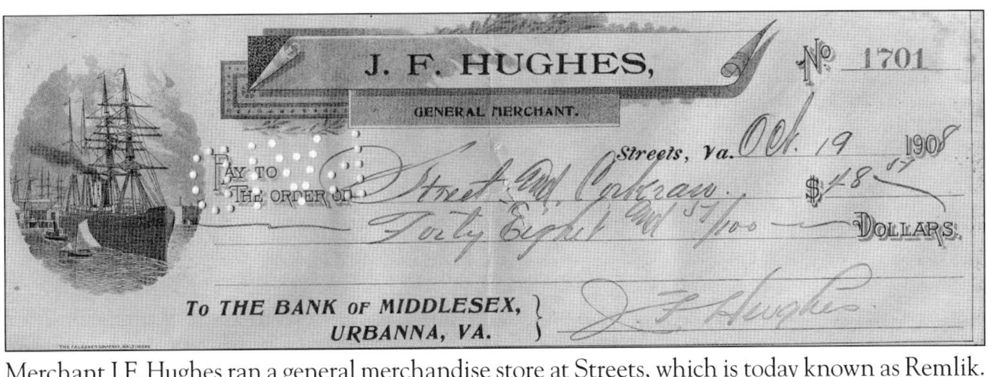

Merchant J.F. Hughes ran a general merchandise store at Streets, which is today known as Remlik. The Bank of Middlesex was only six years old when this check was written. Before modern banking, storekeepers extended "tick," or credit, that was paid back during agriculture or seafood harvest seasons. The local storekeeper was the lifeblood of families who relied on seasonal work to pay their bills. (Courtesy of Mary and Danny Loving.)

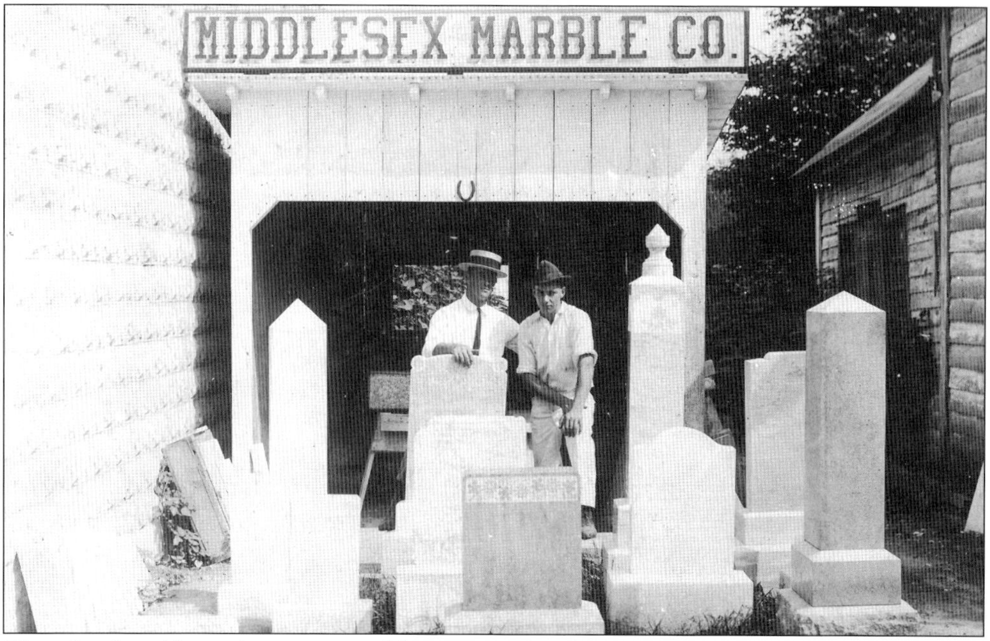

The sale of marble tombstones in Middlesex started in the 1880s. Prior to that, the main marker of graves for poor- and middle-class folk in Middlesex were crosses made of cypress wood from Dragon Run. After the Civil War, marble tombstones were transported by sailing schooners from Baltimore, and around the turn of the 20th century, the Middlesex Marble Co. opened for business on Virginia Street in Urbanna. (Courtesy of Eunice Yesker.)

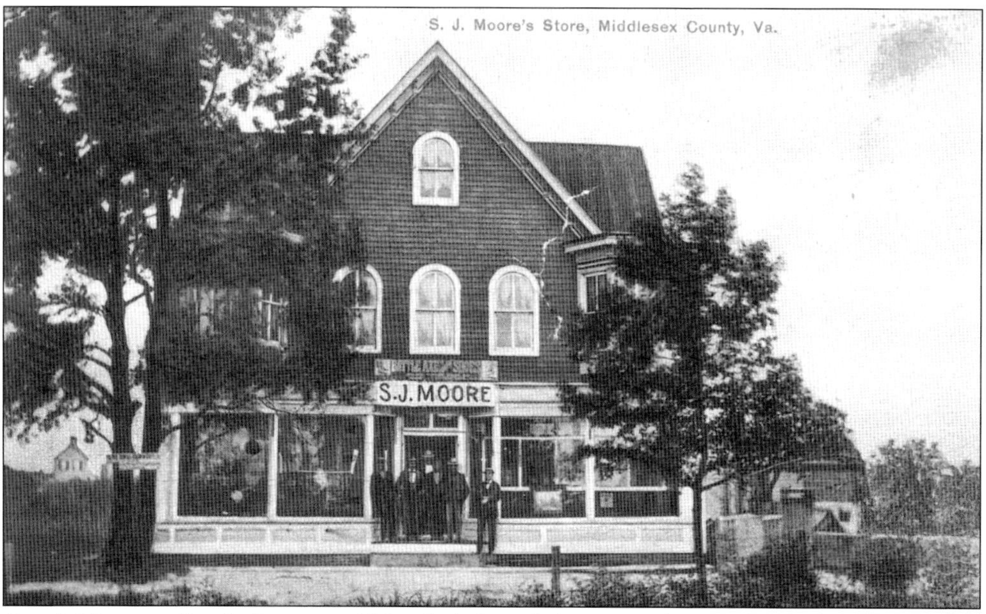

Sam J. Moore in Sandy Bottom sold bottled ale and shoes, as advertised over the front door of his general merchandise store. Moore was a successful businessman who was also involved in banking. Moore and Major Parker Grinels established Packers State Bank in Wake. The bank was formed in 1920 to accommodate a growing economy created by the vegetable and seafood packing businesses in the lower end of Middlesex. (Courtesy of Middlesex County Public Library.)

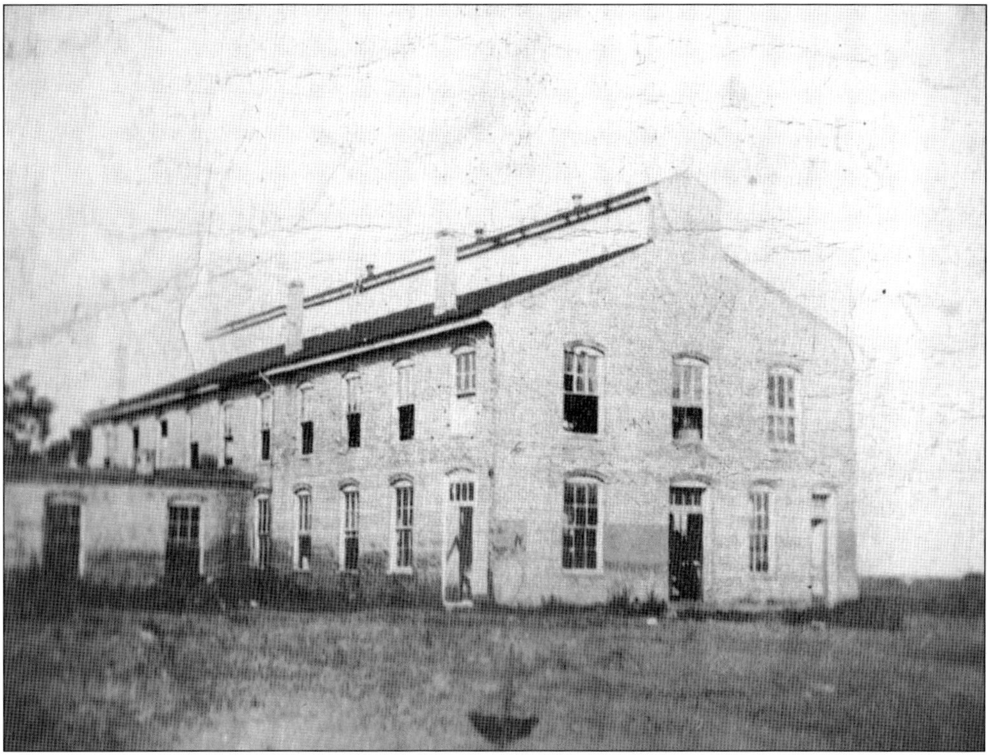

This is a rare photograph of the Urbanna Manufacturing Co. building when it was in operation. Branch Standard Overall Factory was a division of the company that made work shirts and overalls. It was locally called the "Shirt Factory." The plant opened in 1901 and closed about 1915. Afterward, the building was converted into a hotel and operated under the names of Urbanna Beach Hotel and later the Urbanna Lodge and Motel. (Courtesy of Mary and Danny Loving.)

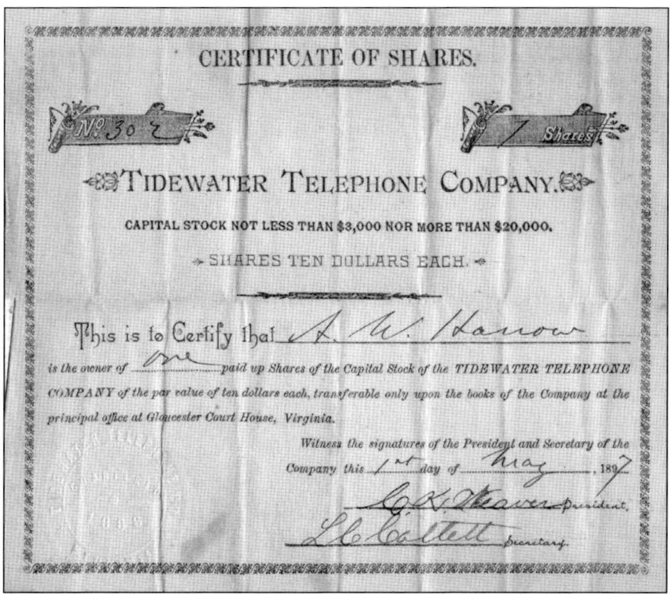

CERTIFICATE OF SHARES.

No. 302

1 Shares

TIDEWATER TELEPHONE COMPANY.

CAPITAL STOCK NOT LESS THAN $3,000 NOR MORE THAN $20,000.

SHARES TEN DOLLARS EACH.

This is to Certify that A. W. Harrow is the owner of one paid up Shares of the Capital Stock of the TIDEWATER TELEPHONE COMPANY of the par value of ten dollars each, transferable only upon the books of the Company at the principal office at Gloucester Court House, Virginia.

Witness the signatures of the President and Secretary of the Company this 1st day of May, 1897

President.

Secretary.

Telephones came to the county by way of Tidewater Telephone Company. The firm was formed in 1894 in Gloucester County, and in 1897, A.W. Harrow of Deltaville was an owner of one share of stock. The first phones were stationary wall crank phones where calls were made through an operator. Direct dialing was introduced in 1958, and by the 1960s, most homes had modern dial-tone telephones. However, many shared neighborhood "party lines" into the 1970s. (Courtesy of Willard and Shirley Norris.)

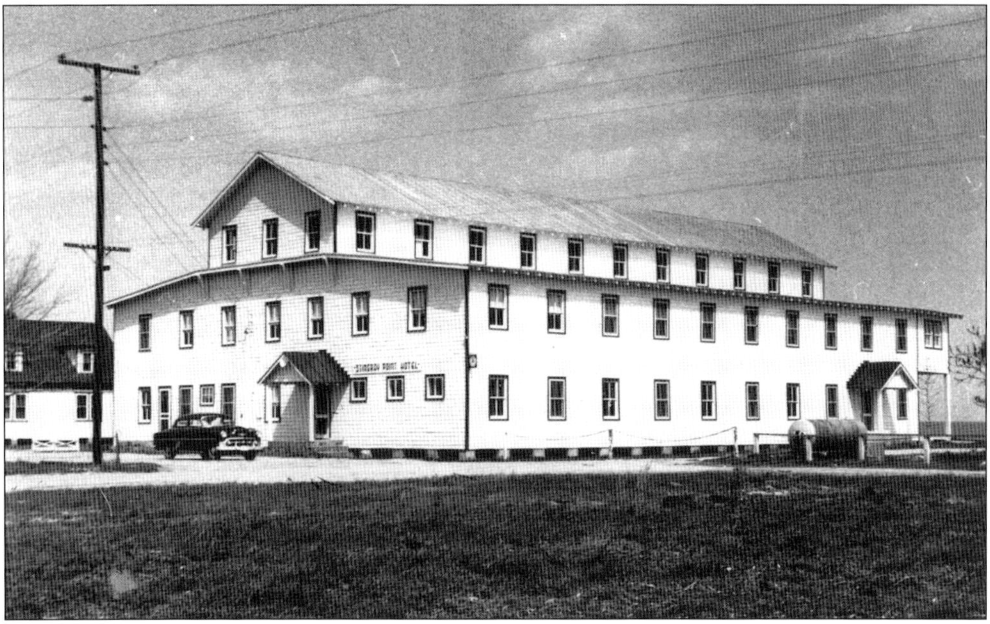

After Sam Moore's hotel Samore burned on Stingray Point, Eddie Harrow built Stingray Point Hotel in Deltaville. During the early years, it was painted white but later was painted red and became known as the "Old Red Barn." The hotel featured a duck-pin bowling alley, a restaurant with fine food, and the delight of being right on the Chesapeake Bay for visitors to swim, fish, and sail. (Courtesy of Edmond Harrow Jr.)

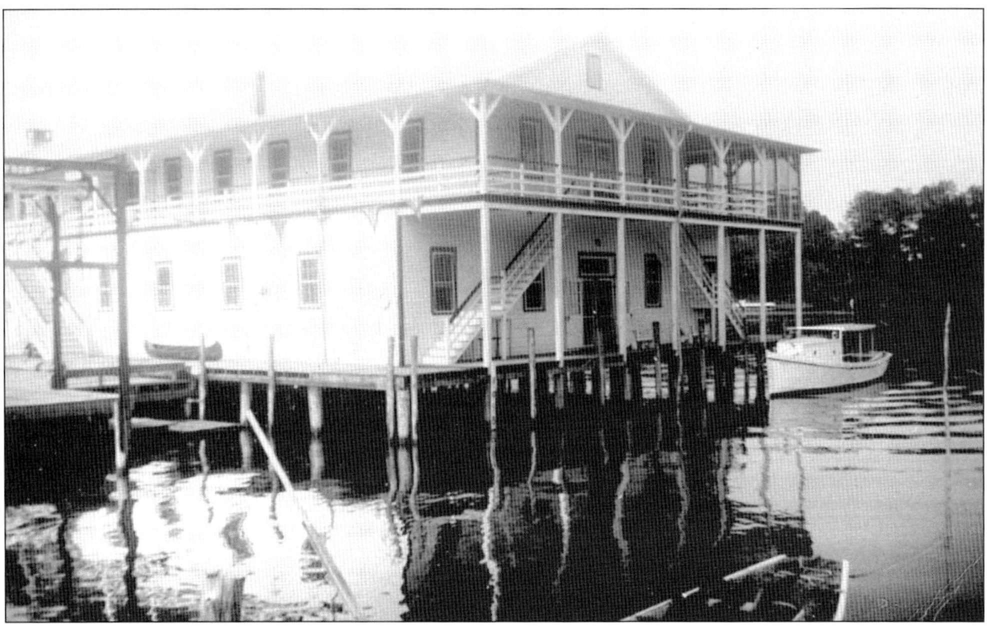

The River Rink was the local entertainment center in the county with a skating rink downstairs and a duckpin bowling alley upstairs. The River Rink was located in Urbanna next to the wooden bridge that entered into town. Until it burned in 1947, young people from one end of the county to the other found the River Rink to be a hot spot for fun and courting. (Courtesy of Betsy Hudgins.)

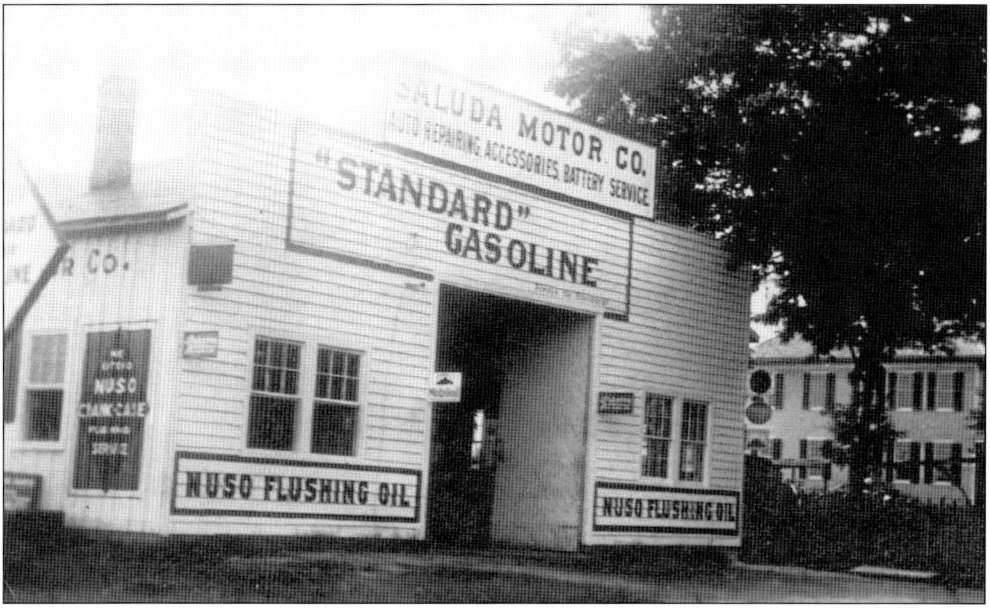

Saluda Motor Co. was an early automobile service station in Saluda. The first cars arrived in Middlesex by steamboat and were delivered to the docks empty of gas. Wharf keepers were concerned that cars full of gas might explode. The first gasoline distributors were country storekeepers, but as cars became popular, service stations such as Saluda Motor Co. provided gasoline and oil and full service for local automobile owners. (Courtesy of Middlesex County Museum.)

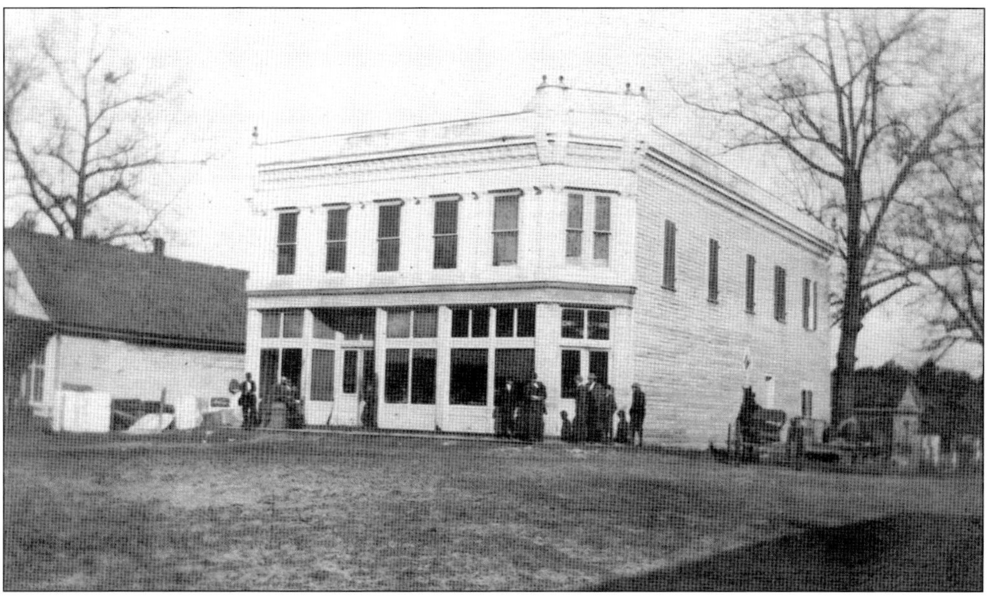

Neale and Smither Store was a busy general merchandise/drug store in Saluda during the early part of the 20th century. Claude Neale and I. Smithers took over full ownership of the store from K.C. Neale in February 1904. The business was operating as Neale Store in 1938, and Claude Neale advertised that year in the *Southside Sentinel* that he had an overabundance of Wilson Heater wood stoves in stock. (Courtesy of Jean Holman.)

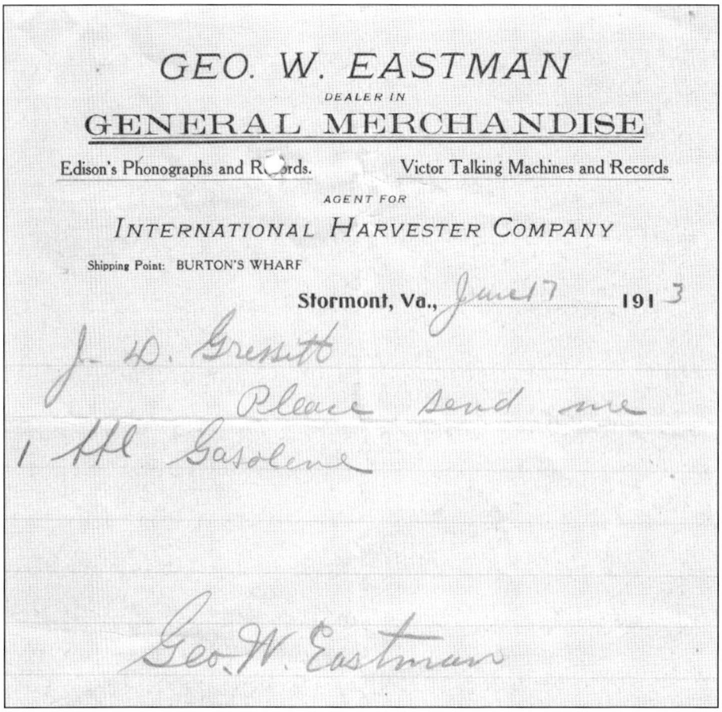

GEO. W. EASTMAN

DEALER IN

GENERAL MERCHANDISE

Edison's Phonographs and Records. Victor Talking Machines and Records

AGENT FOR

INTERNATIONAL HARVESTER COMPANY

Shipping Point: BURTON'S WHARF

Stormont, Va., June 17 1913

J. D. Gressitt

Please send me

1 bbl Gasoline

Geo. W. Eastman

George W. Eastman ran a general merchandise/farm equipment business in 1913 at Stormont. Eastman's billhead speaks to those times, as Edison's phonograph and the Victor Talking Machine attracted buyers to his business. Eastman is requesting one barrel of gasoline from J.D. Gressitt, whose store sold gasoline that came by boat to the Standard Oil Dock in Urbanna. (Courtesy of Middlesex County Library.)

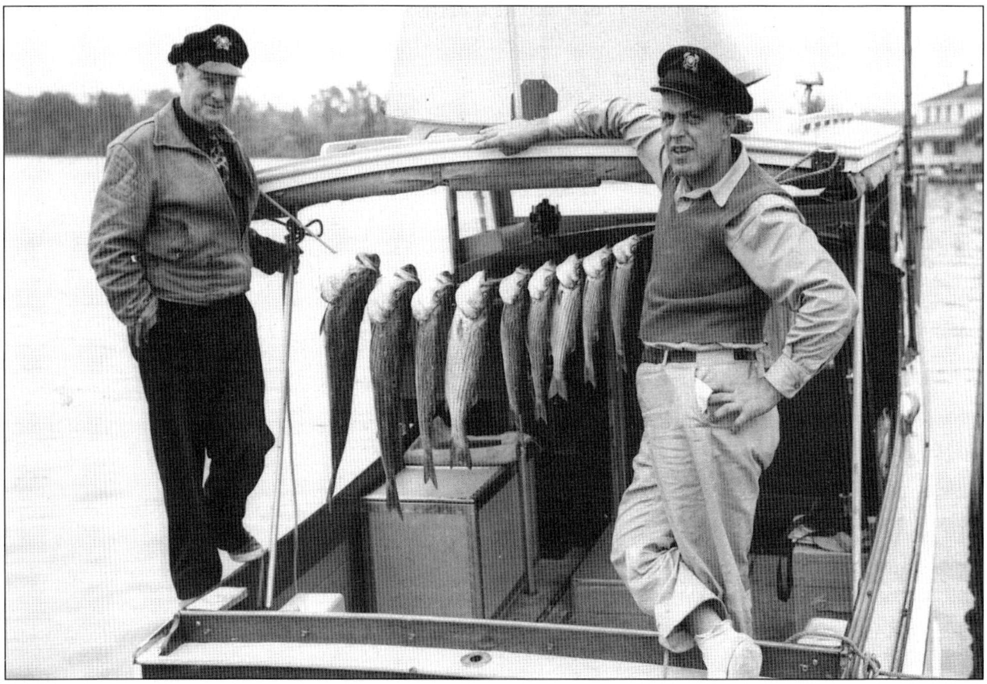

After World War II, recreational fishing gained in popularity, as city people had the means to own boats and to rent boat slips here in the county. The winter and fall rockfish season and spring and summer hook-and-line fishing gave them a good excuse to own a boat and come down on weekends. These happy anglers in the late 1940s had a good day catching rockfish. (C.C. Chowning collection.)

The charter boat hook-and-line fishing business evolved from city people wanting to fish on weekends and holidays and the locals' need to generate income in spring and summer with their oyster boats. This photograph taken in August 1962 of two anglers showing off their cobia catch was a common scene on Broad and Jackson Creeks in the 1950s and 1960s. (Courtesy of Alva Bray.)

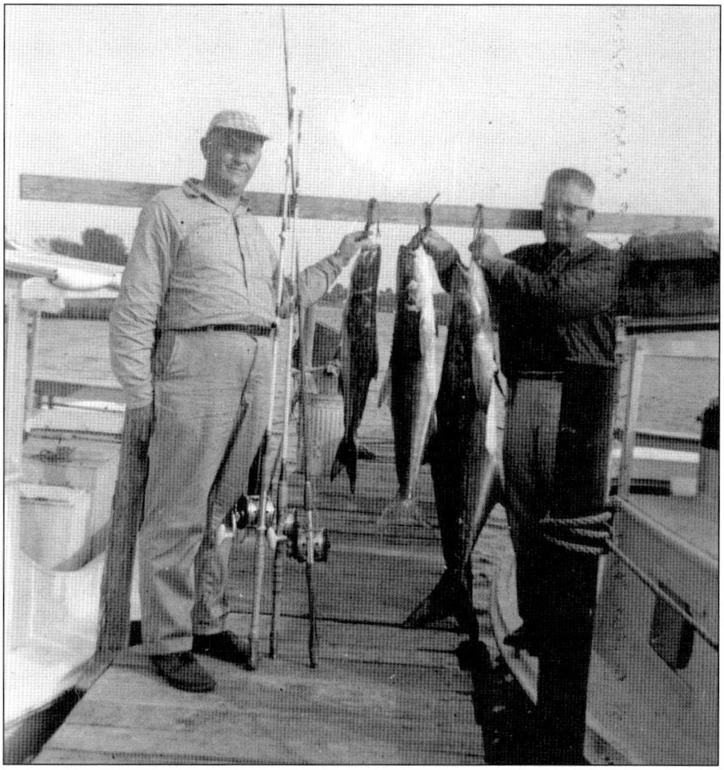

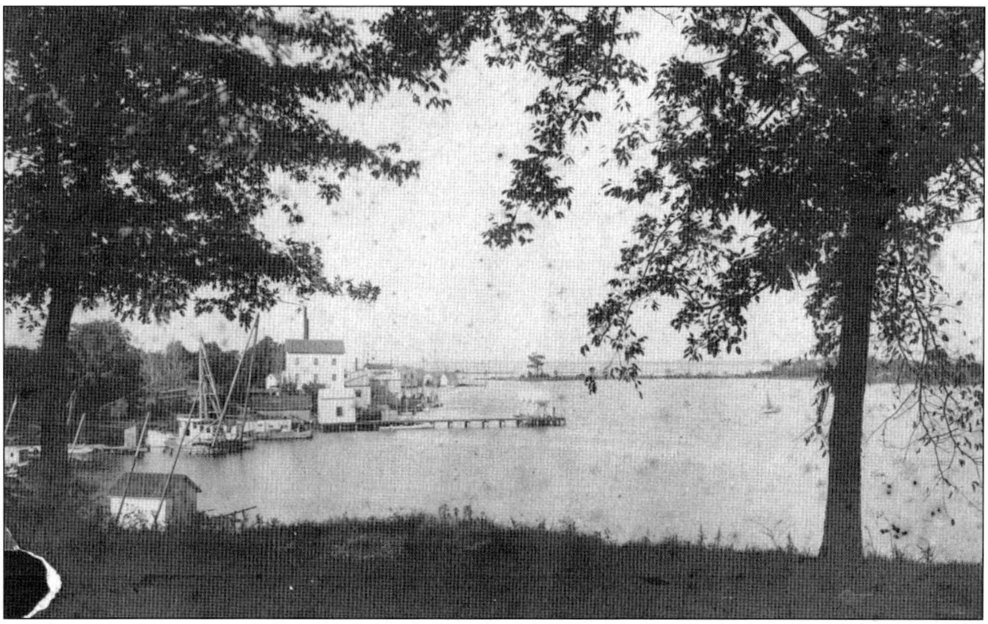

This photograph of Urbanna Creek was taken about 1910. The white two-story building was once the gristmill building on Rosegill Plantation, located on Rosegill Pond. It was moved in 1909 to the town of Urbanna's waterfront and converted into a patent roller mill. The mill business was part of the Middlesex Manufacturing & Mercantile Corp, later called Powell's Mill, which produced the popular Powell's Pride flour. (Courtesy of Buddy Davis.)

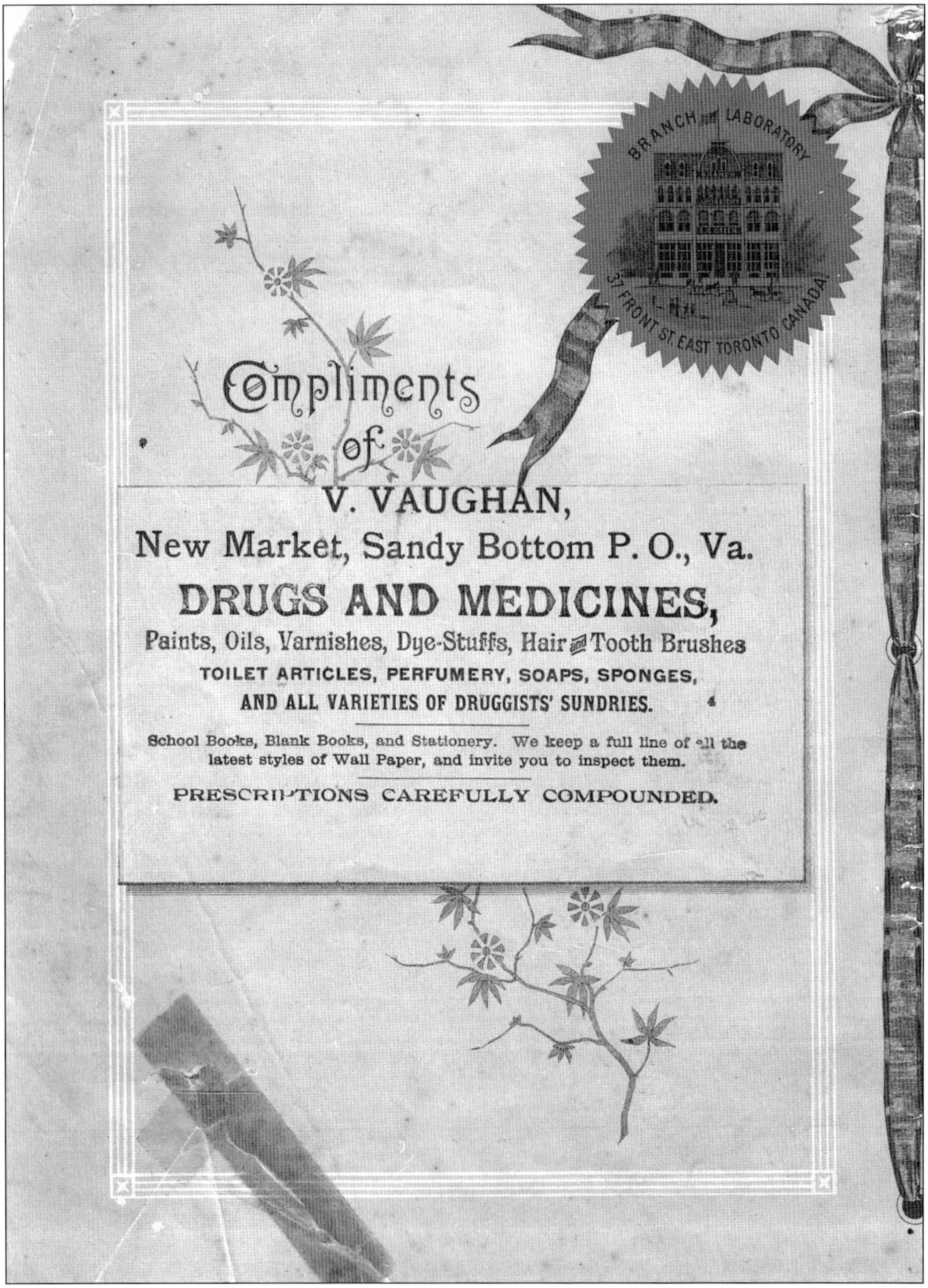

Vespasian Muse Vaughan ran the post office and pharmacy at New Market, where "prescriptions [were] carefully compounded." The store carried a variety of general merchandise, including school books, the latest styles of wallpaper, perfume, soaps, and all varieties of goods. As son-in-law to Capt. David Taylor, who owned several commercial sailing schooners, Vaughan had regular transportation to Baltimore and access to the best goods for his store. (Courtesy of Nola Watson.)

Eight

FACES OF MIDDLESEX

Since Middlesex was settled in 1649, many have lived and passed along the paths, roads, and shores of the county. Some just for a moment, while others spent a lifetime.

The first English settlers were Anglo-Saxons from the southern and western portions of England, and they brought their own culture to a world where Native Americans had lived for centuries.

Throughout much of the county's 350-year history, African Americans made up much of the population as the rich soil along the Rappahannock and Piankatank Rivers shores provided the economic leverage for white landowners to buy slaves. They too brought their own culture, and a blending of the three cultures is part of the county's rich heritage.

Some of the people highlighted in this chapter were born and raised in the county and went away to make their mark on the world. Others lived in Middlesex their entire lives without much notoriety. Others were famous in their own right and came to live in Middlesex.

Many faces are not pictured in this volume, but all are important. Every face in time has been a piece to this 350-year-old story, with each generation making their own endurable mark on Middlesex County's history.

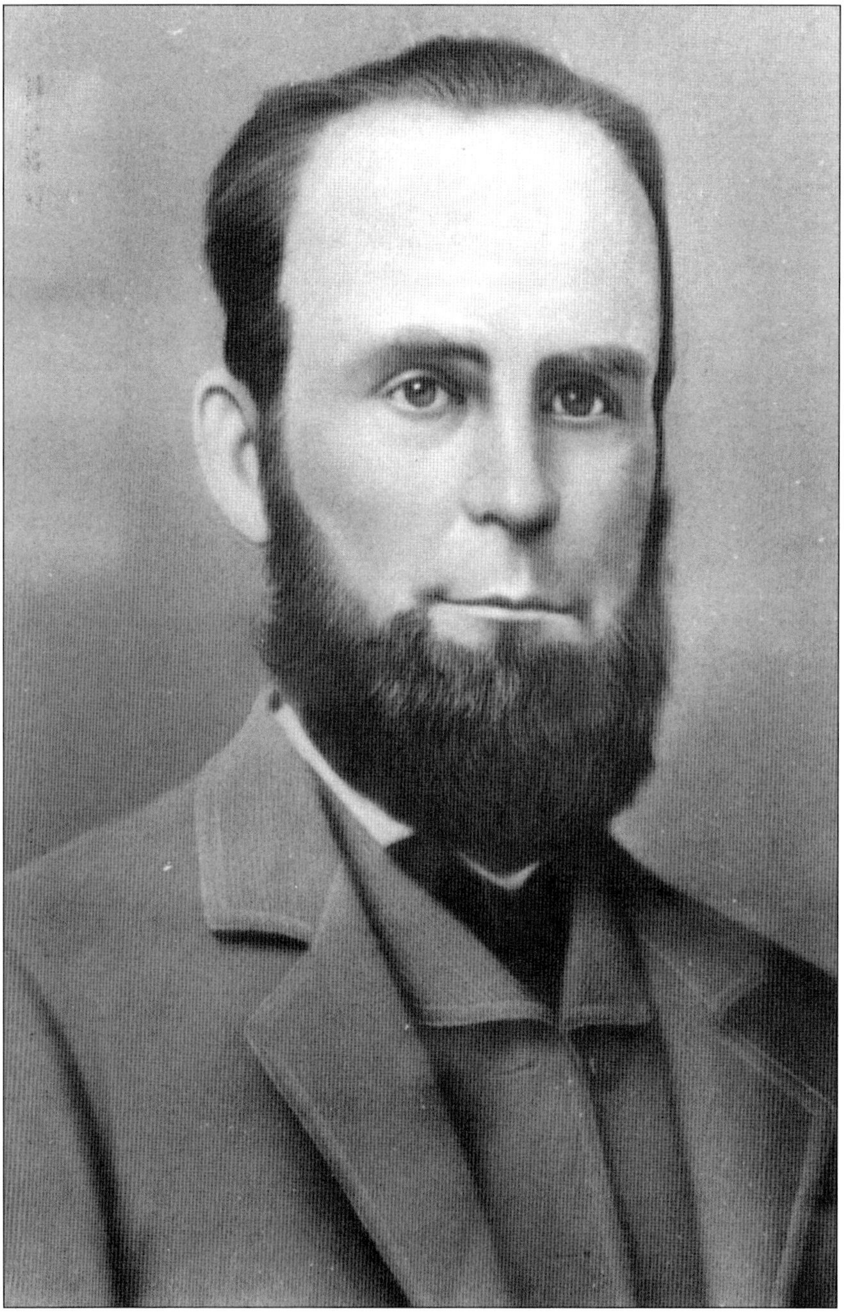

The most famous Middlesex County clerk of court, Philemon T. Woodward, was considered one of the most important figures in county history. He was elected clerk in 1852 and was clerk for 40 years. During the Civil War, the Confederate government in Richmond mandated that county records be brought to the capital of the Confederacy for safekeeping. Woodward refused, and instead buried the records in a secluded area in Dragon Run. When the Confederate army was leaving Richmond on its way to surrender at Appomattox, the soldiers burned portions of the city, and all county records were destroyed. Woodward's defiance of the mandate saved the county's old records that are treasured to this day. (Courtesy of Middlesex County.)

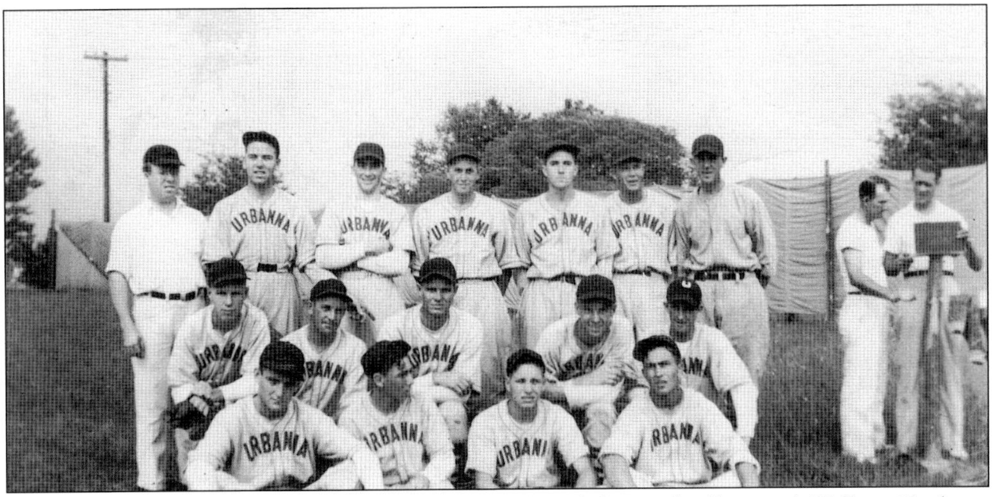

Members of the 1939 Urbanna Baseball Club are, from left to right (first row) William Fitchett, Tyler Thrift, Dick Murray, and Victor Hazelwood; (second row) Richard Moore, John Davis, James Green, Charles Wheeley, and Warner Ashburn; (third row) coach Watty New, Richard Smith, Dorsey Richardson, Lewis Richardson, Woodrow Bristow, Richard Moore, and manager Woodfrin Harwood. (Courtesy of Louise Gray.)

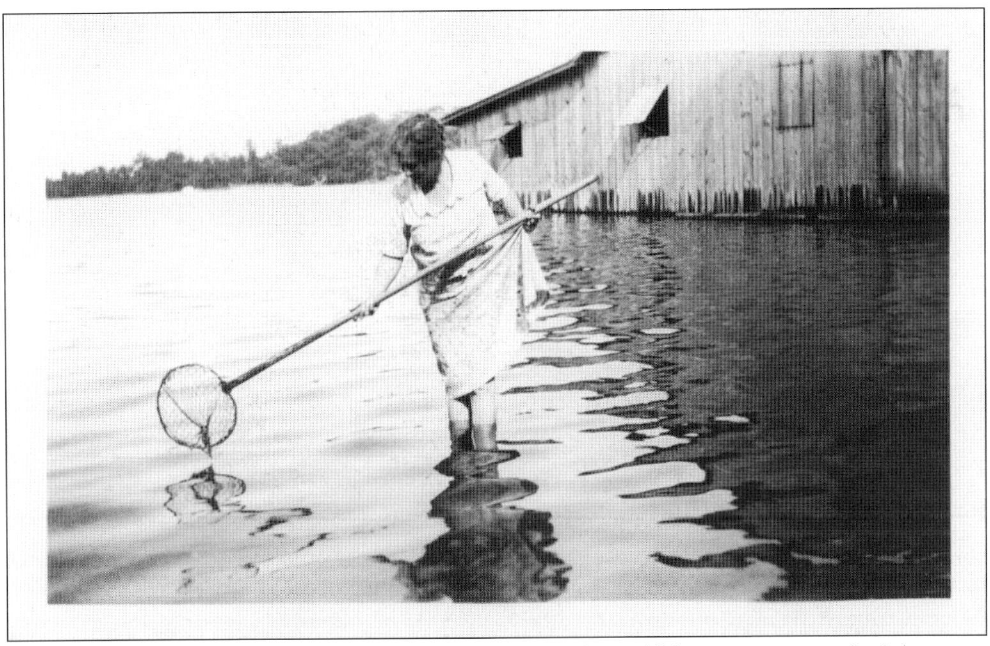

Mary Burton of Urbanna needed a couple more hard crabs to fill her pot, so instead of changing her attire to go crabbing, she just held her skirt up and waded out into Urbanna Creek at low tide and dipped up a Jimmie crab. Fried spot fish and steamed hard crabs were regular seafood delicacies on the dinner tables of Middlesex folk up and down the county. (Courtesy of Betty Burton.)

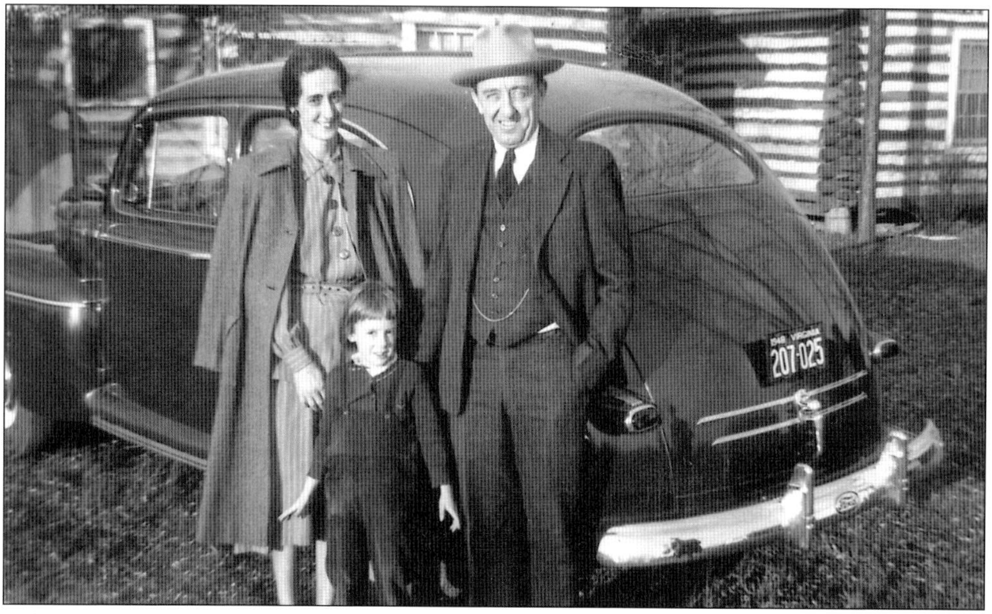

Bob and Elizabeth Bristow and daughter Betty Allen are pictured in 1948. Bob's father, Robert S. Bristow Sr., was born in 1852 at Pleasant View in Stormont. His father, Larkin Bristow, was a farmer, but Robert decided to clerk in his cousin F.A. Bristow's store in Urbanna. Robert established R.S. Bristow and Son in 1876 in Urbanna, and Bob ran the store until he retired in 1988. (Courtesy of Elizabeth Bristow.)

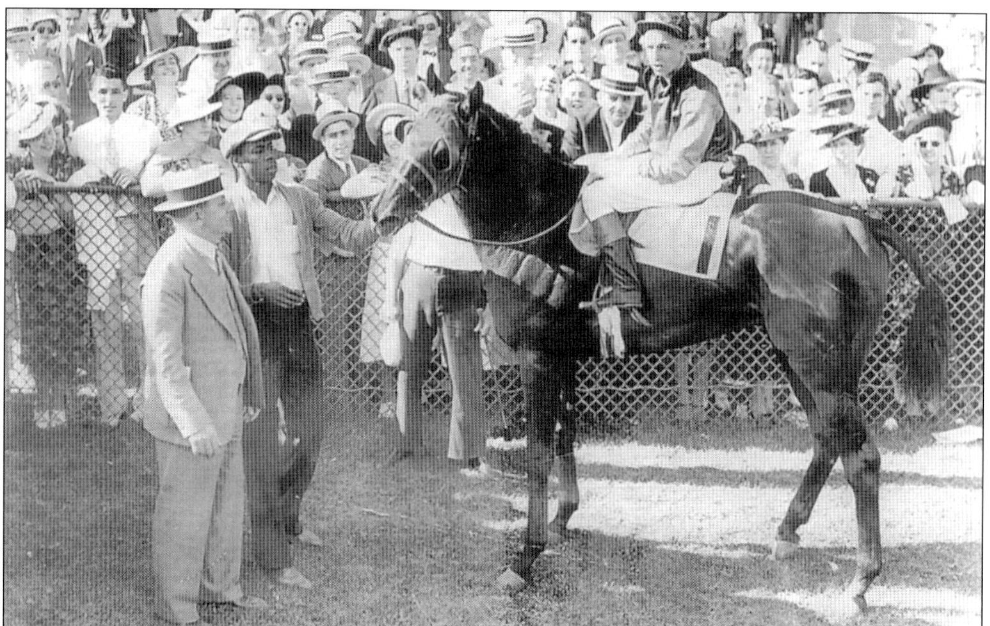

Remlik native Willis Braxton Sr. (second from left) holds the racehorse Nedary in the winner's circle at a Chicago race track in 1938. Braxton was a groom for Willis Sharpe Kilmer, who purchased Remlik Hall Farm in 1909. Kilmer owned such famous horses as Exterminator and Sun Beau, both elected to the National Museum of Racing and Hall of Fame. Braxton and others cared for these horses on Remlik Hall Farm. (Courtesy of Willis Braxton.)

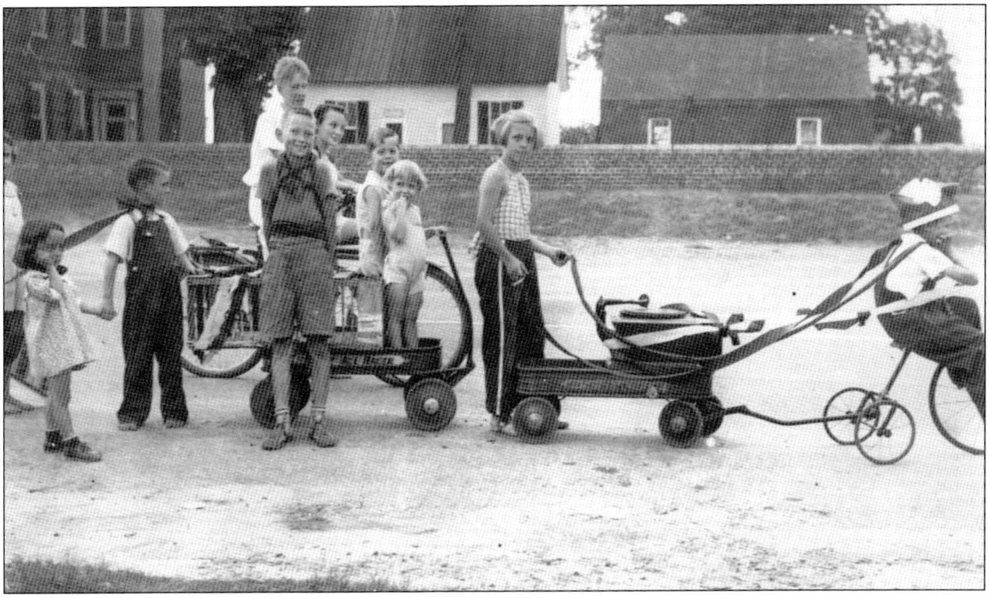

Circus day was annually held in Saluda on Easter Monday. The town children, under the direction of Saluda's Tom Jones, put on a self-styled Barnum and Hayloft children's circus. Performances such as *Snow White and the Seven Dwarfs* were held, with a parade afterward. Pictured in this 1936 parade are, from left to right, Helen Moody, Katherine Kipps, Tom Moody, Tom Jones, Ray Major, Hannah Bourne, Charles Bristow, Jane Royal, Pat (Royal) Perkinson, and Bobby Moody. (Courtesy of Jean Holman.)

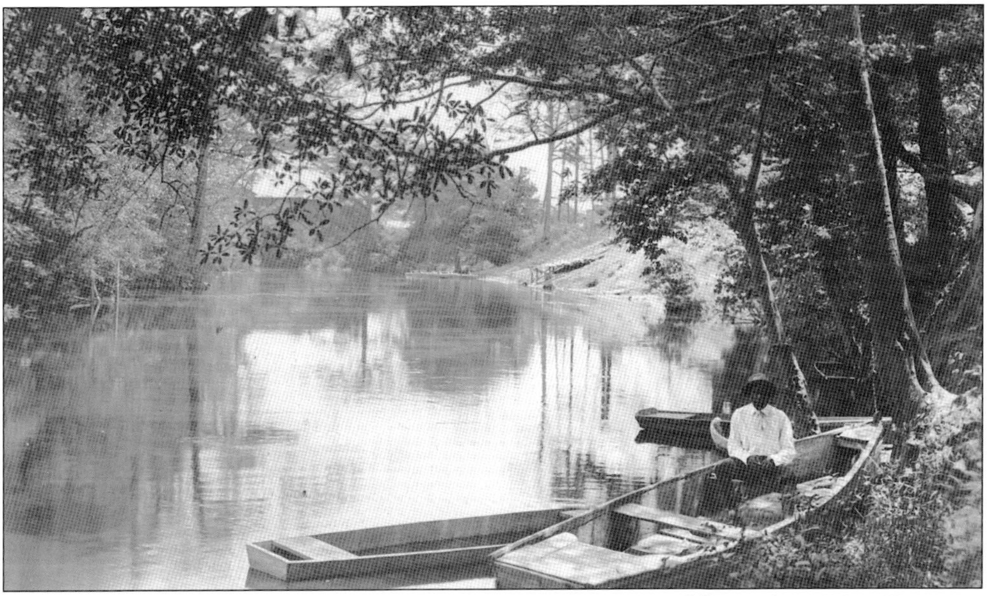

Dragon Run Swamp waters run along the northern edge of Middlesex from Megs Bay near Stormont to Laneview at the Essex County line. Legend has it that the name "Dragon Run" is closely tied to slavery, as white masters suggested that mythical dragons lived in the swamp to discourage their slaves from using it as a hiding place. This old photograph shows a lumber site near Saluda where lumber was loaded onto lighters and poled to awaiting schooners. (Courtesy of Jean Holman.)

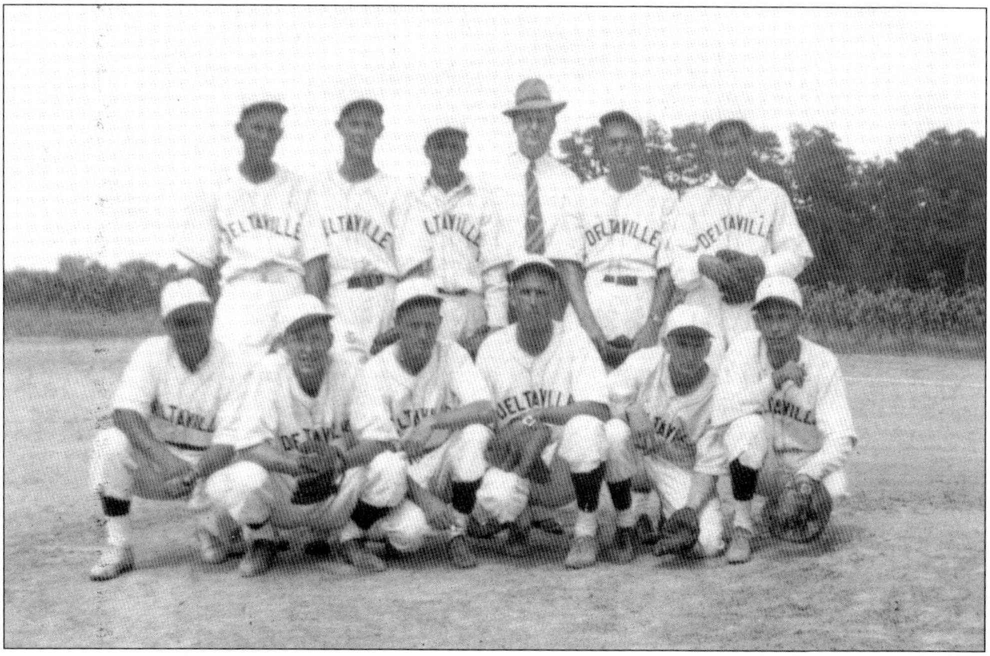

Members of the 1940 Deltaville baseball team were, from left to right (first row) Speck Harrow, Bobby Ailsworth, Raymond Perry, Edward Norton, Norton Hurd, and Mutt Carlton; (second row) Alfred Norris, Clabryn Bridger, Eugene Harrow, John Fleet, Eugene Ruark, and Edmund Harrow. Deltaville is a baseball town to this day, as the Deltaville Deltas, a semipro baseball team, play on summer nights in the community-run Deltaville Ball Park. (Courtesy of Norton Hurd.)

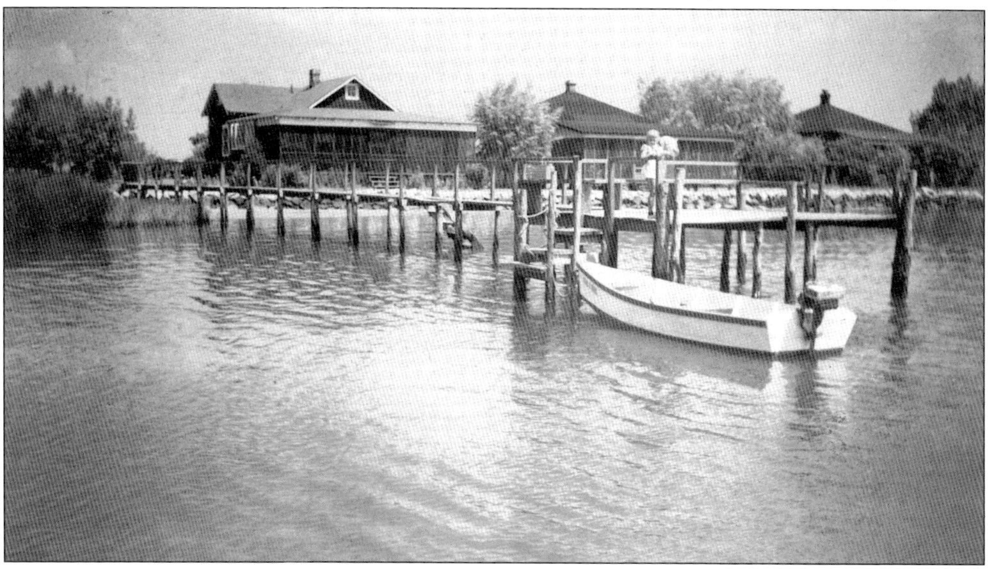

The US Army Corp of Engineers dredged the mouth of Urbanna Creek in 1879. Dredge materials were dumped near the mouth of the creek, creating a man-made point of land. This point of sand and shell eventually became the site of summertime cottages owned by Richmond families, as seen in this photograph. Today, new homes are built upon the footprints of the older cottages as those cottages were flooded and damaged over the years by hurricanes and nor'easter storms. (C.C. Chowning collection.)

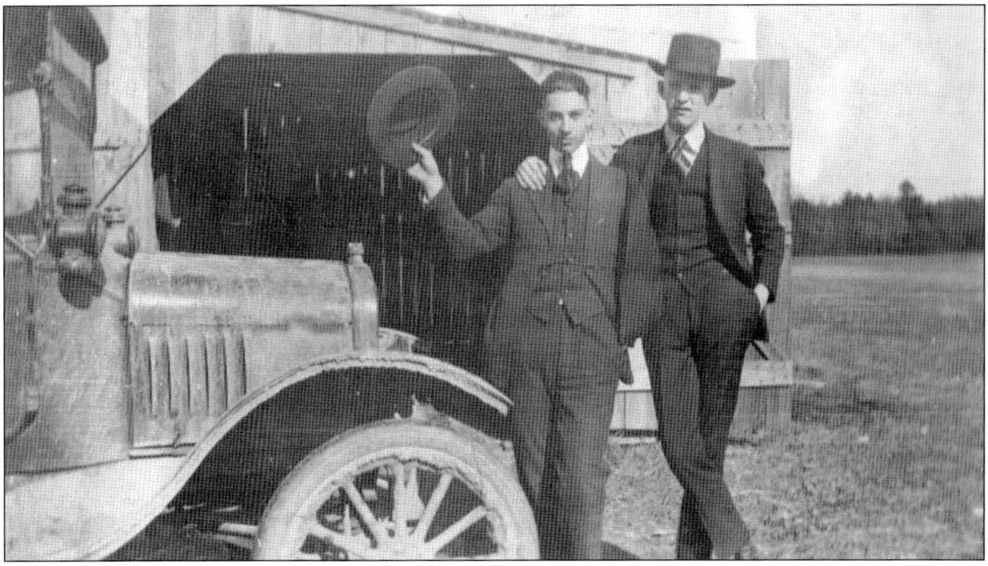

Model T Fords changed forever the way Middlesex citizens traveled. At the turn of the 20th century, the horseless carriage remained a supplemental means of travel. During inclement weather, horse and buggy often maneuvered muddy Middlesex County dirt roads better than the car. When the sun came out and roadbeds were hard, residents dressed in their Sunday best and rode with pride to church in their Model T. (Courtesy of Mary and Danny Loving.)

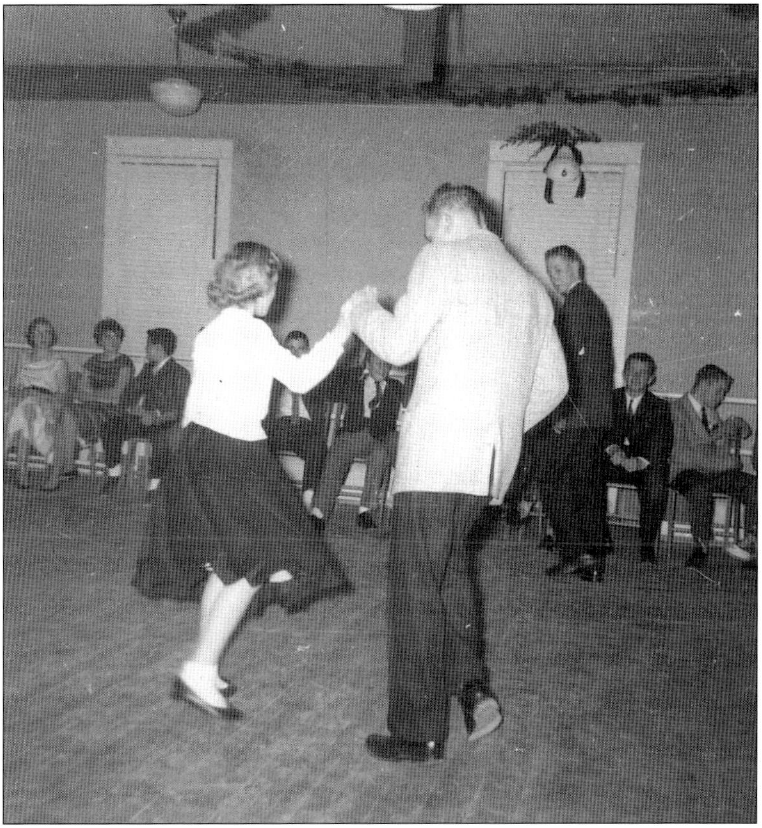

Rock 'n' roll music hit Middlesex with a bang in the 1950s. Dances were held at the Deltaville Community Center and the American Legion building in Saluda for whites. Over the generations, Anglican churchwardens and, later, Baptist church officers, enforced the moral authority of their times. This new style of dancing was frowned upon by some conservative Baptists. (Courtesy of Louise Gray.)

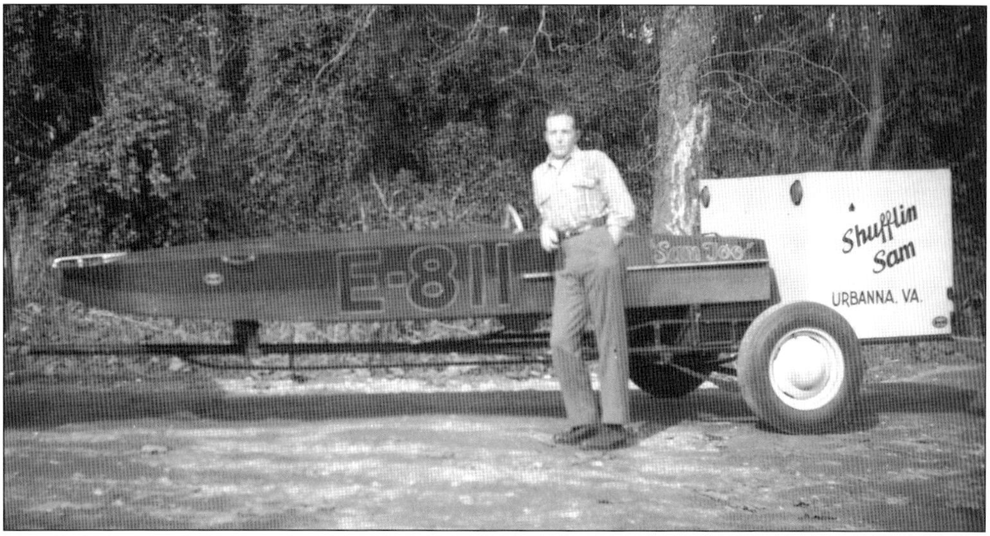

The Urbanna Labor Day Boat Races was an annual event in the town of Urbanna from 1938 until 1966. For Urbanna residents, *Shufflin Sam*, built and owned by Urbanna's own Walter Boyd Hurley, was the town favorite. In 1941, Hurley and *Shufflin Sam* won the handicap race, to the roar of friends and family standing along the shore. The family still cherishes the silver embossed plate won at that Labor Day race. (Courtesy of Walt Hurley.)

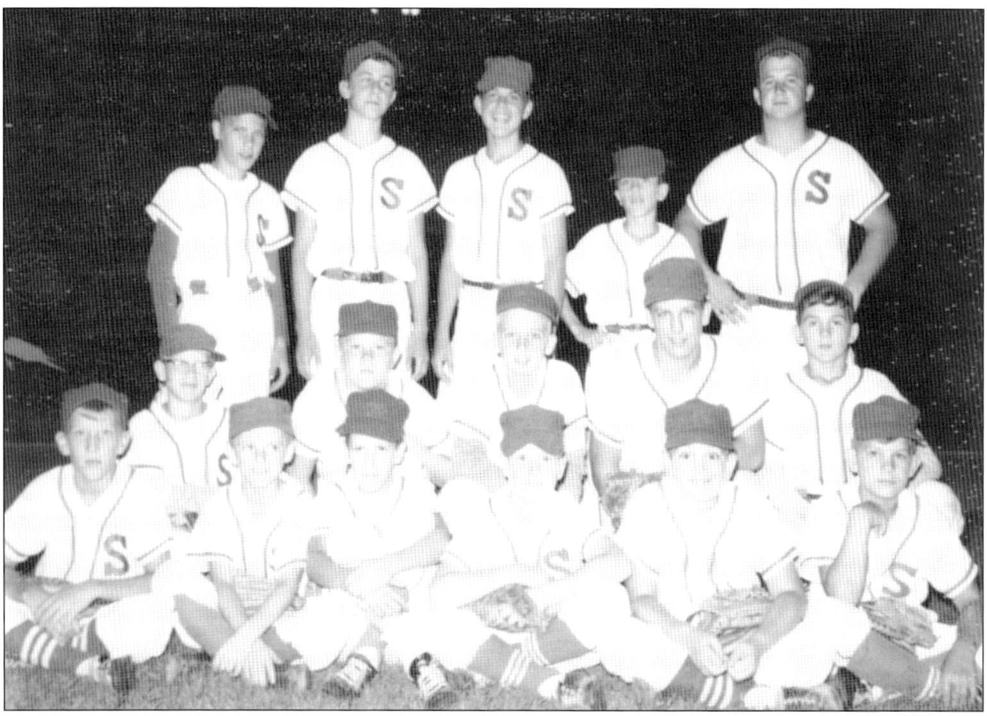

Members of the 1964 Syringa boy's league team are, from left to right (first row) Gary Estes, Glenn Mathews, Charles B. Miller, David Blake, Tony Jackson, and Larry Maul; (second row) Jimmy Lucas, Bill Maul, Johnny Revere, James Allen Whitaker, and Hugh Dunlevy; (third row) Meredith Miller, E.G. Fleet, Eugene Snead, Jimmy Rose, and manager Johnny Fleet. (Courtesy of John M. Bareford Jr.)

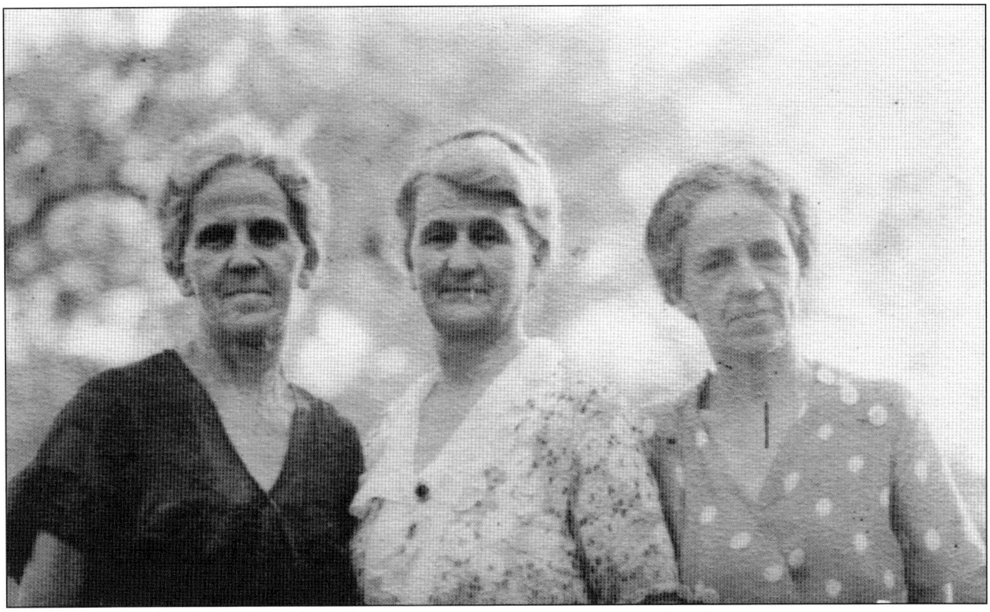

On August 18, 1920, the 19th Amendment to the Constitution finally gave women the right to vote. Women in Middlesex soon made their way to the courthouse in Saluda to register. Susan D. Lawson was the first woman to sign on September 6. The next day, F.E. Bristow and Flossie B. Eastman registered. These three sisters, from left to right, Gay Ward Wright, Lena Ward Blakey, and Emma Lee Ward Bell, all signed up on the same day. (Courtesy of Jean Holman.)

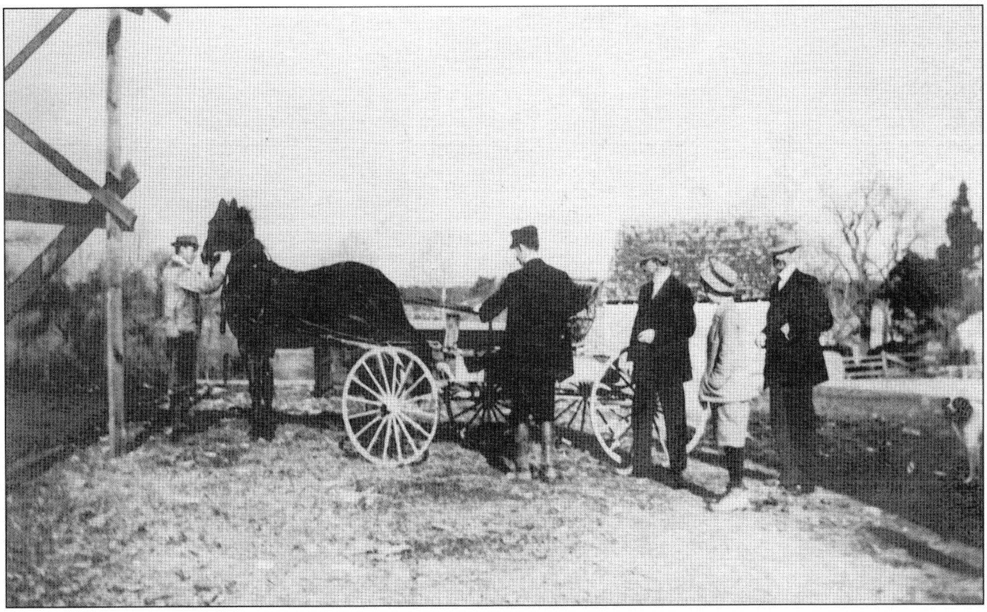

This horse and wagon belonged to the Gray family of Oakenham near Saluda. The wagon was used to carry the family to social functions and church on Sundays at Clarks Neck Baptist Church. James Clarke Gray and Florence Parrish Gray purchased Oakenham in 1902. Gray, a native of Tiverton, Rhode Island, had come to Virginia after Capt. John Bailey of Rosegill died to manage Rosegill for his aunt Eliza Hughes Bailey. (Courtesy of Louise Gray.)

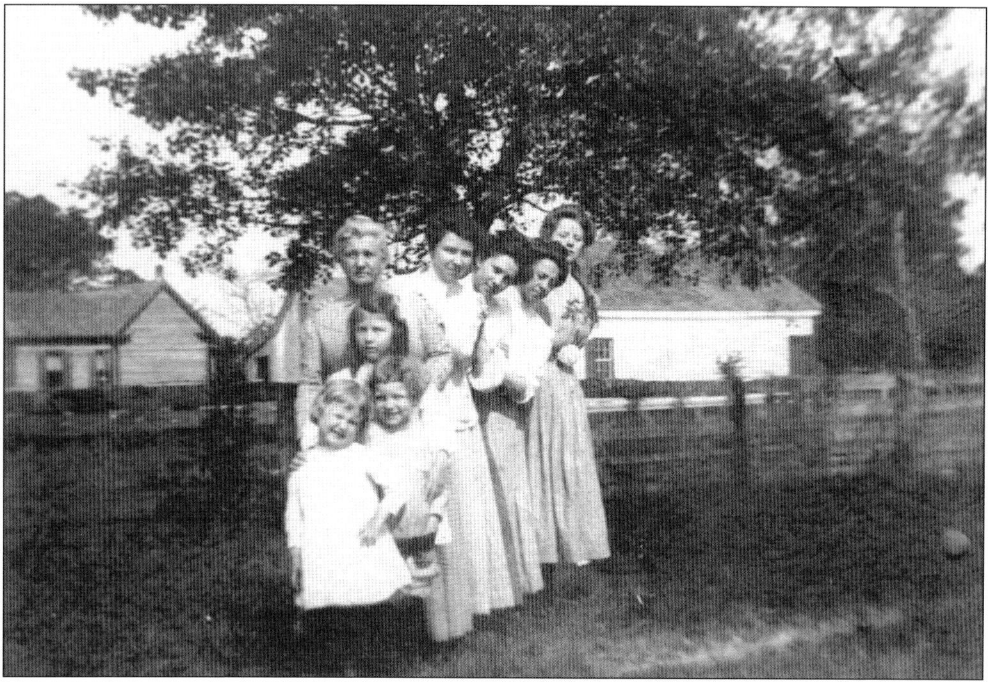

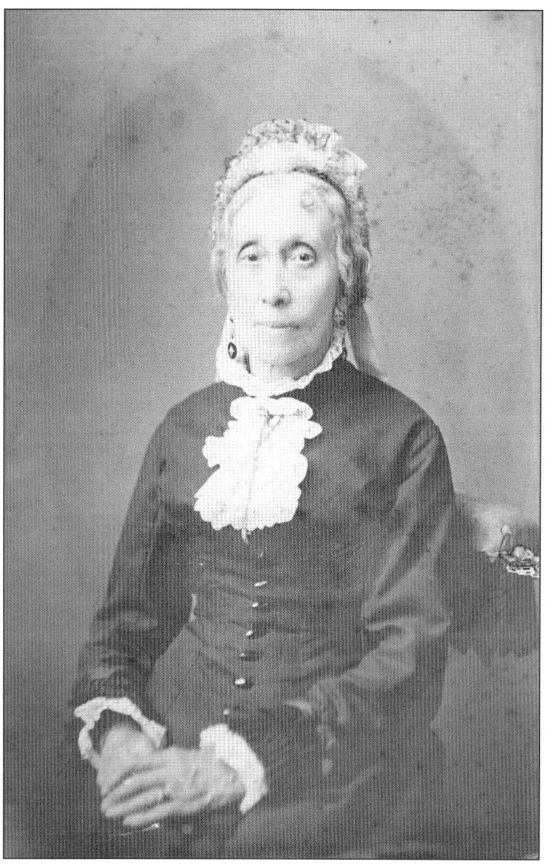

The Vaughan girls of New Market are all lined up in front of Vespasian Vaughan's store (white building). Vespasian's wife, Julia Maria (Boss) Vaughan, with gray hair, was the first female postmaster of Sandy Bottom Post Office. She took over as postmaster in 1894 when Vespasian died of an injury related to a bullet wound to his stomach that he had received during the Civil War. (Courtesy of Lola Watson.)

Elija Bailey became the mistress of Rosegill when her husband, Capt. John Bailey, purchased the farm in 1849. During the summer of 1863, John Taylor Wood, a nephew of Confederate president Jefferson Davis, launched a series of naval raids along the Middlesex shores. On Sunday, August 23, Wood's troops captured two Union vessels, resulting in wounded Confederate and Union sailors and runaway slaves. Rosegill was converted into a hospital, and Elija insisted that all wounded, white and black, would be treated. (Courtesy of George Temple.)

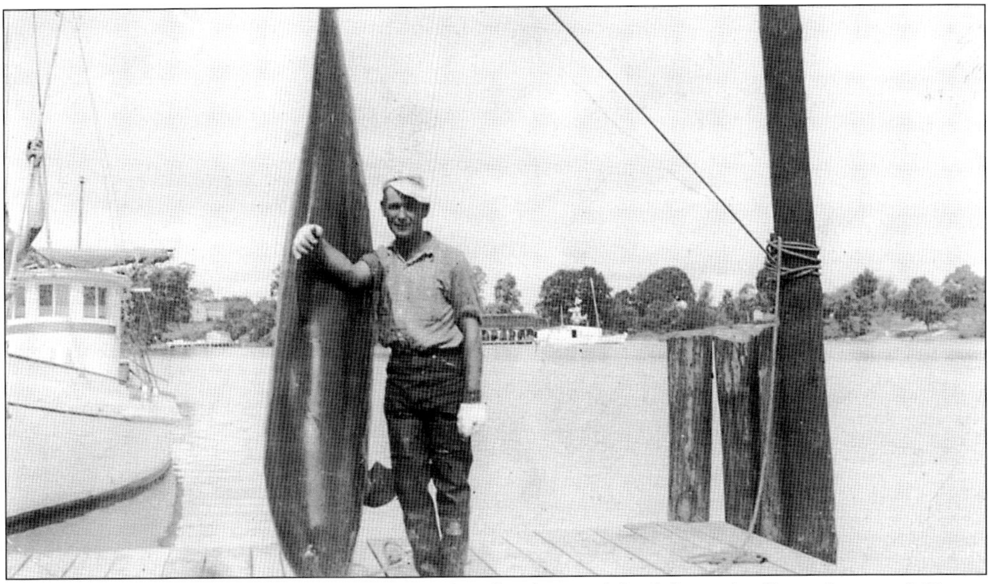

Willis Wilson of Deltaville and his father, Obie, haul seined for fish on the Rappahannock River. One year, they caught a dolphin and took it to their dock on Broad Creek and sent a boy out into the neighborhood to tell all the people. When people started coming to the dock, Obie stopped them at the shore and charged each person a nickel to come out on the dock. They had 160 people come and made $8. (Courtesy of Willis Wilson.)

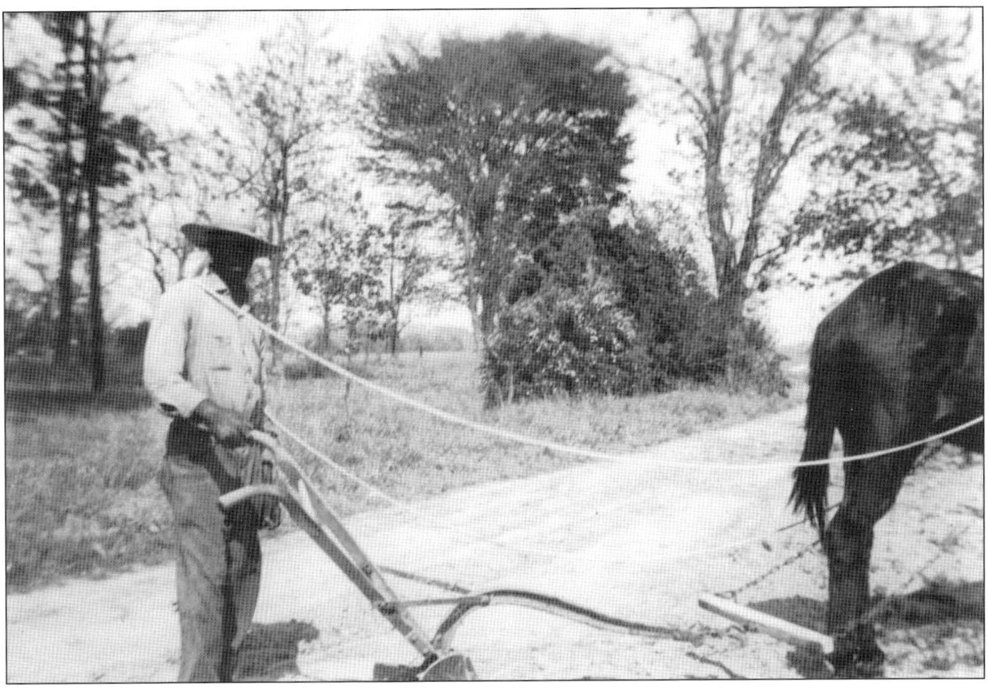

For much of the county's history, families were able to grow most of their own food from the land; raise hogs, chickens, and beef cattle; and catch oysters, fish, and crabs from the rivers. The horse and plow were essential tools in working the fertile soils of Middlesex County. (Courtesy of Louise Gray.)

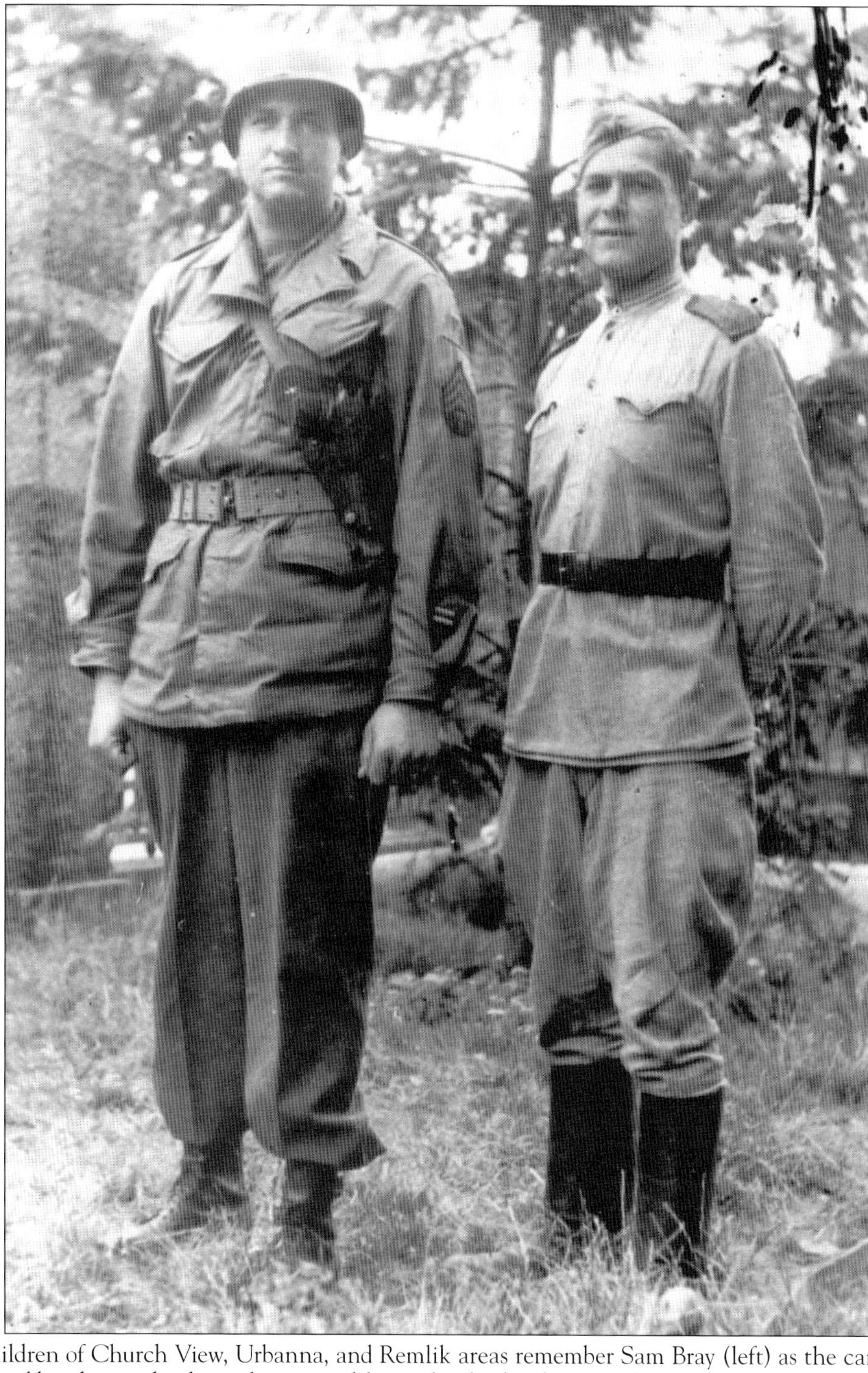

Children of Church View, Urbanna, and Remlik areas remember Sam Bray (left) as the caring school bus driver who drove them to and from school. They knew nothing of the man who, during World War II, participated in five major battles in the European Theater and was selected to go to Potsdam, Germany, to serve as an honor guard for the Potsdam Conference, where the future of Germany was determined. (Courtesy of Jerry and Alva Bray.)

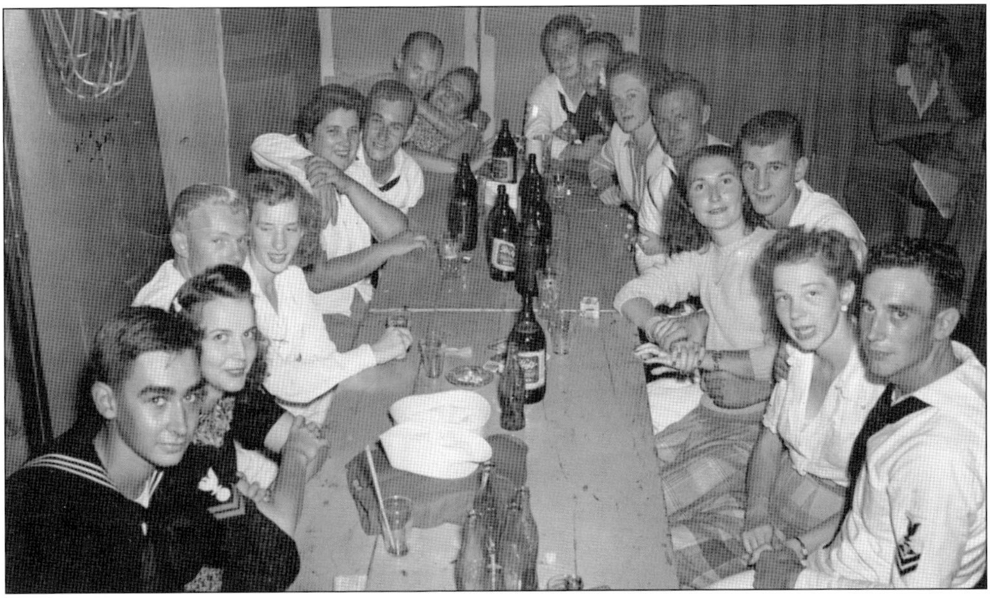

Carroll Chowning Jr. of Saluda (seated at front left) graduated in 1941 from Christchurch School. The next year, he went to the Naval Academy Preparatory School in Norfolk. This photograph was taken in 1943 after he was transferred to Saybrooks College in New Haven, Connecticut, where he continued training in the US Navy. Most Middlesex boys of those times were a part of the "Greatest Generation," who fought the Germans and Japanese in World War II. (C.C. Chowning collection.)

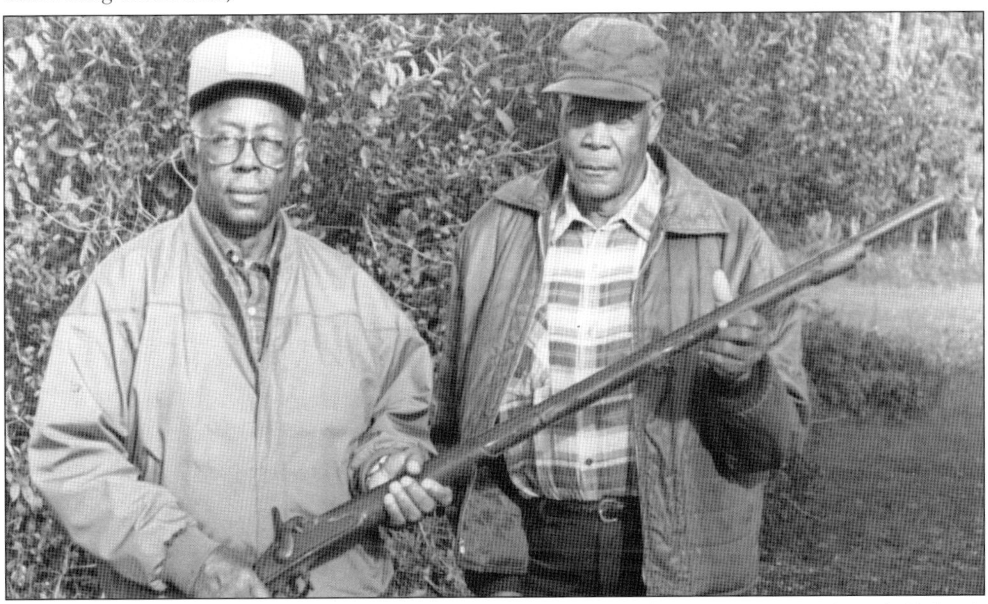

During the Civil War, Charlie Smith was a slave on Nesting plantation. Master Joseph Eubank gave Smith this gun to protect Nesting from Union soldiers. Descendants of Nesting slaves William Dickerson (left) and Clemon Brown hold the old gun. There were four guns allotted to slaves, used to guard "Big Gate" (the main entrance), a point on Mud Creek, Percifull Landing, and a beach near Punch Bowl. When freedom came, Eubank told his former slaves to keep the rifles. (Author's collection.)

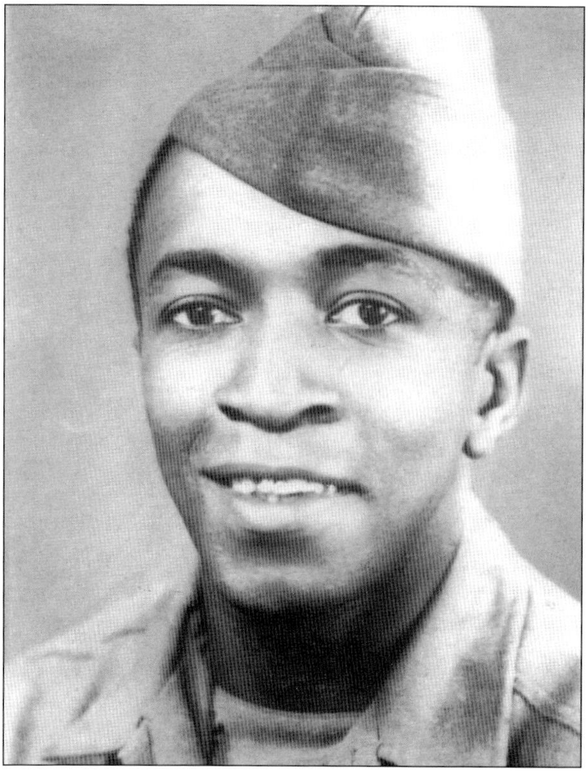

In the winter of 1944–1945, Raymond W. Burrell of Deltaville was fighting with the now-famous segregated Black Panthers of the 761st Tank Battalion, which saw extensive action at the Battle of the Bulge—Hitler's last desperate effort to stop the Allies. The 761st was the first African American tank battalion. The famous baseball star Jackie Robinson was in the battalion and bunked three bunks down from Burrell. (Courtesy of George Robinson.)

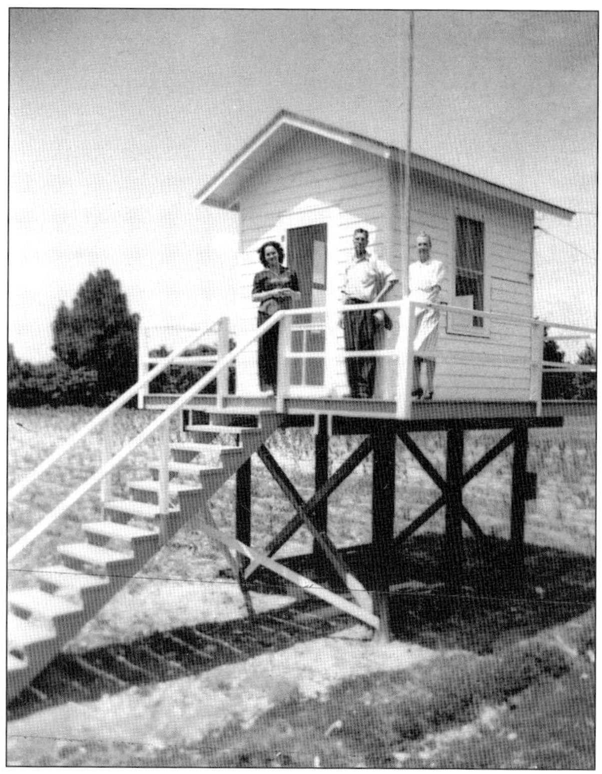

Air raid spotter stations were built during World War II up and down the county. The governor of Virginia named Lt. Cmdr. William Harris Booth of Urbanna Civil Defense coordinator for the county. Harry Vail of Deltaville, Raymond Jones of Saluda, and Carroll Chowning Sr. of Urbanna were assistant coordinators who oversaw the construction and manning of stations. This station was located in Urbanna. (Courtesy of Pat Marshall.)

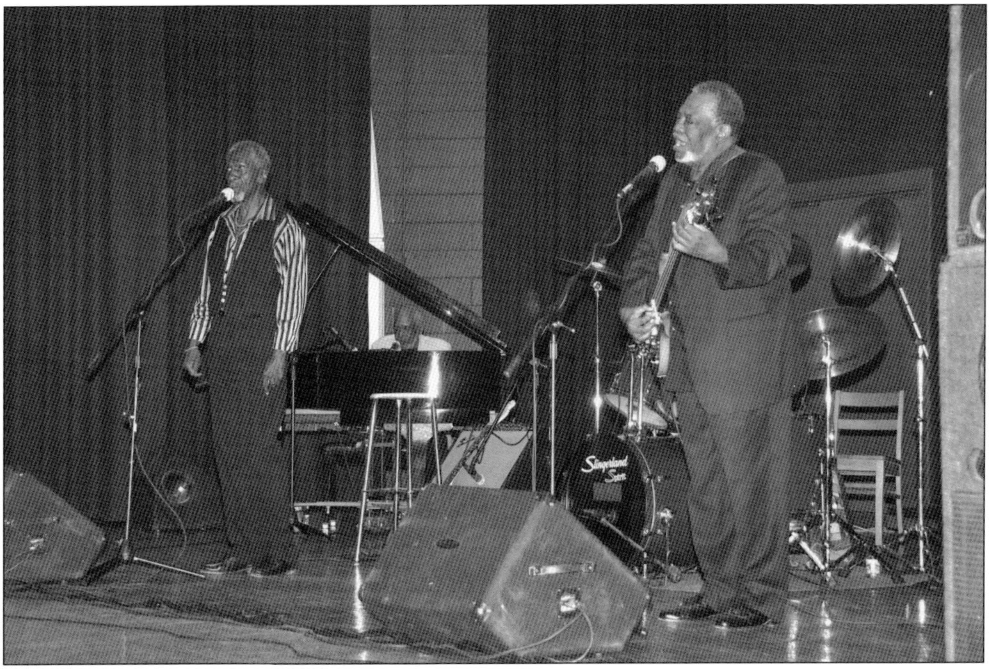

Sherman (guitar) and Wendell Holmes (piano) grew up at Christ Church and started their music careers singing for the Calvary Baptist Church choir. The Holmes Brothers gained international fame for their vocal and instrumental talents singing and playing soul, blues, gospel, and country music. They appeared on the *Late Show with David Letterman* in August 1990 and performed for Pres. Bill Clinton. A member of the band, the late Popsy Dixon, is at the microphone. (Courtesy of the *Southside Sentinel.*)

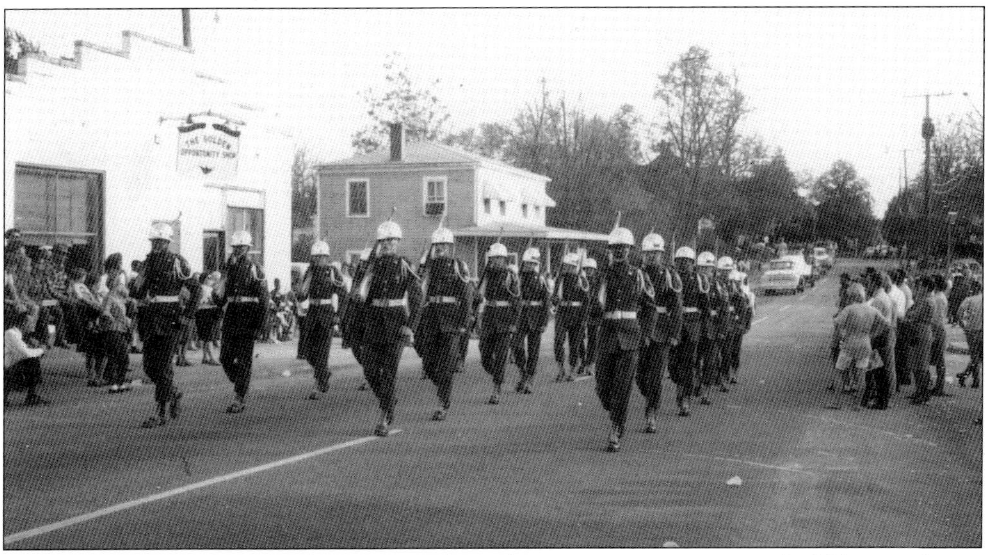

The event that has brought the most people to the county at one time is the Urbanna Oyster Festival. Started in 1957 as Urbanna Days, the event has grown into one of the largest festivals in the area. This 1964 photograph of a military marching band was a highlight at that festival. The Urbanna Oyster Festival is held annually on the first weekend in November. (Courtesy of John M. Bareford Jr.)

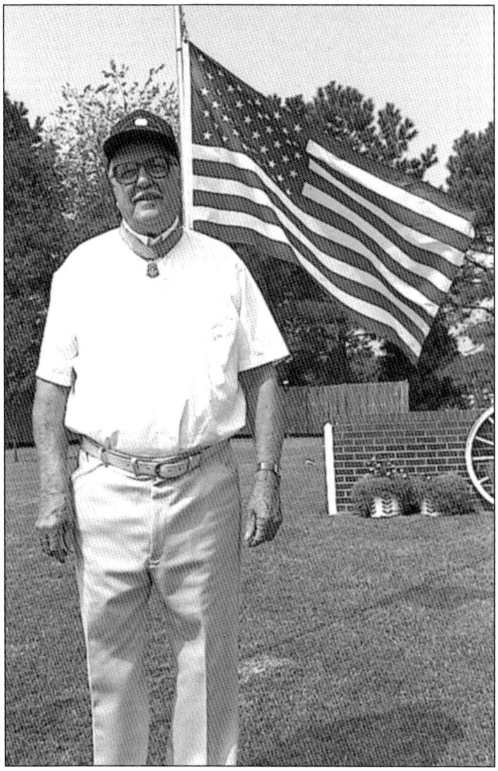

Lt. Beryl R. Newman of Remlik was awarded the Congressional Medal of Honor on January 15, 1945, for his heroics in World War II. Lieutenant Newman captured two enemy machine gun nests, killing all but two Germans, who fled into a house. He attacked the house, calling for the occupants to surrender. Eleven Germans surrendered to Newman, who did not realize until the shooting was over that he was alone. His platoon had not advanced with him. (Courtesy of the *Southside Sentinel.*)

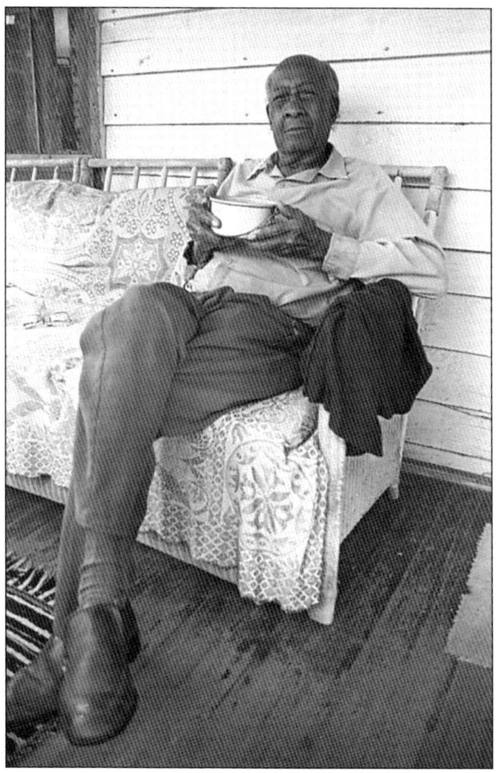

In 1991, Callie Richardson of Jamaica was 95 years old and the last surviving World War I veteran in the county. In 1918, he had just arrived in France when the armistice was signed and the war ended. Richardson stayed a year after the war, digging up battlefield graves of American soldiers and moving them to proper burial sites. In one graveyard where Richardson carried the dead, there were 85,000 Americans buried. (Courtesy of the *Southside Sentinel.*)

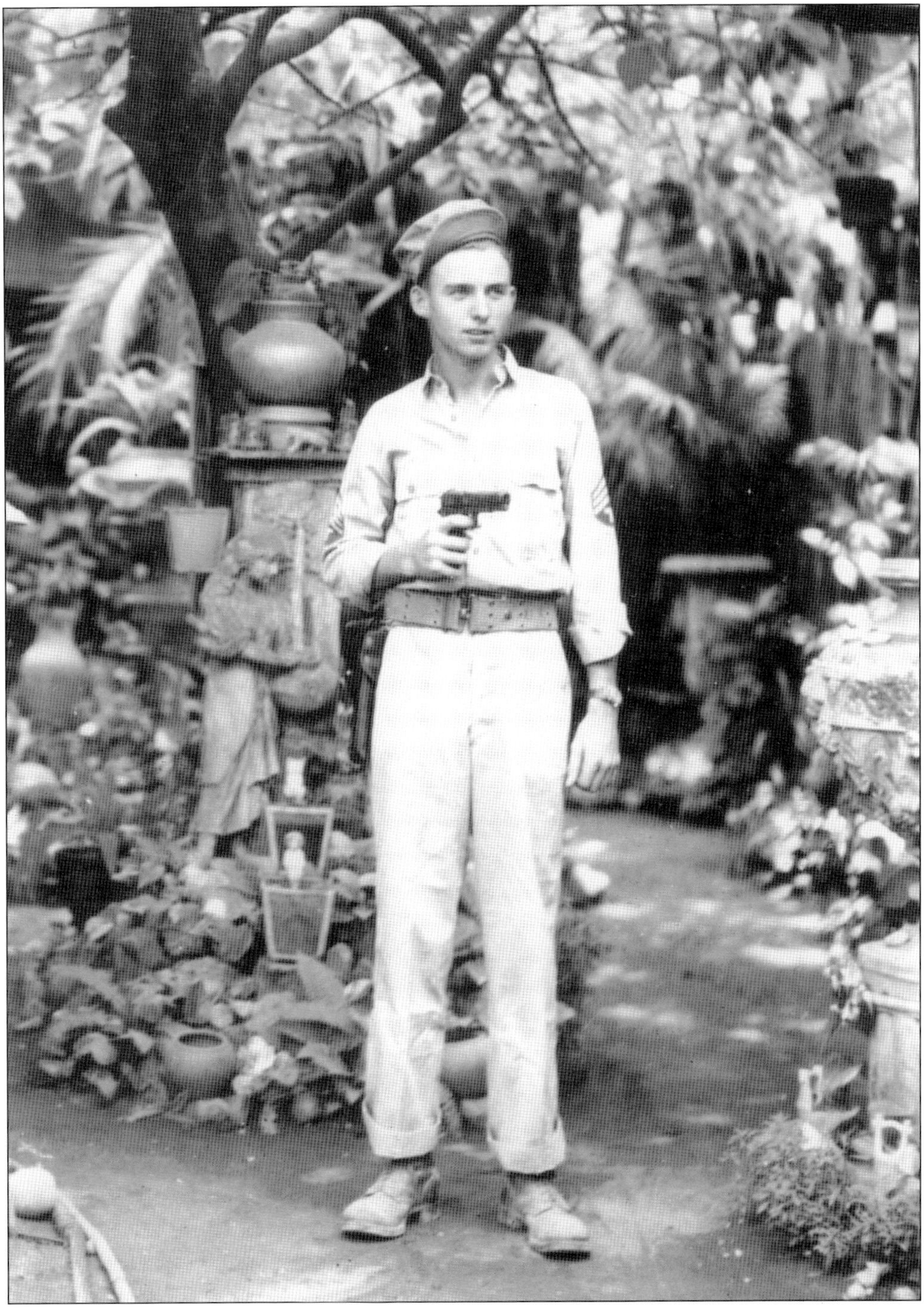

Ed Deagle of Deltaville was in the South Pacific when a Japanese kamikaze ran a boat loaded with explosives into an American ship. The explosives hit near the mess hall where sailors were eating and killed hundreds. Deagle was on shore when he spotted the Japanese soldier swimming. He took a boat and went out to the swimming man and shot and killed him. It was an event he carried with him the rest of his life. (Courtesy of Ed Deagle.)

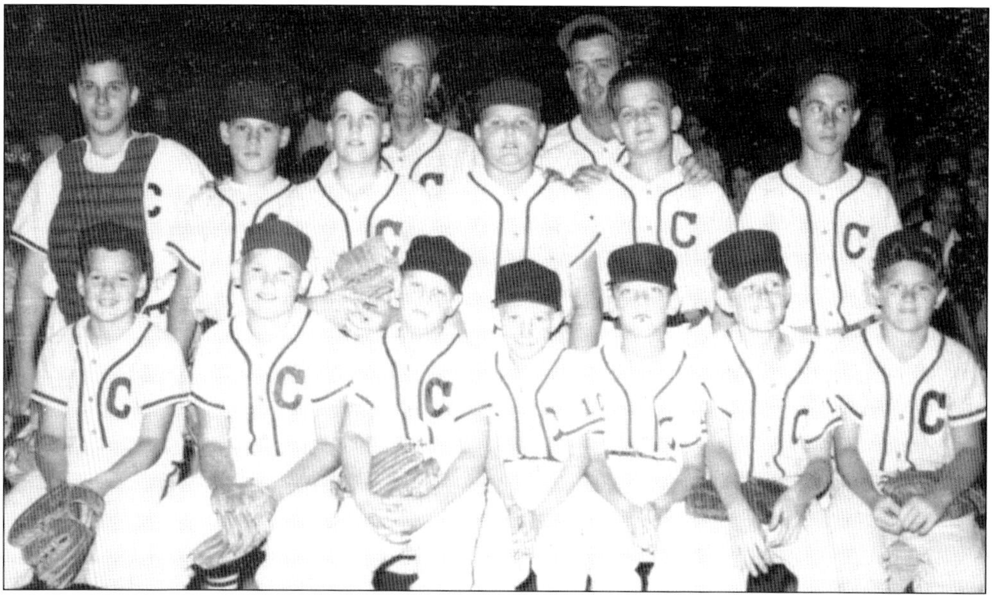

The Middlesex all-white little league baseball league started in 1958 with four teams: Urbanna, Deltaville, Syringa, and Church View. Members of the 1964 Church View team are, from left to right, (first row) Larry Burch, Thomas Powell, Mark Bray, Dennis Hogge, Wilton Marshall, Calvin Langford, and Deane Sickal; (second row) Monty Newbill, Thomas Williams, William Thrift, Donald Williams, Jerry Bray, and Chuck Leasure; (third row) manager Raymond Carnell and coach Bernard J. Sickal. (Courtesy of John M. Bareford Jr.)

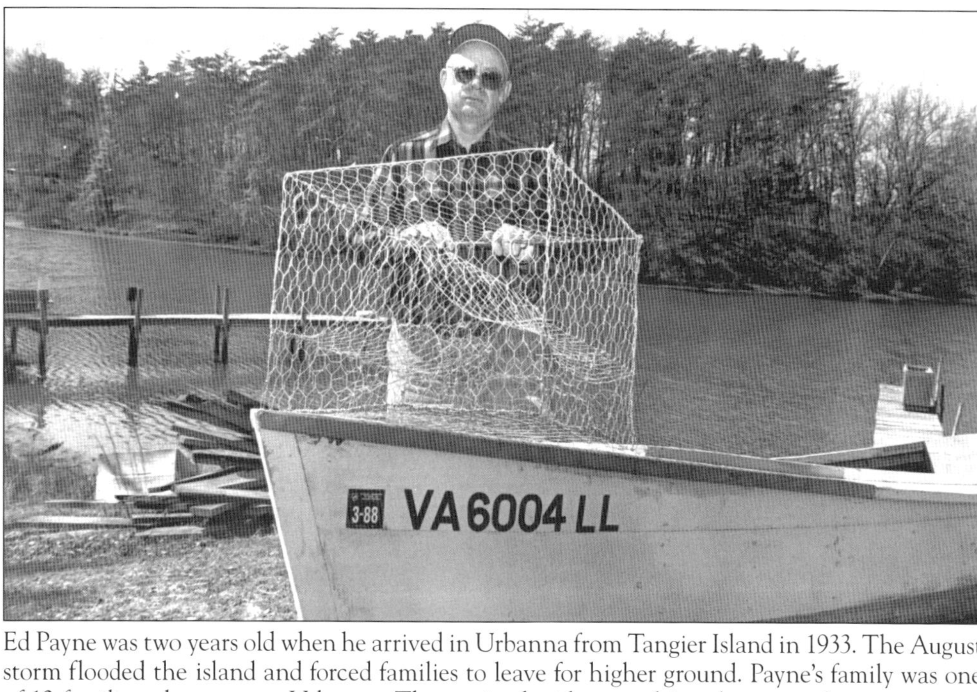

Ed Payne was two years old when he arrived in Urbanna from Tangier Island in 1933. The August storm flooded the island and forced families to leave for higher ground. Payne's family was one of 13 families who came to Urbanna. They arrived with everything they owned in a convoy of small boats. They brought with them island knowledge of crabbing and oystering. Ed made crab pots behind his home on Perkins Creek. (Author's collection.)

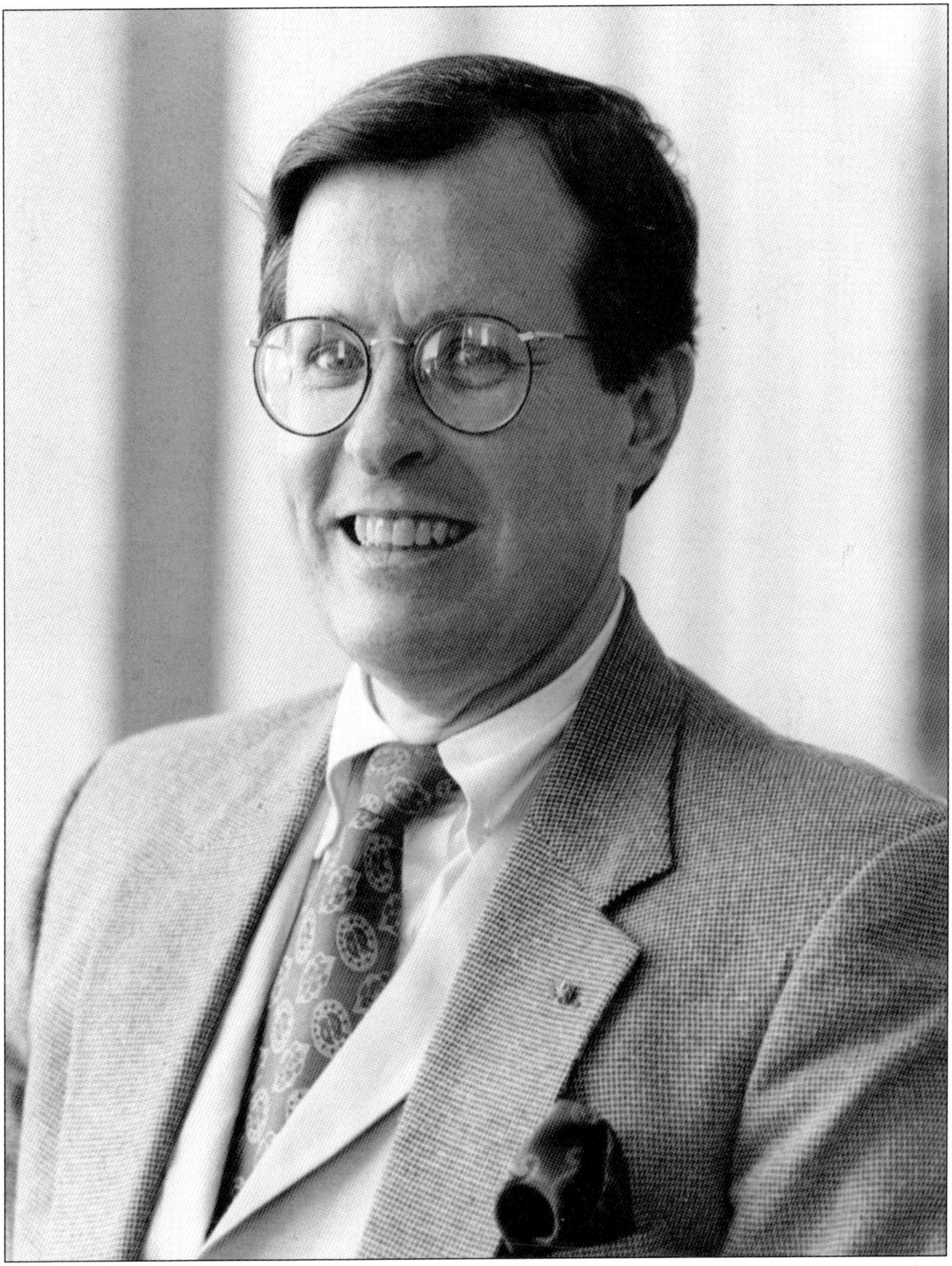

Lewis Burwell Puller Jr. won the 1992 Pulitzer Prize for his autobiography *Fortunate Son*. His father, Lt. General Lewis "Chesty" Puller, is the most decorated marine in the history of the US Marine Corp, and when he retired, the family moved to Saluda. Chesty Puller is buried in Christ Church cemetery, and hundreds of marines come each year to pay homage to the great general. Lewis Jr. was the 1992 grand marshal of the Urbanna Oyster Festival, attended Urbanna Grade School, and graduated from Christchurch School in 1963. (Courtesy of the *Southside Sentinel*.)

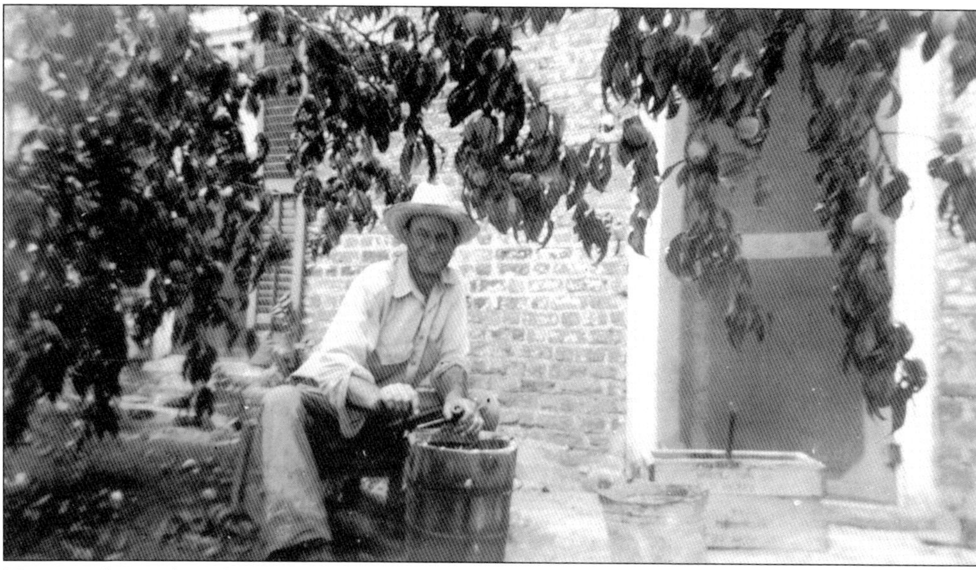

Homemade peach and apple brandy and mint juleps were staple drinks for Middlesex households. Each household grew peaches and apples for making homemade brandy and spearmint for making mint juleps. The arrival of the Baptists in 1772 brought on a temperance movement that changed the county's culture toward drinking alcohol. If not for brandy, peaches were grown for making homemade ice cream. This photograph of a man making ice cream was taken at Clifton on Dragon Run. (Courtesy of Jean Holman.)

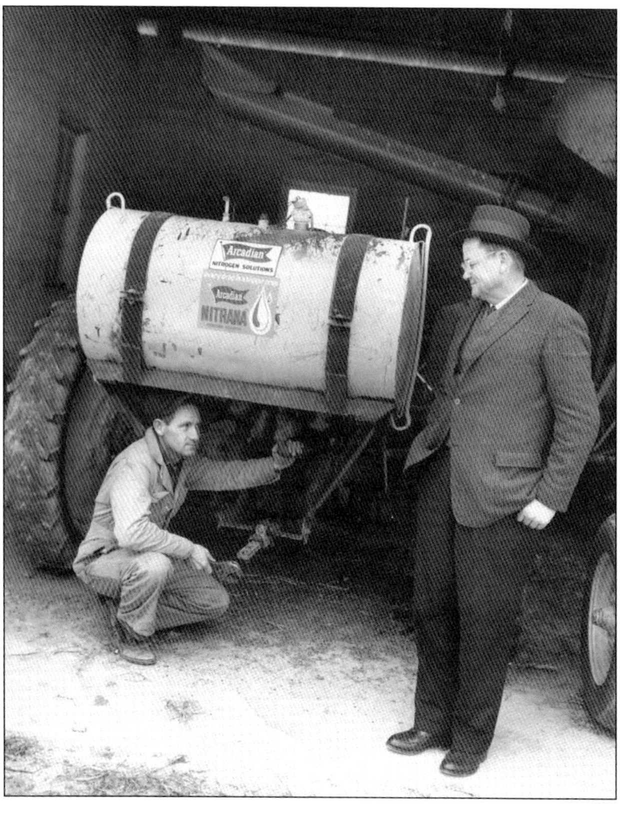

Rufus Harrell (right) purchased Corbin Hall Farm in Samos in 1959. Corbin Hall is the largest single tract farm in Middlesex. When he bought the farm, it was being used primarily to grow sweet potatoes. His first year, Harrell grew peas for Lord-Mott Cannery. After that, he grew corn, wheat, and soybeans. Farm manager Olden Russell (left) came with Harrell in 1959 and managed Corbin Hall until he retired. (Courtesy of Ronnie and Cathy Russell.)

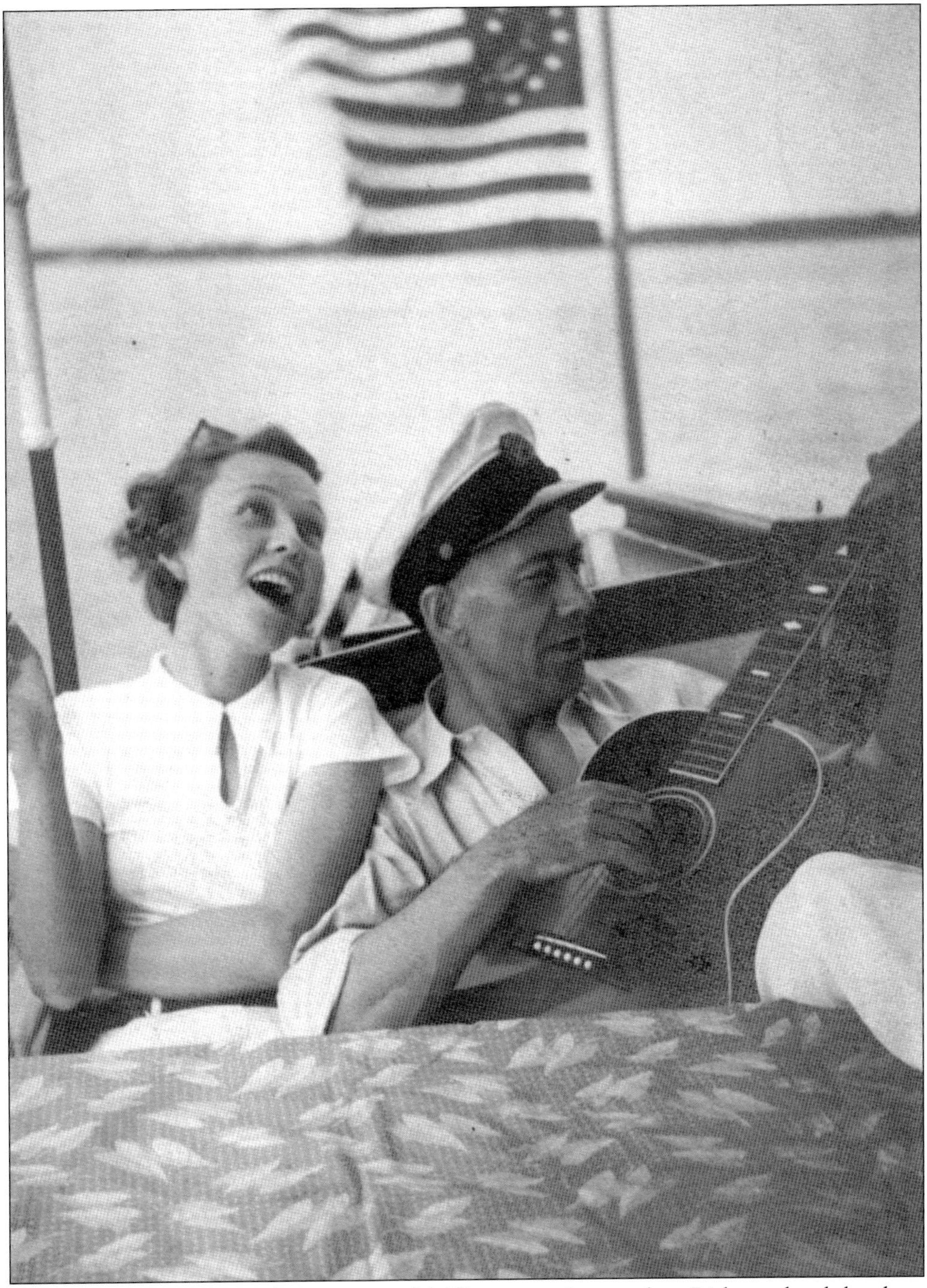

After World War II, a revived spirit came to Middlesex as yachtsmen from Richmond and elsewhere brought their families down on weekends to relax, enjoy a day of bottom fishing, an evening of dinner and song, and overnight stays on their boat. The next generation of weekenders preferred entertaining and spending nights in cottages that they built along the shorelines. Many of the next generation transformed those cottages into substantial homes and have retired to the county. (C.C. Chowning collection.)

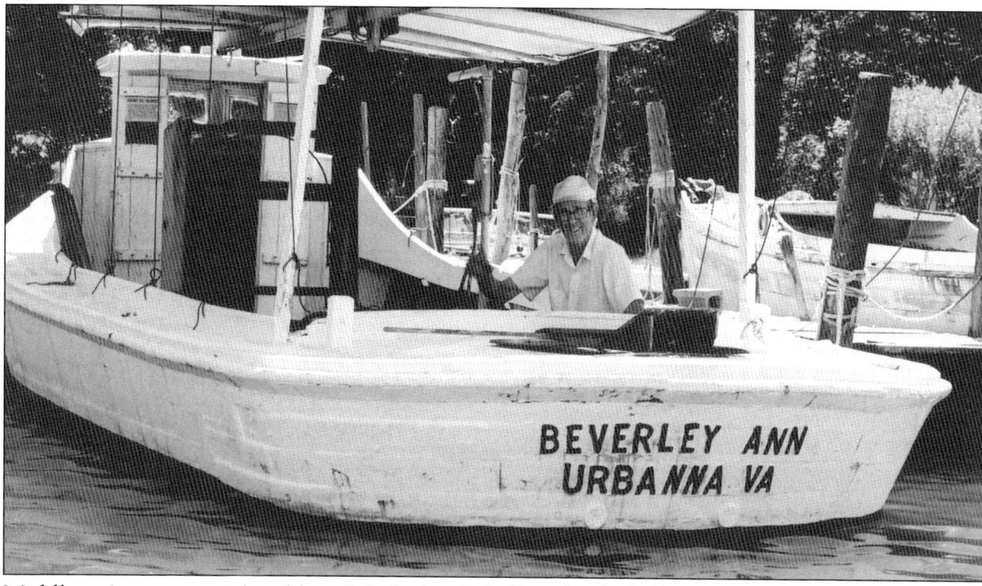

Middlesex's commercial crabbers fish for hard-shell and soft-shell crabs. Jimmies (male crabs) are preferred for steaming and picking, while soft-shell crabs are battered and fried. Roland Didlake worked crab pots in Rappahannock River for decades in the classic wooden deadrise *Beverley Ann*. The rounded stern is made of layers of blocks or "chunks" of wood, a style of shaping the stern developed by 19th-century log canoe builders. (Author's collection.)

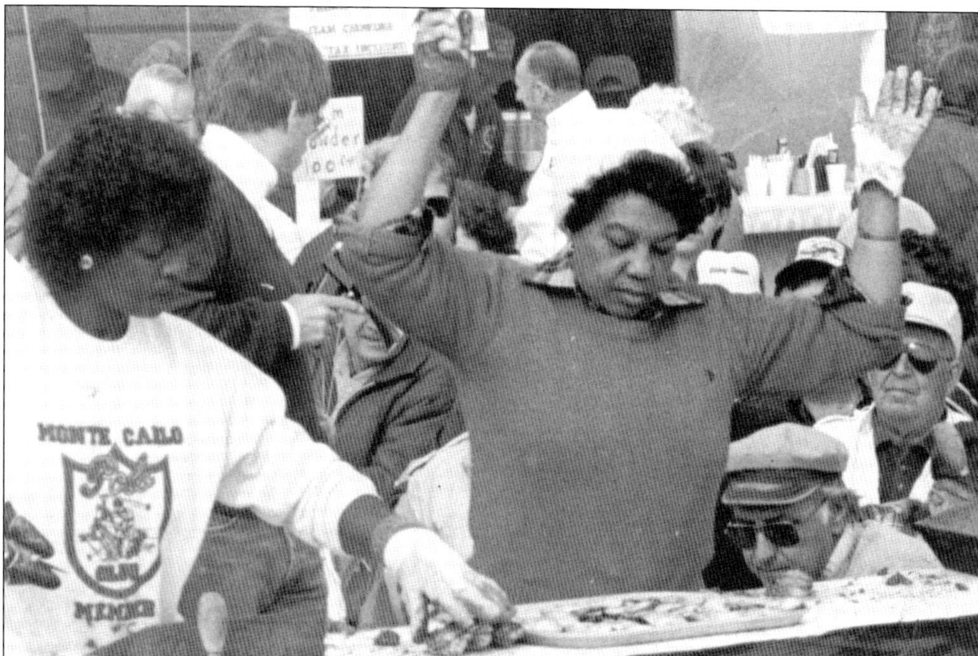

African American women have dominated the Virginia state oyster shucking competition for decades. Sara Hammond was the first Virginia shucker to win the US oyster shucking title in Leonardtown, Maryland. She competed in the International Oyster Shucking Contest in Galway, Ireland, in 1984 and finished third. Here, she is winning the Virginia women's title in 1983 at the Urbanna Oyster Festival. (Courtesy of the *Southside Sentinel*.)

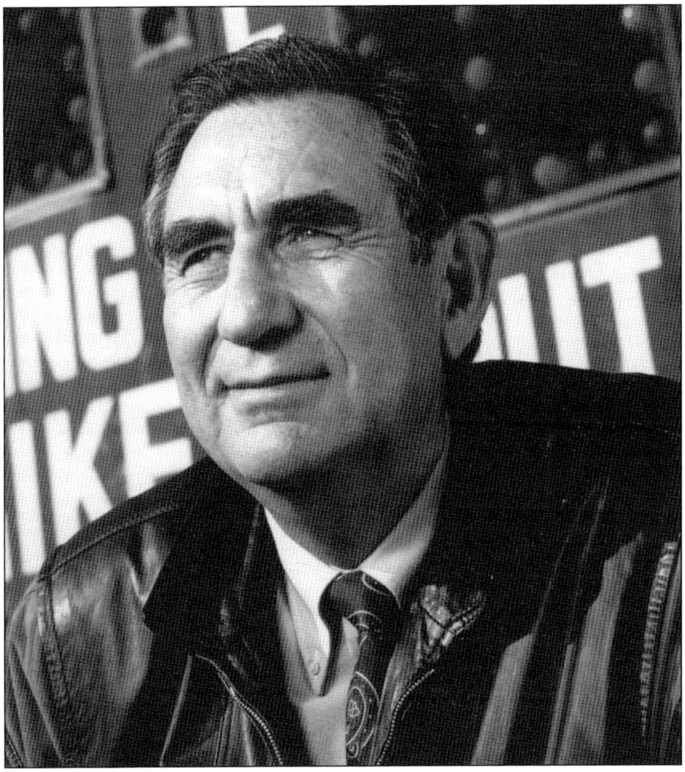

Syd Thrift was born in 1929 at Locust Hill. He graduated from Syringa High School and coached baseball at Middlesex High School for one season. After a stint as a player in the New York Yankees organization and a long career as a baseball scout, he was named general manager of the Pittsburgh Pirates in 1985, and by 1988, the club finished second in the National League East to the New York Mets. He hired manager Jim Leyland, who won three straight division titles for the Pirates in 1990, 1991, and 1992. (Courtesy of Dolly Thrift.)

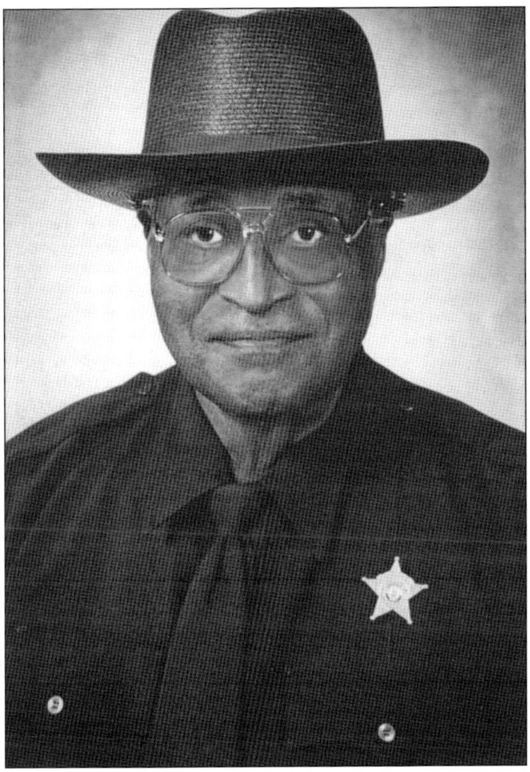

Born in 1914 in Locust Hill, Josh Holmes started working on the Rappahannock River as an oyster culling boy at the age of nine with his father Zachary on a 28-foot log canoe. With little education, he rose to the rank of sheriff of Middlesex County in 1979, becoming the first black to be elected sheriff in the history of the county. By using a common-sense approach to the job, he was considered a very competent sheriff. (Courtesy of Middlesex County.)

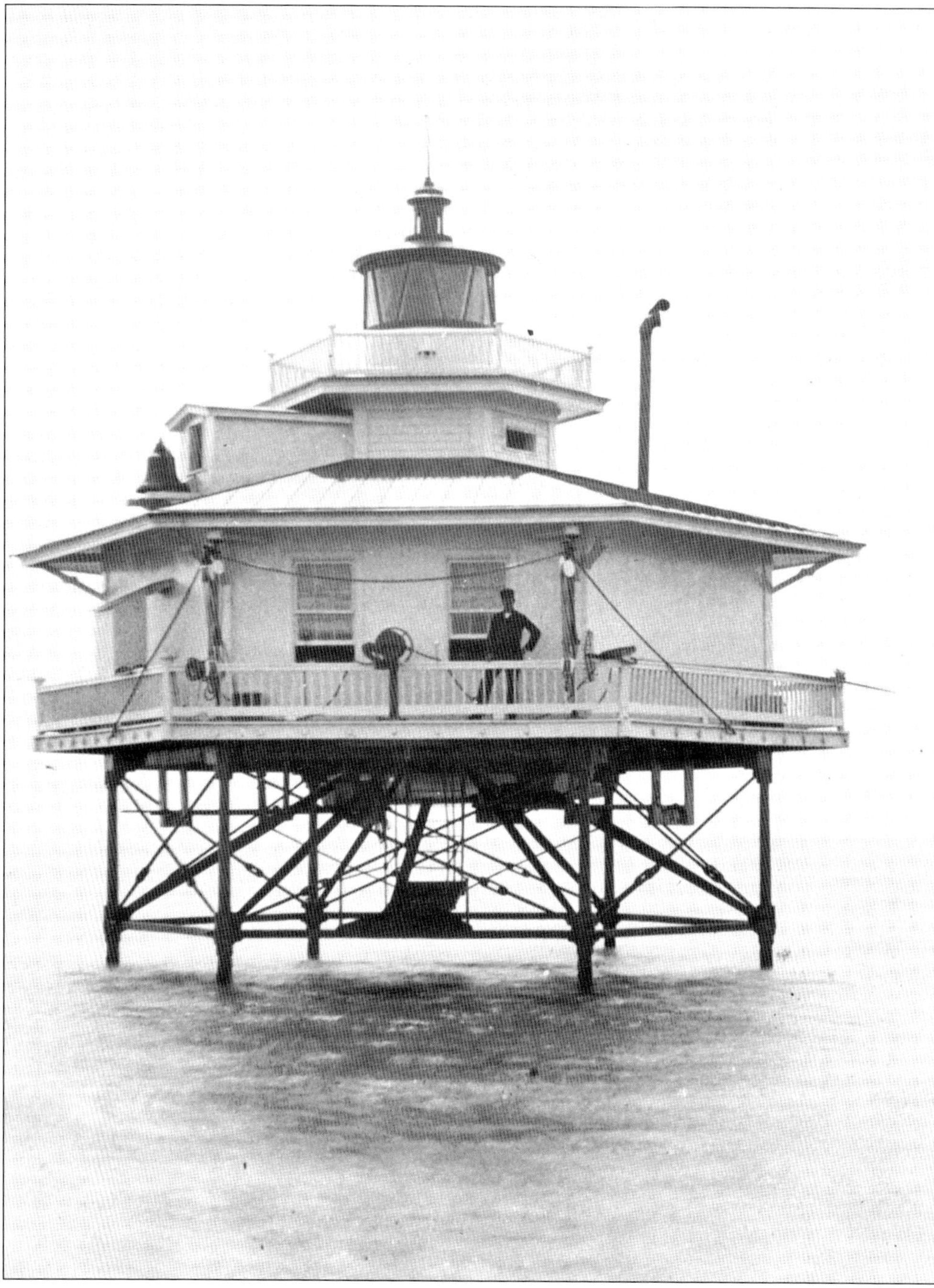

Stingray Point Lighthouse was completed in 1858 and was part of the county's waterscape for 94 years. Mrs. Lit Wilson, a granddaughter of James Parks, lighthouse keeper during the 52-day 1917–1918 freeze, told of the time during the freeze her grandfather ran out of food. He walked across the ice, dragging a boat to shore. Parks loaded up with food and, with the help of several local people, dragged the boat back to the lighthouse. The hexagonal lighthouse was dismantled in 1965 and taken down to make way for an automatic beacon built on the foundation of the old lighthouse. (Courtesy of Chesapeake Bay Maritime Museum.)

Bibliography

Bogger, Tommy. *A History of African-Americans in Middlesex County, 1646–1992*. White Stone, VA: Nohill, 1994.

Chamberlayne, C.G. *The Vestry Book of Christ Church Parish, Middlesex County, Virginia, 1663–1767.* Greenville, SC: Southern Historical Press, 2006.

Chowning, Larry S. "Pitts Lumber: 100 Years Old and Still Thriving." *Southside Sentinel*, November 5, 1998.

Chowning, Larry S., Archie Soucek, and Pat DePina. *Signatures in Time: A Living History of Middlesex County, Virginia*. Middlesex County, VA: Middlesex County, 2012.

———. *Soldiers at the Doorstep: Civil War Lore*. Atglen, PA: Schiffer Publishing, 2016.

DeBusk, Jessie M. *Family Histories of Middlesex County, Virginia*. Urbanna, VA: Ralph Wormeley Branch, APVA, 1982.

Fischer, David Hackett. *Albion's Seed: Four British Folkways in America*. New York, NY: Oxford University Press, 2015.

Gray, Louise E., Evelyn Q. Ryland, Bettie J. Simmons, Richard A. Genders, and Walter C.C. Johnson. *Historic Buildings in Middlesex County, Virginia, 1650–1875*. Lancaster, VA: Anchor Communications, 2003.

McKann, Homer Alton. "History of Early Education in Middlesex County 1669–1890." Thesis for master of science in education at University of Richmond, 1942. Unpublished.

Nugent, Nell Marion. *Cavaliers and Pioneers; Abstracts of Virginia Land Patents and Grants, 1623–1800*. Richmond, VA: Virginia State Library, 1934.

Perkinson, Pat Royal. *Cemeteries in Middlesex County, Virginia*. Saluda, VA: Middlesex County Cemetery Survey Committee and the Middlesex County Board of Supervisors, 2001.

Rutman, Darrett B. and Anita H. Rutman. *A Place in Time: Middlesex County, Virginia, 1650–1750*. New York, NY: W.W. Norton and Co, 1986.